Hot Blooded

A Sexual Resurrection

Karin Grace Wares

PAGE PUBLISHING, INC.
Conneaut Lake, PA

First originally published by Page Publishing 2020

Cover drawing and design by author.

ISBN 978-1-64584-991-9 (pbk)
ISBN 978-1-64584-992-6 (digital)

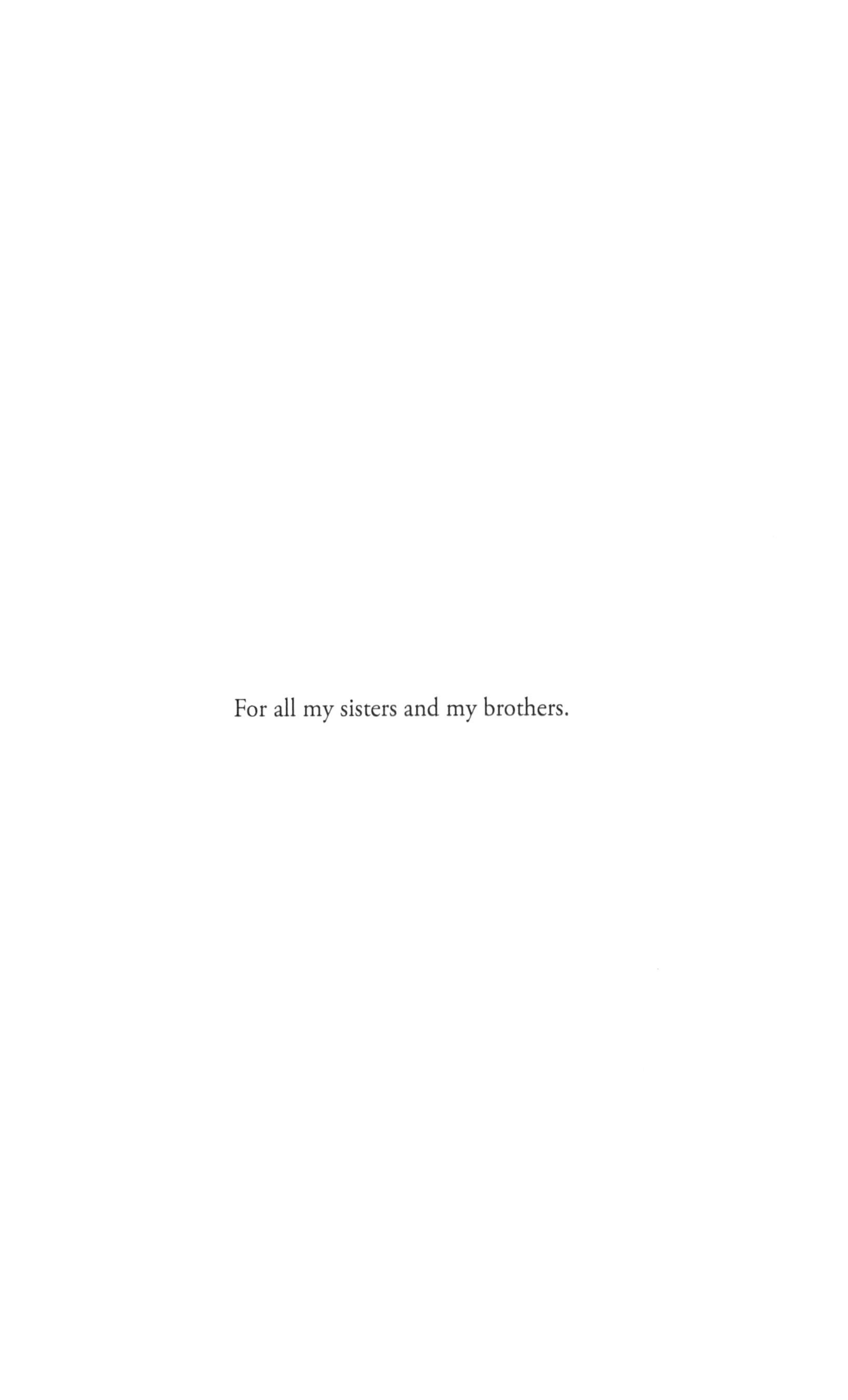

For all my sisters and my brothers.

Certainly no aspect of human biology in our current civilization stands in more need of scientific knowledge and courageous humility than that of sex. The history of medicine proves that in so far as man seeks to know himself and face his whole nature, he has become free from bewildered fear, despondent shame and arrant hypocrisy. As long as sex is dealt with in the current confusion of ignorance and sophistication, denial and indulgence, suppression and stimulation, punishment and exploitation, secrecy and display, it will be associated with a duplicity and indecency that lead neither to intellectual honesty nor human dignity.

—Dr. Alan Gregg, preface to
Sexual Behavior in the Human Male,
by Alfred Kinsey (1948)

CONTENTS

(Under Pressure)

ACKNOWLEDGMENTS

From the depth of my heart, my unspeakable appreciation goes out to all the people who shared their bodies with me sexually, and sometimes their hearts and souls. I could not have learned about myself, my sexuality, and sex in general without their willing participation.

I owe just about everything else between the covers of this book to my spiritual support network who, collectively, held my hand from day one, teaching me that it's not only okay but also vitally important to open my mind, my heart, and my legs to discover what sex is (and is not) and what it can be. It took some convincing!

Special homage to my fierce and loving soul sister, Virginia Roberson, for withstanding the relentless pains of conventional society to pull her into the fold. A deep bow to the integrity of Danny Goldsmith, my spiritual brother, for standing strong on his own principles when caving to traditional demands would have made his life easier and secured his sexual outlets.

My immense gratitude to Glen Torbert for his time and energy spent poring over my early manuscript, cleaning up my messes! His enthusiastic interest in all that I've produced on this topic has fueled, inspired, and sustained my endeavor.

A big thank you to the individuals at Page Publishing. Brian Droste reeled me in with his no-nonsense communication skills, Steven Matthews generously attended to my mile-long list of questions, and Holly Ickes, efficient, reliable and responsive, delivers even better than the postal service!

Additional thanks to David Hildes for his astute questions and perspective, to Karolina Waclawiak for her initial encouragement and advice in the daunting publishing world, to Janet Hardy and Tod Davies for their early critique and input, to Michele Reed for later inspiration, and to Marty Klein (in addition to his fabulous work in the field of sexuality) for being both forthright and forthcoming, injecting the energy I needed to publish my website.

And finally, a nod to each of my parents: My mother's understated, deeply personal feminist sensibility and lifelong yearning for equality affected me more than I realized; my father's pure, sweet love set the tone for my attitude toward men, my experiences in relationship, and burns on inside me like an Olympian torch.

INTRODUCTION

Is it just me, or do you notice we're all wandering around in a war zone when it comes to dealing with sex? I couldn't sit still any longer watching the bodies fall all around me, so I silently took to my keyboard and wound up with this book.

In it, I share some of my most personal experiences to animate my pointy social critique. The feedback from much of the publishing industry was to separate these two ingredients and write a different book, but I refused to do so. If I'm going down spread-eagle to the publishers, inviting the whole world to ogle up the speculum, I'm going down swinging with both hands! There are plenty of good books out there presenting the cultural data, but nothing that brings it back so close to home as I do here. And what use is the spectacle of my carnal escapades outside a much greater framework? Separately, you get the usual limitations; together, the possibilities are, quite frankly, limitless. Fusing these two things allows me to act as a living example to body forth the more cerebral theoretical discussions, ultimately delivering a new vision of sexuality and sexual functioning.

At the moment, publishers in the sexuality genre are much more enamored with books about sexual deviance and fringe identity, rather than the words and works of a vanilla jane like me. So I ran into another snag in trying to share a story with the potential to speak to so many people on so many levels—that I'm too ordinary. But *normal* doesn't mean *normative*, so please don't let any stray fears of that battleground keep you from the universal carnage of this book!

What I give you here is *relevance*, something both deeply personal and broadly inclusive. My experience as a woman has shaped my journey, but I identify as human! So while on the surface our activities may appear very different, underneath we all deal with similar experiences because, as sexual beings, we live out our lives through cultural traditions that deny and distort sexual expression at every turn. This perspective diminishes the tiresome emphasis on all our distinctions, allowing the focus to remain on this simple (and far more significant) area of common ground. And this is why I call my philosophy and approach *sexual humanism*. So, as I delve into discussions involving things like misogyny, its evil twin, misandry, and the labyrinthine psychology of sexual conditioning and repression, please hang in there with me. I'm not here to rant and rave, choose sides and pick fights. I *am* here to cut deep where it counts (which can get grisly) and to package and present things in a new, hopefully enlightening, way.

A seismic shift is heaving under foot around female empowerment. Spurred by the MeToo movement, reflected in recent Hollywood movies, published materials, media, and even changes in social standards and governmental policies, we are seeing a trend toward women stepping out and embracing their power more boldly. Potentially—*and only if we seriously revamp the realm of sexuality*—I see this as one of the most critical components in bringing forth the well-being of humanity at large. But in order to make this a genuine, meaningful, and enduring reality we have to ungird our tender loins and let it all hang out! And we can't do it alone.

Far beyond gender, we *all* have work to do on this front, serious work inside and out around sex. Due to the troubled sexual history of our cultural inheritance, we all have to turn over some heavy stones and poke around in some pretty rank places in order to set ourselves straight and move forward in a way that really works. We're all in this thing together, and we have to get a grip on the deeper layers of the logjam if we ever want to be truly free to get along and have a really good time. The layers exposed in *Hot Blooded* I believe to be some of the key missing links preventing us from getting there. Along the way, I reference materials published for the lay public that most aptly reflect these key features forming the uneasy, erratic pulse of our common socio-sexual world.

But sex is a primal force of our humanity that we can tune into and manifest just like we do so well with music—bridging differences, healing wounds, empowering change, generating energy, and finally, establishing rhythm and harmony. We're in for, I sincerely hope, a rocking romp through a topic that, at its essence, unites the living experience of humankind. Welcome, and thank you for joining me…

*It is no longer possible to stand aside and to say, "Forgive them for they know not what they do." **It is time that we all know what we do—and why we do it.***

—Mary Higgins,
foreword to *The Discovery of the Orgone: The Function of the Orgasm,*
by Wilhelm Reich (New York, 1961)

WHAT'S GOING ON?

Sex is the original rock and roll—radical by nature, tuned to the throbbing pulse of life, all you have to do is give yourself to it and let the spirit move you. It's the natural order of things; it's revolutionary.

Ah, but revolution is hard work, and finding the natural order of things can be a highly contentious endeavor, especially when it comes to something as loaded as sex, the beast of burden that it's become. So much for any floaty inspirations I might have gotten about being a lover and not a fighter from one of the musical genre's classic themes. Setting out to answer serious questions about what's actually going on around sex, I learned I had to be *both*.

So, with the rebel song in my throat and the warrior spirit close to my heart, I went about surrendering and opening every part of my being in order to locate the real goods of natural-born sexuality. I'd have to tap the full spectrum of my capacities to get to the bottom of this thing—involving a deep dive through the complex layers of culture, the feminine legacy, and my own lineage…

My mother was a nun. Growing up as she did, life's structure and meaning had not been nebulous affairs. From an Air Force family, raised on the standard series of military bases and educated in Catholic schools, she knew what was expected and what to expect. Seeing little other promise in life as a presixties-era woman, she joined the convent out of high school to devote her budding life to the cloister. Her best friend even followed suit, but the rebellious, irreverent practical joker didn't last long, promptly receiving the "left foot of fellowship" right in the posterior. My mother, however (Sister Mary

Grace among the nuns), was very serious. She diligently pursued her studies and dutifully followed the conventions of the order with a sincere interest in leading a devotional life. But there was something under her skin…

As resentful as she was about her own womanhood and the lack of options it afforded, she identified intensely with her gender and looked to the Blessed Virgin Mary for inspiration. Yet what she found in that venerated figure of femininity was so far removed from her own grounded sense of reality that it became one of the early seeds of her ultimate alienation from the church itself. For my mother, a pragmatic, real-life woman looking for a genuine role model, there was not a shred of earthly inspiration to be found in the holy Madonna.

Frankly, I'd bet Jesus himself would positively plotz bearing witness to the historical transformation of his own mother, at the hands of his followers, into an altogether inhuman mythological figure. Apparently, those overzealous, female-fearing celibates of subsequent Christendom[1] could not as easily dispense with their messiah's own mother as they could with the other real (quite empowered and highly respected) women of Jesus's circle, thus opting for a full makeover instead. Had *the man's own* views formed the basis of the church canon, however (assuming the religion's same success), my mother would certainly have grown up in an entirely different cultural milieu and would have had no reason to seek refuge from a world lacking in gender equality, nor to then run far and fast from an institution fostering such anathema within its own confines.[2]

---

[1] One scholar points out that the notion of celibacy arose not from anything Jesus actually said or proposed in his day but from a mixed-up interpretation of his response to the Pharisees on the issue of *divorce*, his denunciation of which would have been a gesture that would have actually protected women from the abusive practices of his fellow Jews (Uta Ranke-Heinemann, *Eunuchs for the Kingdom of Heaven: Women, Sexuality, and the Catholic Church* [New York, NY: Penguin Books, 1990], originally published in German in 1988, translated by Peter Heinegg, 32–33).

[2] Uta Ranke-Heinemann, in *Eunuchs for the Kingdom of Heaven*, writes, "Jesus was a friend of women, the first and practically the last friend women had in the Church. He caused a stir by the fact that he had dealings with women, that he was surrounded by 'many women' (Lk. 8:3), which for a rabbi and

Inevitably, two years later she left. Try as they might, the elders were unable to persuade her to stay. And so, wearing the frumpy and ill-fitted street clothing rustled together among the nuns, the promising young novice was ushered out of the institution under the stealthy cover of darkness. She kicked the "habit"—and she never looked back.

Needless to say, I was not raised Catholic. Besides the erratic option of joining my grandparents on their Sunday excursion to Mass and a sputtering dabble in Bible studies, I was raised with no direct religious influence whatsoever, which spared me the more blatant onslaughts comprising the Catholic conscience. As for the nun, on the other hand, you can take the girl out the habit—and bury it in the hamper—but you can't take the *habit* out of the girl. Catholicism and its sex-negative misogyny had left in her (as throughout much of the world) its indelible impressions. The guilt of original sin is irremediable; the shame of possessing the reprehensible anatomy of the original seductress goes to the bone.

And then, of course, the apple doesn't fall far from the tree. My recognition of these features in my mother would only come with the gradual unraveling of my own rendition of it as I uncovered the hidden attitudes, deep within my psyche, forming the basis of my confused, misguided relationship with my own sexuality.

I, like most people, didn't even realize how badly bent out of shape it all was until I started the shaky adventure of finding out. But somewhere inside myself, I'd discovered a gyrating force—a trembling truth and shuddering energy that would rock my world and send the apple rolling into regions far afield! In search of hard

---

teacher of Jewish law was absolutely inappropriate and unprecedented for his day and age. We all know that he had twelve male disciples, but he also had many female disciples, including society ladies such as Joanna, the wife of a high official under Herod Antipas. Nowadays these women would be called 'liberated,' because they did not accept traditional female roles, but on the contrary financed Jesus and his group 'out of their means' (Lk. 8:3)....Jesus' followers, however, have not followed him on this point. His openness to women, the respect he showed them, was replaced after his death, on the part of male church officials, by a peculiar mixture of repressed fear, mistrust, and arrogance" (Ranke-Heinemann, 119–20).

answers, I galvanized my will to go against every grain of my good-girl existence and went rogue—through the jungle of open relationship, across uncharted stretches of the playing field alone, into the mineshafts of celibacy and monogamy, up and down the brass pole on the public circuit... Sacrificing my own comfort and my entire identity, I reduced my ill-conceived world to rubble, rediscovering, reviving, and rebuilding my sexual self at the core of it all, according to the laws of nature rather than those of man.

The hidden attitudes I found in myself are reflections not only of immediate family upbringing but also, more extensively, of the entire culture. The profoundly distorted messages that educate us about sex, sexuality, and gender have fostered a malignant malaise infecting the individual, our relationships, and society as a whole (so that now, essentially, what we've got on our hands is a bunch of rotten apples!).

In order to gyrate forever out from under its thick, sprawling limbs, though, I had to figure out the roots of that old twisted tree. What follows is my theory about what's been going on, under the surface, to get us to where we're at now.

The basic problem boils down to economy and human nature. Biologically, we are *social-sexual* animals. That's the foundation of our human nature, driven and sustained by inherent natural desire. Economics is an inevitable result of our social functioning, and we have a system comprised of hierarchical power over limited resources. Along with this precarious position of power comes the irksome challenge of maintaining that position, so things do get nasty.

Women are needed, and valued, the world over for the reproductive capacity that represents economic power (through generating the pawns of productivity and furthering the accumulation of wealth). In a matriarchal system, with inheritance passing through the maternal lineage, female sexuality is no big deal since it is impossible to mistake, under ordinary circumstances, who is the mother of a child. In such societies, it has been observed that sex tends to be an openly shared cultural pastime to the joyful benefit of all.[3] However, in a patriarchal system—as in those dominating most of our modern world—since paternity is a much more dubious determination, *female sexuality then becomes something that must be carefully controlled to maintain the order of things*, something that we can see has been quite an obsessive endeavor. (Throughout this book, I'll highlight the nuances of how this still has us hogtied in ways we rarely recognize.)

Adding sexual desire to the mix jacks up the already inherent fear factor (that of losing what's been obtained), because when there's a demanding desire to access the subjects of subordination (men not only need but also *want* their women in the worst way), the stakes become that much higher. Then comes the fevered battle to further subordinate and secure the element of control. The power of women in such a situation has often been relegated to their willingness or resistance to acquiesce sexually, prompting furious resentment of that power and the ongoing, frequently violent, struggle of the sexes to this day.

Finally, adding religion to the mix (which we've done in spades), you get brimstone and fire. You've got a collection of highly sexed creatures building a world based upon acquiring and securing power, and now, trying to wrest the spirit free within a moral institution thoroughly embroiled in that same context, you've got a real messy dilemma.

The irrepressible force of passionate desire takes on staggering significance in this realm, since God himself is demanding your chastity in exchange for the promise of heaven. So you focus on the issue of sex (and its counter-representatives) because it appears to be the quintessential obstacle in the way of spiritual deliverance from eternal hellfire. (When sex is sin and Satan is behind all temptation, it only makes sense—from a heterosexual male perspective—that, therefore, woman must be the wily-eyed Devil himself.)[4]

---

[3] Christopher Ryan and Cacilda Jetha, *Sex at Dawn: How We Mate, Why We Stray, and What It Means for Modern Relationships* (New York: HarperCollins, 2010), 133–34.

[4] Furthermore, God's purported instructions on reproduction in the Bible, coupled with the growing demands of agricultural development, fuel the immense

Judaism, Islam, Hinduism, and even benevolent Buddhism have, along with Christianity, lent their own robust contributions to the misogynistic mind-set entrenched in cultures around the globe, since men have been the predominant figures forming, writing, translating, and promulgating popular religion and its taut hierarchy throughout much of the history of civilization.

Religious guidelines tend to be based upon particular ideals of virtue, all of which require restraint, since desires (and their relentless onslaught) are generally in conflict with those high-minded ideals. Desires conspicuously plague the mind that is seeking freedom, salvation, or redemption in any context (even pure hedonism). Apart from the basic bodily desires (food, shelter) directly linked to individual survival, which are generally accepted and moderately accommodated (except in extreme asceticism), sex is the linchpin of desire, representing to the puritanical pious a carnal abomination that must be conquered and obliterated. The unruly agitation stirred up in the mind and body by passionate desire is directly opposed to the harmonious composure and control being sought. It's very real to the serious seeker. And when the object of one's desire is animated (a person versus, say, a bowl of rice) and operating under its own volitions, it is that much more threatening and, therefore, that much more easily viewed as evil incarnate, *pointedly and deliberately* undermining the chaste and dispassionate ideal.

Thus, one's own spiritual endeavor foists moral implications upon the unsuspecting objects, in this case, women. The outcome, then, of this intensely personal struggle is a misdirected moral imperative fobbed off onto the masses as doctrine and dogma (which now forms the unspoken, malformed basis of our collective "moral sensibility" around sex). As a result, the coveted chastity of mind, interpreted as the absence of sexual content of any kind, comes to represent true virtue and the epitome of innocence, posing no threat to the devout. *Since sex is the ultimate threat, innocence can be nothing*

---

movement to multiply fruitfully and intensify the massive oppression of women. In *Prehistory of Sex*, author Timothy Taylor says archaeological evidence shows "vigorous widespread use of contraception" prior to the agricultural era (Timothy Taylor, *Prehistory of Sex* [New York: Bantam Books, 1996]).

other than asexuality. Then come the impossible caricatures of this ideal (that Blessed Virgin), placed upon pedestals for veneration and emulation by the rest of us who have no basis for understanding, let alone attaining, such a demeanor.

And the farther a common woman strays from the model, the more she is feared, distrusted, and hated, even today, in the mainstream culture. (If you don't believe me, try it.) In this way, the moral ideology is enforced, and vast, intricate networks to further its execution have taken shape, and root, in society, exacting a magnificent price for *all* concerned. Everybody suffers because of the social-sexual nature of humanity; any overarching problem in one area is going to affect the other. Yet devotedly, we keep trying so damn hard to exorcize the sexual demon from the equation and get rosy results.

Are we having fun yet, or did I miss that memo?

Witchy Woman

Twenty-five years ago, I would have insisted that the demonization of women is an antiquated notion here in the USA (in fact, I would have been annoyed by the suggestion of it). But what I personally encountered as I broke away from convention has shown me that it's not; it is only masked by PC modernity and buffered, admittedly, by growing pockets of alternative minorities. This is my first heavy stone to turn, so as I grease up the elbows, please note that much of its mass is actually due to the illusion that we've already moved beyond it.

Just sitting at home with a computer, you don't have to look far to see clues to the extant remains of this notion. Interestingly, on a Google search for something else entirely, I found that the first instant web-engine prompt to typing "are women" was "evil," and the barrage of sites clamoring to answer, in the affirmative, this apparently burning question of my fellow web surfers reveals a vibrant culture of modern misogynists of all ages.[5] After taking an irresistible

---

[5]   I also scanned related blogs and comment threads that severely admonished even the *basis* of the question (frequently asked by women themselves). These come

detour through the relevant blogosphere, I decided, primarily, that this current attitude is squarely based on the clashing of the sexes on real, contentious issues happening between men and women and, in these cases, men having gotten sorely—often repeatedly—screwed by the women in their lives. The game that's going on out there is brutal, and neither side is any longer an innocent victim, so I am not about to plead the case of tender, blameless women being vilified without warrant. However, it is the labeling of women as "evil" that stands out in the fray to me, because this particular notion is embedded deeply in the religious substratum of patriarchal philosophy still widely informing our cultural psyche. It's not being plucked out of a vacuum.

Evil, as we in the West regard it, is fundamentally a Judeo-Christian religious construct, the general understanding of its common meaning shaped by theological doctrine. This idea (albeit rooted in human pondering as old as human consciousness itself) evolved through the ancient Israelite religion beginning with "the Satan" (or *Shatan*) as one of God's divine council members. It later on became that fallen angel, "the Devil," or God's mortal enemy,[6] forming the original duality of "good" and "evil," now naturalized throughout the language—and in the minds—of religious and secular society alike.

---

from a section of the population who are quite certain about the irrelevance of the whole query (as I used to be), and they provide examples—from ancient Hindu and Celtic goddesses, Mary Magdalene, and other biblical women to modern cinematic and comics heroines—to prove that the notion of woman-as-evil is a cultural nonissue and that the scales are in fact balanced. Most of these comments appeared to be written by intelligently articulated, well-educated, emotionally balanced, and personally empowered men and women. My point is not to argue that our history and current society are entirely based upon and singly composed of misogynistic purpose. Rather, it is to look at what the manifest reality has been and currently is, including the fact that there are remnants in our midst that are still taking a toll—and much more than we may consciously realize.

Also, as an interesting side note, when I next experimentally googled the words *"are men..."*, among the top instant prompts that arose were *"...and women equal,"* *"...better,"* and *"...smarter."* Draw your own conclusions.

6   Bart Ehrman, *God's Problem: How the Bible Fails to Answer Our Most Important Question—Why We Suffer* (New York: HarperCollins Publishers, 2008), 165.

It's almost become a commonsense conclusion that the greatest transposition of *evil* onto the entity of women took place in the Book of Genesis in the story of Adam and Eve. But the original meaning of the myth (whatever it may truly have been) has clearly become colored with deep-seated assumptions we have since fostered about its inherent she-devil message, because a look at the English translation presents us with an Eve that, although perhaps a little dumb (not unlike Adam himself), does not overtly suggest she is the devil.

It is really through the elaborate journey of translation and interpretation of the Old and New Testaments, by the proponents of Christianity, that has bred such assumptions about the evil of woman (much thanks to writings attributed to its earliest evangelist, St. Paul, who never actually met the man Jesus and whose chauvinistic, misogynistic opinions have been immortalized and proselytized by the canonization of these writings). This historical journey has been defined by traversing through an environment fraught with the tension—the fear and the hostility—between sex and power. (Stripped down, misogyny is the logical sum, in a patriarchal culture, of the fearful condemnation of sex plus the fanatical struggle for power. If you think about it, it adds up to little else.)

Christopher Witcombe, author of *Eve and the Identity of Women*, writes, "Whether or not you believe the Bible was divinely inspired, the Book of Genesis has served as the primary source in the West for definitions of gender and morality [...] this view of Eve and of women in general has been insinuated into the culture to such an extent that both men and women believe it defines a <u>natural condition</u> of women."[7] He says that through the millennia, Eve's story has represented the fundamental character and identity of all women telling us all what women are really like, warning men not to trust them, and women not to trust themselves or each other. He also says that this negative perception of Eve has been extraordinarily tenacious, and the extent to which it continues to subtly influence our view of women must not be underestimated.

---

[7] Christopher L. C. E. Witcombe, "*Eve and the Identity of Women*," (Sweet Briar College, 2000).

As Witcombe points out, whether or not we buy into Western religion and the Bible at all is neither here nor there. The zeitgeist takes care of it for us. The last two thousand years, dominated by Christianity, have nurtured within us all the suspicious view of women as represented by a hinky bitch like Eve. It lurks around pretty well hidden much of the time, but it's there. My point is, the fact that modern men and women are both inspired to question whether *evil* is the "natural condition" of women should give rise, *at least*, to an eyebrow. Women embattled in the war of the sexes will often say all men are assholes, dicks, pricks, douchebags, what have you, but you will not generally encounter use of the term *evil* in their description. This is because the age-old cultural evaluation of the inherent "God-given" quality of men rests, within the same background of religious ideology, upon the smug certainty that *he* was created in God's image, not as an afterthought, a comfort, or a servant-turned-sinister-temptation.

Back on the personal front, I found this fearful misogyny (drummed into *both* men and women) awaits just beneath the veneer of the updated facade for the right stimulus to roust it from its hiding place. All you have to do, as I did, is stretch the envelope in just the right places and the earth begins to tremble…then you have a very immediate personal reality. What is that stimulus? Nowadays, it is a single, unattached (especially childless) heterosexual woman operating as a free sexual agent, going after what she wants and manifesting it as she wishes.

Such a woman cannot be controlled, and she cannot be understood according to any of the creaky old models: she is not the virginal innocent to be taken, guided, and protected by a worldly man; she is not the virtuous moral pillar that will tame the soulless beasts of men; she is not a rebellious adolescent or confused deviant that will, in due time with proper guidance, reenter the anointed fold; she is not the mother, the wife, the widow, or the godforsaken spinster of yore. She will be called a slut and a whore, but the venom within these labels tells us pointedly that she has gotten under the thin skin of an ailing mass. Such a woman yet defies comfy categorization. She cannot even be mockingly cursed with a jab of the elbow as the deluded lesbian who simply needs a good deep dicking to sort out her ways—she's messing with things much more serious, things not so "other" and more close to home. Even in this day and age, such a woman is likely to find herself regarded with nervous suspicion, both by men *and* by women, as if she presents a threat to the civilized world as we know it. (Ooh, yes she does. Later on I'll tell you a story about modern pharma.)

For me, the experience—of breaking from convention and being assaulted by the fallout from the outside world—has forced me to examine the hidden pockets within, unwittingly packed with my own internalized misogyny.

To punctuate this shameless tirade, I have a wacky little story from less than a week ago at this writing.

I paid a twenty-year-overdue visit to my last landlord in my hometown of Baker City, Oregon. Having spent the past couple decades cleaning out my secret closet (not that of my sexy lingerie, of course, but rather of my stinky old skeletons), I realized I still owed an apology to that generous woman whose carpet I had damaged with a hot candle and, as per my own recollection, had surprised her with upon my departure. She was well into her seventies back then, so as I drove up in front of the house I'd known her to inhabit at that time, I wondered if I would find her—forget living *there*, but living *at all*. I pulled out the two-hundred-dollar offering I had stashed in my purse to emphasize my sentiments and crossed the street to her front yard. Before I reached the door, it opened, and out she popped, mail in hand, tinier than I remembered but still the sprightly woman I recognized.

After a friendly bantering exchange in which she insisted I owed her nothing and I insisted that I did, I managed to wheedle her into accepting my apology with at least half of my wad of cash. After reluctantly, though graciously, taking it from my hand, she peered hawkishly into my eyes through the thick lenses of her spectacles and asked me pointedly if I was still a *Satan worshiper*.

Well, damn, that floored me for a minute. But since the burning of candles is generally regarded as a pretty innocuous activity within both religious and profane realms, I can only assume that whoever chose to inform her of such a harebrained fable had simply become privy to some of the incendiary local legends stimulated by my unconventional lifestyle as a solitary "free electron": childless, unwed, sexually active, female.

I will exemplify and elaborate on such a woman in a later chapter. For now, suffice it to say, women (most, if not all, of us) are carrying a cleverly hidden misogynistic affliction within us (whether or not we've knowingly adopted the mind-set), *wrapped tightly around our sexual identity* as we have internalized it from the world, and passing it along, mother to daughter, sister to sister, generation to generation.

Us and Them

So, yeah, this is about the scourge of us wretched women. And…it's also about the bane of those mangy men, because, in the ongoing drama of "us" against "them," they have in turn been reviled, condemned, vilified. Although I suppose that could be seen as somewhat gratifying in the name of retaliation, it is, nevertheless, as Joan Jett might howl, "Dead-End Justice": *nobody wins.* The ever-shining yet oft-forgotten truth beyond all this drama is that we are all the same species of creature, with all the same human frailties, vulnerabilities, insecurities, fears, and the same hopes, dreams, needs, and desires. Yet the bickering and fighting continue, and divisive attitudes prevail.

Howard Bloom, author of a fascinating book called *The Lucifer Principle*,[8] says that the "us" versus "them" behavior pitting in-group against out-group is as old as civilization itself, acting as a force that not only fissures but in fact fuses society in significant ways—united we stand, divided we fall, united, divided…and round we go. It also serves as a "functional release valve," he says, for the underlying fury of mankind. This fury arises from frustrations with the natural lim-

---

8   Howard Bloom, *The Lucifer Principle: A Scientific Expedition into the Forces of History* (New York: The Atlantic Monthly Press, 1995).

itations of reality intensified even further by the inevitable role-playing in our human lives.

In the war between the sexes, it's obvious how the gender roles (as we've set them up) present exasperating limitations on both sides, and the genders themselves present exceedingly convenient group categorization. In other words, it's easy to distinguish ally from enemy. In a sense, we have just fallen into a natural default system of fighting out our primal frustrations, tribe against tribe.

But it's more than mere frustration that drives us; it is also fear. In his Terror of History lectures, Dr. Teofilo Ruiz[9] suggests hostility provides an escape from the terrors of *real* life. Identifying an enemy gives a welcome focal point within the frightening ambiguity of reality (and then, of course, banding up against it makes us feel tough). During the witch craze, in the midst of the deeply unsettling upheavals of the Christian Reformation and counter-reformation, the chasing of witches was a comforting occupation (like ratting out all those "commies" purportedly haunting every shadow during the McCarthy era—or, to quote Monty Python, "I can see [Brezhnev] peeping out of my wife's blouse!"). Having an enemy, even an imaginary one, helps to focus the anxious mind. Defining an *us* and a *them* tends to anchor those worrisome loose ends that incessantly plague our lives, and when it comes to things as powerful as sex, the fear and neurosis bred within our culture sets the stage for high drama—bring on the moral crusades!

But the collateral damage of the theatrical "war of the sexes" just sweeps across the board of humanity, taking innocent lives for ransom without anyone being able to clearly specify what concessions are to be demanded on a person-to-person basis, just because it's such a colossal mess. And until we thoroughly examine the difficult reality of who we are (the lives we are living, the roles we are playing) and adequately address the most critical components—first and foremost of which is sex and sexuality—this insanity (and its rein of terror) will not cease.

---

[9]   Professor Teofilo F. Ruiz, *The Terror of History: Mystics, Heretics, and Witches in the Western Tradition* (UCLA, the Teaching Company, 2002).

The "obscure" etiology and uncertain prognosis of the malaise between the sexes is wrapped up in a highly convoluted morass of early formative experiences reinforced throughout a lifetime of exposure to a hostile antisexual environment—then, frequently, reinforced again within the very activity of sex. The fears and superstitions surrounding sex create painful vulnerabilities, which naturally call up psychological and emotional defenses that all too easily get dumped onto the sexual partner, inevitably turning the pair into adversaries—or "haters" rather than "lovers."

What I hope to do in the following chapters is expose and tease apart more specifics in the matted mare's nest surrounding the issue of sex. With sexuality operating at the core of our social existence as a species, the fallout of sexual dysfunction is naturally going to be ubiquitous and extensive. Given what I've learned about the depth and subtlety of my own derangement (which, as it turns out, falls quite comfortably within the troubled bounds of "normal"), in addition to what I've encountered in intimate relationships with others who have addressed theirs, I am convinced that anything less than rigorous self-examination and aggressive overhaul (basically a full-on gut rehab) is temporarily palliative, at the very best. Therefore, throughout the rest of this book, understand that I'm talking about revolution—deeply personal, experiential revolution. This is not armchair philosophy. So as you read my story and commentary, please watch closely your own reflection moving in the mirror.

My cry from the heart is to women who have an interest in unearthing concealed layers of sexual disempowerment, expanding their perspective, discovering the more subtle features of sexuality and activating a more vital identity as a result.

My overture is to men (and any others) who want a clearer understanding about what's going on in this realm, who care for women (even for *a* woman), who may be perplexed or frustrated by them, by sex in general, or who simply want to get more out of sex, life, and their relationships.

This is a personal story within the larger sphere of human sexuality. It is neither discriminatory nor politically correct. It's my honest and passionate attempt to share the perspective gleaned from an eccentric, extensive excursion that goes far beyond the territorial demarcation and disputes between "us" and "them" and, instead, treads deep into the dark recesses of the matter at hand via personal exposure, examination, discovery, and transformation.

More, it is about the way we humans have utterly deluded and robbed ourselves—tragically for all of us—and how we perpetuate the delusion in spite of our own misery. For what?

"For the sake of the little children," it is often said.

LET THE CHILDREN PLAY

I remember, at the age of three, playing with my sister's doll with the long blond hair that pulled out of a hole on the top of her head and wound back inside her with a turn of the knob protruding from the middle of her back. Her anatomical oddities didn't faze me; in fact, all the hair truly meant to me was that the color was like my own which allowed me to identify with the doll. My interest in her capacity to instantly change the length of her white-gold hair was obliterated by my fascination with her bottom. I couldn't wait to be alone with her, to remove her panties under her little dress, exposing the subtle implication of a crack.

"Nobody knows how naughty she is, going without her panties," I would imagine, sitting in the closet, as the waves of pleasure coursed through my body like the warmth of the sunlight through the window hitting the carpet and filling the room with a radiant red glow.

The stillness and the tingling vitality are as vivid to me now as they were then, forty-five years ago. In fact, now these sensations have returned. After many years of diligently removing the obstacles, it is clear that what was going on then was the free flow of vibrant sexual energy that occurs naturally in the body when there are no psychological barriers in the way.

But even back then, I sat in the closet for a reason: I was hiding. At three, there was already shame and secrecy surrounding my pleasures, even though the supple surge of the energy in my body was not yet blocked by crystallized inhibitions. I have no recollection of precisely where these insidious notions came from (probably oodles of preverbal impressions), but I behaved according to an unquestioning certainty that what I was enjoying must be a secret. I felt a rush of adrenaline when I heard my mother's footsteps approaching the room, and I felt my face flush red like the carpet when she mused aloud at how quiet I was…and how odd that I played in the closet.

There's a great phobic, fastidious fuss over the matter of protecting children from any and all notions pertaining to sexuality. It's as though we were staving off a dreadful, disfiguring disease for as long as possible to preserve the unblemished (asexual) essence of their tender youth before it is inevitably infected by a foreign airborne pathogen. I visualize parents frantically swatting away the "malarial" mosquitos carrying instead…the sex virus.

Well, to be direct and to the point, these are our innocent children: unborn fetuses are masturbating in the uterus, infants (feared to be having seizures) are convulsing in orgasm, toddlers are molesting the furniture, tweens are humping their beds…and towheaded tykes are dallying with their dollies.

Truly, this is the reality of it, but we choose to deny and suppress it, parents believing that "exposure" to sexuality itself will damage the asexual innocence of their children *when it is the child's innocence alone that leaves their natural sexuality intact*. Virtually every human being is innately "infected" by way of being alive, so there is nothing to be done along the lines of protection. That's an exercise in futility—and a destructive one at that.

What we're really doing is inventing and projecting onto children a fantasy of sexual "innocence" (or asexuality) as an escape from confronting the disaster that's been made of our own sexuality throughout the centuries—millennia—of cultural confusion. This conversation brings us down to touch the bedrock of that mutilated definition of innocence we've enshrined as a result of our deep suspicions of sex. Because we simply do not trust it, innocence by definition must be asexual. But since that sexuality is inseparable from our very nature, what does that do to us? It makes us all quite pitifully twisted, of course.

Yet, rather than healing "thyself," we play the imprudent part of the physician, pinning our hopes (and our weighty psychological burdens) on the hapless kids. So many messages, spoken and unspoken, based upon adults' discomfort with and alienation from their own sexuality immediately begin to distort the *real* innocence of children; the misguided attempts to protect the *imaginary* innocence are the very things that destroy it, by instilling contaminated attitudes toward their own bodies and bodily impulses.

The undeveloped person utilizes input from the outside world to build a functioning identity. Therefore, because their innocent existence is inherently a sexual experience, messages from the outside world that deny the child's fundamental essence can only result in a fractured psychology. And this is the root of our most significant widespread human dysfunction. (Dr. Wilhelm Reich was onto this, and the early psychoanalyst's radical ideas landed him in prison until the end of his days with several tons of his publications burned by court order.)

Even the best parental intentions cannot prevent the damage that will absolutely be done by their own profoundly injured attitudes toward sexuality. My own parents were quite liberal, in fact—scientifically minded and educated. My mother, after the convent, did gratefully live through the sixties, established some fresh distance from her Catholic roots, studied biology in college and married a man from an open-minded family background. They both spoke very matter-of-factly about the details of the reproductive process.

In addition, from the age of seven, I was raised on a ranch with a very clear visual—and strategic manipulation—of mating among numerous species of animals (my mother still cherishes the childish renderings of our mating sheep comprising the portfolio of my nascent artistry). I did not lack a clinical understanding of the rudiments of sexual reproduction. Nevertheless, like most people, I still wound up damaged and disfigured around my own sexuality (and completely oblivious to this fact).

Even something like the sixties cannot cure a disease that is deeply impressed within the being via culture and family upbringing (what did happen to the sixties, anyway?). It can only put different ideas into the head, and ideas cannot be turned into an abiding reality without a concerted effort to do so. In this case, it requires the total reorganization of fundamental principles (those attitudes again), which involves the entire repertoire of insight, understanding, motivation, willingness, capacity, and strategy to make it happen. (This is why revolution *en masse* doesn't generally result in a profoundly enduring phenomenon…hence, the vanishing sixties…besides the fact that this repertoire is a far cry from just getting stoned.)

What hasn't been learned cannot be taught; what *has* been learned *will* be conveyed thoroughly, the teaching beginning in the preverbal stages of development with the *unspoken* messages forming some of the deepest obstacles in the psyche regarding sexuality. The impressions absorbed are deeply subconscious and form the bedrock of foundational attitudes that will govern our navigation through life both consciously and unconsciously.

Communication Breakdown

By the time the day approaches when parents are forced to concede that the topic of their children's own personal sexual activity must be broached with them, it's usually far too late for this angle of discussion. The subject has already become enshrouded in embarrassment and the communication is awkwardly stilted and ineffective, just an obligatory formality poorly timed.

Late in my freshman year in high school, I had my first "boyfriend." He wasn't my dreamboat, but he was a good friend and I loved him as such. We spent many a long, heated evening making out heavily in his Volkswagen Rabbit to the sultry voice of Stevie Nicks, the windows steaming and my panties soaking wet. I took my shirt off once with him on the living room floor at his house, only to hurriedly put it back on. His disappointment was palpable, but he didn't push. I never touched his penis; he never even really felt me up.

I knew my limits at the time; they were chiseled out of petrified heebie-jeebies, so when my mother approached me to have the conversation about sex (probably after finding my slippery undergarments in the laundry), I brushed her off as abruptly as possible, emphatically assuring her she had *nothing*(!) to worry about, and it was never mentioned again. It was, indeed, too late for me to be open, receptive, and interested in discussing the topic of her concern. By this time, the whole world and all its perverted implications had crawled up inside my panties and twisted them into a tight little wad.

When children are quite young, long before puberty, they are full of curious fascination about sex. This is when they begin exploring and asking the questions that make adults squirm inside as they come face-to-face with that sense of parental protective responsibility: that of preserving the child's sexual *innocence* (which ultimately amounts to preserving only their sexual *ignorance*). And this is where the problem begins its more overtly manipulated manifestations, as what emerges from the mouth (obscure innuendos, insinuations, "squeamish euphemisms,"[10] etc.) is the distorted result of so much confusion and skeeter-borne social disease.

When I was around the age of eight, we acquired a new ram of a different breed to service our evolving flock of ewes. He was what is called a Rambouillet, a hardy breed with fine wool, distinctive rolls of skin around the neck, and long, thick, curling horns. He was a proud new addition to the ranch, and he needed a proper name. As I listened to the adults batting around various potential monikers, I looked at this magnificent animal with his impressive headset and blurted out that of course his name should be Horny.

The resounding laughter among everyone, including my sister (a year older but far more worldly-wise), was intensely perplexing to me. No one would venture to respond directly to my requests for clarification around the humor of the matter. While observing that I had certainly made a funny joke, I also felt confused embarrassment around the sense that, in my isolated ignorance, I was actually the ultimate butt of that joke, and I couldn't understand why nobody

---

[10] I took this descriptively apt phrase from an article by Ellen Barry, "90-Year-Old Sex Columnist Shatters Taboos in India," *New York Times*, International, the Saturday Profile, August 9, 2014.

was willing to let me in on it. The name stuck, and that ram lived a happy, horny life among green pastures and ewes in estrous.

To this day we all smile about it together—now that I get the joke—but it is also an unremarkable example of the finer little inadvertent fibers from childhood that spin into larger cords and get woven, as we grow and mature, into the fabric of this disproportionate problem we have about sex. I'm not suggesting we swaddle the subject in sepulchral tones of sobriety—healthy humor toward all aspects of our outrageous human situation is vital, and sex itself is inherently joyful—but it's got to be good, clean fun, not the too-typical smirking, shirking from open transparency that turns the topic of good, clean fun into something shameful and uncomfortable. The simple way to steer such an incident into the former, far superior, realm is to have a good, hearty laugh and then embracingly inform the child about the basis of the joke. No child will suffer damage from such inclusion!

But this is not the way we choose to function, and—in this awkward, random, and unintentional way—so goes the more overt distortion of young innocence as the child absorbs the communicated information (*at every level* as children naturally do like little sponges), telling them that sex is an embarrassing topic that must be approached at oblique angles as indirectly and obtusely as possible. And such is the education in how they are to speak about and address the topic among themselves and, eventually, with their own children.

Paint It Black

In 2014, in Fremont, California, heated debates were burning up the pages of newspapers regarding the appropriateness of a certain textbook, *Your Health Today*, issued for the ninth-grade health and sex education classes of the Fremont Unified School District. Hundreds of parents, petitioning to have the book removed, complained that its contents, frequently addressing college kids, are too advanced for ninth graders, that the anatomy drawings are offensive and "not necessary for these children," even that the book itself is *pornographic*. Some were offended that the textbook doesn't adhere to the "cultural values of the community," comprised of a majority Asia and Asia Minor population. Others believed that the kids should be taught that abstinence is the best choice for their sexual health. District officials argued that the students actually need the comprehensive information well before they get to college, that sex is already happening among their freshmen and parents "need to take their blinders off." Touché.

But wait a minute…we're actually still debating whether or not to explicitly educate fourteen- and fifteen-year-old kids about sex?! To quote the *Encyclopedia Britannica*, puberty "usually occurs between ages eleven and sixteen," generally *peaking* at twelve in girls and fourteen in boys; we're already way overdue here. By the ninth grade, almost all girls have grown their breasts and are regularly menstruating and ovulating. Boys have begun producing sperm and ejaculating fully viable semen. Hormones have been seriously raging through their developing bodies for several years now, profoundly *enhancing* their deepest sensations, thoughts, and emotions and directly motivating their actions. (Note my emphasis on *enhancing*, since the person as a human being has been experiencing a sexual existence all along, much to our holy fucking chagrin.)

The bottom line is that all the prudish insanity around the subject of sex education is obviously not for the children's sake.

It has been conclusively proven in study after study that the efforts to destroy comprehensive sex education, ultimately striving to prevent kids from having sex, *doesn't* work. They who are doing this do not want to remove or even mitigate any negative consequences of "unauthorized" sex (i.e., disease, teen pregnancy), but instead want to *increase* those risks and dangers, because they so desperately want to discourage promiscuity on moral grounds. (Widespread use of the remarkable drug Gardasil, which protects young men and women with a 90% success rate against HPV,[11] a virus linked directly to can-

---

[11] In girls and women ages nine to twenty-six, Gardasil 9 protects against the seven types of HPV that cause about 90% of HPV-related cervical and vulvar cancer cases, and about 85% of HPV-related vaginal cancer cases. In males and females, Gardasil 9 protects against the seven types of HPV that cause about 90% of HPV-related anal cancer cases and the two types that cause about 90%

cer, has been successfully thwarted for this reason.) So what we're all getting as a result is actually a much more aggravated problem: more kids who are suffering more consequences due to lack of information, lack of protection, and lack of support.

In fact, the very people who keep insisting on the same failed strategy *have* this conclusive proof of its failure because it has, in many cases, been proven *by their own* studies. It seems that in spite of their lack of success in scaring kids out of having sex, they are self-righteously fueled by an indignant (practically outright malicious) satisfaction that more people are at least suffering negative consequences—a shameless revel in a disaster of their own design.[12]

So, no, it is certainly not for the children's sake. It is as Marty Klein says in his unflinching book *America's War on Sex*: "The battle over sex education…isn't about what's safe and healthy for the children. It's about what's comfortable (and politically advantageous) for the adults. In the War on Sex, children are cannon fodder. The welfare of our children is being sacrificed so that adults can sleep better at night. It is, of course, supposed to be the other way around."[13]

---

of HPV-related genital warts cases. (There are forty genital HPV types altogether; types 6, 11, 16, 18, 31, 33, 45, 52, and 58 cause the majority of HPV-related cancers and diseases) (www.gardasil9.com).

An assessment (through peer-reviewed articles on observational studies from 2007 to 2016) of the global effect of quadrivalent HPV (4vHPV) vaccination on HPV infection and disease shows "maximal reductions" of approximately 90% for HPV 6, 11, 16, 18 infection, 90% for genital warts, 45% for low-grade cytological cervical abnormalities, and 85% for high-grade histologically proven cervical abnormalities (Oxford Academic) (academic.oup.com).

[12] Dr. Wilhelm Reich articulates it very clearly: "Healthy children show a natural spontaneous sexuality. Sick children show an unnatural, that is, perverse sexuality. The alternative with which we are confronted in the matter of sexual education is thus not: *sexuality* or *abstinence*; but: *natural and healthy*, or *perverse and neurotic sexual life*." *The Discovery of the Orgone: The Function of the Orgasm*, translated from German by Theodore P. Wolfe (New York: The Noonday Press, 1942, 1948, 1961), 203.

[13] Marty Klein, *America's War on Sex: The Continuing Attack on Law, Lust, and Liberty*, 2nd ed. (Santa Barbara, CA: Praeger, 2012), 7.

In Michael Moore's movie *Where to Invade Next*,[14] he films a teacher in France speaking about *how to be good lovers* to the expectant faces of rosy young innocence seated in her classroom. She describes to them how to respect and honor one another's sexual experience, attending mindfully to their pleasure and well-being (of course, I immediately reflect on the nature of my own freshman course, its clinical presentation of anatomy and overwhelming preoccupation with disease). When Moore interrupts the teacher's compassionate discourse with the question, "Why not teach them abstinence?" she stops short, obviously stunned by the absurdity of the question coming from another adult. After a moment's incredulous pause, she bluntly admonishes, "Because that's too dangerous."

The infliction of sexual ignorance, either deliberately or mindlessly, upon children and adolescents is abusive.

In any cultural context, it is abuse. In India, where conservative groups (like those in the US) fight against sex education in schools, a government survey showed that only a fifth of young adults have received any type of sex education whatsoever.

There, the massive job pours into the hands of advice columnists in popular publications. These are the people who step in to combat the shocking sexual ignorance bred out of a culture rife with sexual prohibitions based on a history combining Victorian (from the British Raj), Muslim, and Hindu influences. These writers field questions from people (adults) wondering about the most basic of things, such as if pregnancy may be caused by masturbating together, if a man can get pregnant by anal sex, whether masturbating causes disease, and so forth.

Ninety-year-old Dr. Mahinder Watsa, with nine years into writing his column, Ask the Sexpert, in the *Mumbai Mirror* (the first daily newspaper in India to contain such a section), said, "They don't have much choice."[15]

Ignorance is not innocence, and innocence is not naivety. Sexual innocence is the freedom from guilt and shame around healthy, nat-

---

[14] Michael Moore, *Where to Invade Next,* 2016.

[15] Barry, *New York Times*, August 9, 2014.

ural processes and impulses, and only this kind of freedom, *coupled* with informed understanding, allows a person—throughout life—to make intelligent, responsible, and healthy sexual choices. I emphasize *coupled* in that last sentence since the effective application of the factual knowledge requires a healthy attitudinal construct within which to happen. With insight based upon his American studies of male sexuality, Dr. Alfred Kinsey stated, "The so-called sex instruction which is given by parents and schools usually consists of a certain amount of information concerning the anatomy and mechanics of reproduction. As far as our present information goes, this has a minimum of effect upon the development of patterns of sex behavior and, indeed, it may have no effect at all. *Patterns of behavior are the products of attitudes, and attitudes may begin shaping long before the child has acquired very much, if any, factual information*"[16] (italics mine).

Just as birds and other animals are known to imprint (socially and sexually) on the parental entities present upon their arrival into the world, humans have their own psychological mechanisms of imprinting upon contact with various impressions. Since humans have an extended juvenile development, the period of time during which the child is subject to such imprints ("impressionable") is therefore extended. When and upon what the child imprints is a pretty random and chaotic affair, something that cannot be controlled, only—hopefully—modulated to some degree by the more stable aspects of their environment. These imprints will be the guiding force subconsciously shaping the development of subsequent behavior and attitudes throughout their lifetime.

This force will continue, largely unaltered, throughout adulthood unless brought to the surface of conscious awareness and subjected to the rigors of deliberate effort to do so. (Be clear, we're talking about treating an infection everyone's bent over backward to incubate. Adults must work on curing their own disease in order to prevent passing that disease along to their children, and to reverse

---

[16] Albert Deutsch, "The Sex Habits of American Men: Some Findings of the Kinsey Report," *Harper's Magazine*, December, 1947.

the old adage, it probably requires about a pound of cure to get that ounce of prevention.) At this point, in order to reverse the direction of this mighty force, *information* is the first rudimentary requirement necessary before beginning to approach the deeper layers of the troubled construct of sexuality.

Sexual information disseminated to children is a threat only to parents who are ill-equipped, and ill-inclined, to answer the questions it may stimulate in their kids. And it is only *potentially* a threat to kids who are not provided with a milieu that nurtures and supports their own sexual existence, *although it is probably much more likely to be a tremendous boon to these children*, even under such circumstances.

Either way, it's a parent's job to educate, guide, and support their child throughout development, the most deeply significant and thoroughly pervasive aspect of which is sexual. In fact, sexuality is so central to humanity I would conclude that well-rounded sexual information for children is as critical to healthy development as proper nutrition.

American Girl (Ball of Confusion!)

My own journey through female adolescence was mostly uninformed and unsupported, and this I attribute largely to my mother's discomfort with her own femininity. Thankfully, she had not held to any illusions of holy purity or blessed virginity. Nevertheless, having cultivated no sense of compassionate or nurturing acceptance toward her own female form, she was prevented from extending that supportive hand to her daughters.

Whereas my sister (at the very least) had her Judy Blume and Sweet Valley High books as background reference for girls her age, as well as a cadre of girlfriends for support, I, as a somewhat solitary "tomboy," had my Jim Kjelgaard dog stories and First Blood Rambo series going on—not so very handy in the female puberty department.

All through adolescence (and well into adulthood) I was very ashamed of my sexuality and my changing body. At age twelve, I wanted to deny the fact that I was beginning to develop breasts. A sixth-grade acquaintance privately approached me, kindly telling me that I needed to start wearing a bra. Mortified but compliant, I reluctantly purchased one—and wore it—but I didn't know which was more embarrassing: little swelling nipple buds showing through my knit shirt or having a visible bra line. I remember the shopping experience with my mother and grandmother, and honestly, I can't imagine I would have felt any more alienated embarrassment had I been a twelve-year-old boy forced to go shopping for brassieres.

I resented my body for putting me through this; there was absolutely no joy or excitement involved in my pubescent development. I wanted to stay like the little boys. The future looked even grimmer because I had heard things about periods where you bled through your crotch, and I had the impression that I would be bleeding all the time and was sure I would have to give up all the activities I enjoyed such as swimming and horseback riding.

My fear of the whole affair enormously impaired my cognitive process, and the translation from textbook knowledge to my subjective body was lost in a vortex of silent panic. I should have deduced from observations of the females around me (hello!) that my ideas were distorted. I could have asked questions, but my shame was too overpowering. I think mostly the issue was having no idea how *I* would handle it myself because the practicalities of it were completely inconceivable to me. Like my whole worldview at the time (that everyone else knew exactly what was going on except me), my inmost sense was that I was doomed to grope my way, alone, through the endless tunnel of uncertainty. Yikes.

The worst imaginable scenario was to have an accident at school where you bled through your clothing—"nature loves her little surprises"—and young women new to the process and not yet tuned into their cyclical rhythm frequently find themselves in just such a situation. I'd seen it happen to some poor girls, and the abuse was brutal. The boys made horribly condescending remarks, and the other girls were so glad it wasn't them that they, too, chimed in. I just watched in horror and approached menstruation with dread.

At age fourteen, when I did start bleeding, I wanted to use tampons to minimize the "mess" and the infuriating discomfort of wearing what felt to me like a diaper. I locked myself in the bathroom at home and got out one of my mother's austere little OB tampons. I was terrified of putting something into my vagina and squeamish about having to poke around in the general area with my fingers. First of all, not knowing subjectively exactly where it was located, *having never seen it or touched it*, I feared putting the tampon into the wrong hole. Secondly, I thought once I got it in there that it might just keep migrating deeper and deeper inside my entrails and get irretrievably lost (surely that string couldn't possibly be long enough!). The last thing I wanted to have to do was ask for help, and subject myself to such insufferable humiliation. Using a hand mirror, I desperately figured it out, all the while in a cold sweat, feeling wretchedly nervous, disgusted, and ashamed, afraid of being "caught" as if I were doing something I really should not be doing.

The whole experience confirmed the suspicion that my mature female anatomy was just a smelly, messy, and embarrassing corpus. Not something to be proud of. I certainly couldn't fathom, for the life of me, how a boy could have any interest in being involved with it without some kind of elaborate sterilization procedure beforehand.

My experience, unfortunately, rather than being isolated and unique, is actually located well within the bell-curve norm. For me, it cut a deep channel in my being that I have spent most of my adult life working to fill in for a seamless, healthy attitude toward my body, my sexuality, and my inmost relationship with myself. I can only imagine how a more supportive environment may have altered my own life and that of so many others. (Author Naomi Wolf, in response to reading the ornately affectionate language honoring female sexual anatomy in ancient Chinese educational "pornography," commented in *Promiscuities*, "Just imagine how differently a young girl today might feel about her developing womanhood if every routine slang description she heard of female genitalia used metaphors of preciousness and beauty.")[17] I can only visualize the increased well

---

[17] Jonathan Margolis, *O: The Intimate History of the Orgasm* (New York, NY: Grove Press, 2004), 187.

being of humanity fostered by generations coming of age in a bona fide sex-positive environment.

Mr. Mojo Risin'

While girls encounter the more generally demeaning and derogatory messages (with the weightiest historical reinforcements) about their shameful, unclean anatomy and physiology, boys and girls are both socialized in a culture plagued by the syndrome of sexual stupidity.

So, even though males are cultured for more personal pride in their phallic endowment—its power and its cleanliness—the social interface offers a painful twist of fortune. For males, an analogous issue to the menstrual accident is the disgrace of finding themselves with an untimely erection. And, of course, this distressing scenario can occur at any moment 24-7, any given time of the month. There is so little training in sexual intelligence that boys are made to feel as though they are guilty of some heinous offense. Obviously, that offense is having "inappropriate" thoughts and motives—and something that they "ought" to be in control of—even though the behavior of the penis often (or perhaps usually) has nothing whatsoever to do with anything conscious or cerebral.

Girls learn that boys are sexually vulgar and predatory, and so witnessing their counterparts in this infelicitous moment of delinquent bodily function can be confirmation of that fact in their minds. An "inappropriately" erect penis can instantly conjure up the anger and resentment that stem from underlying anxieties about male sexual aggression, as well as the nasty social ridicule that kids enact when confronted with the awkwardness instilled into them around sexuality.

Knowing this, in sheer terror, the boy can feel as though this momentary ungovernable instant is a death sentence to his social and therefore sexual existence. This inculcation of guilt for his overt sexual responses follows a man throughout his life as the women around him continue to carry their ingrained beliefs, fears, and judgments about men into adulthood.

A friend of about my age recently discussed an experience he had at a dance class. After a session of contact improvisation with an attractive female, he suddenly became aware that he was sporting a plucky (oh-so-unlucky) erection, and not only that, a visible wet spot on his pants revealed the further extent of his pre-ejaculatory arousal. This grown man's description of the shame, horror, and anguish that he experienced as a result of this incident (abusing himself with the social admonitions of his training) distressed me to tears.

Mama Weer All Crazy Now

One woman has her work cut out for her. Bat Sheva Marcus is an Orthodox Jewish sex counselor who helps struggling wives smoke out their elusive sexual desire.[18] With a doctorate in human sexuality (and described as "an Einstein of our days" by the rabbis who discretely send her patients), Marcus counsels Orthodox women unable to get sexy in their marriages due to, literally, apocalypse-proportioned fears.

She guides these women to reconnect with bodily sensation through *memories* (perhaps like my own memory with the doll)—memories they may have never even recognized as sexual. Their vague memories are often all that remain tenuously within reach after the utter obliteration of their natural erotic impulses through a tradition that saddles women with the trivial task of preventing cosmic cataclysm by assiduously guarding their own physical modesty and sexual chastity. In spite of this inordinate social burden, some heroic women successfully recover a modicum of sexual functionality, others do not. Though they are *told* they should suddenly discover divine sexual rapture once married to a man they may hardly know, this tidbit somehow just doesn't manage to deliver the godly goods.

The hokey notion that we can squelch sexuality throughout development and then expect it, miraculously, to blossom into tran-

---

18 Daniel Bergner, "Flesh of My Flesh: The Sex Guru Who Tries to Help Orthodox Women Find Pleasure—Without Breaking the (Talmudic) Law," *New York Times*, January 25, 2015.

scendent heavenly glory as soon as we tie the knot is as good an example as any of complete ignorant delusion about sex, nature, and human psychology. (It doesn't *really* take a genius of theoretical physics to figure this out.)

But this kind of superstition is not limited to the realm of strictly orthodox religious sects. Klein describes a watered-down version being thrust upon American children through the nation's abstinence movement (which has infiltrated to an alarming extent the public and private educational system) teaching kids to fear sex as a ruinous force to their present and future lives that is somehow all supposed to change on their wedding night. He says the abstinence project transforms eroticism from a normal part of life into an estranged enemy and quotes sex educator Sol Gordon saying sarcastically, "Sex is dirty—save it for someone you love."[19]

This crackpot strategy lays the foundation for considerable social strife. With our most essential living feature—at the root of our social humanity—twisted so badly out of shape, how can we possibly get along famously? I will not mince my words: to love and to honor one another, we first have to know and honor ourselves, which is thoroughly impossible if our only view of sex is askance and askew.

While girls are clobbered by misogynistic messages about their femininity, boys endure their own difficulties coming of age, and then they must contend with girls who are probably screwed up even worse than they are (not to mention the snakepit many gay teenagers still have to navigate). The confusion of adolescence brought on by the hormonal cyclone is compounded by our culture's neurotic delusions around sex, and as a result, the possibility of salvaging any scrap of innocence through the foray into sexual activity is almost completely obliterated.

In spite of all the strutting around and bloviating about the innocence of our poor children, we continue carrying and propagating the most crippling contagion. By not cleaning up our own individual and collective affliction, we *all* end up being the worst perpetrators of sexual abuse. There may not exist a more sweeping offense

---

[19] Klein, 11.

to innocence than the way we continue subjecting our youth to the unnecessary angst, shame, ignorance, confusion, and fear around sex and sexual development that results from our own avoidance of the problem at the deepest personal levels.

And, since sexuality forms the core of our person and our social existence, shaping internal well-being and outward relationships, this becomes a psychological wrecking ball, rolling through time, wreaking havoc on all fronts of our human relations. We really underestimate and downplay the size of it all, and we have to stop fooling ourselves. Until we seriously heal ourselves and sort out this rampant sexual catastrophe, we stand in no position to serve or protect the children.

LIKE A VIRGIN

Early in my freshman year of high school, 1985, I played in the school marching band. Our lead drummer was a tall and lanky sophomore, with a shoulder-length tousle of a blond mullet floating around a sweet, clear-skinned face. He wore torn Levi's and heavy-metal T-shirts, smoked pot and cigarettes, partied heavily, and was generally gregarious, rebellious, and obnoxious—just like I liked them. I couldn't have been more dissimilar: quiet, shy, and solitary, sighing romantically into my flute.

But he thrilled me. I was totally smitten, and he didn't know I existed…or so I thought. Much to my disbelief, on one of our marching band trips, he noticed me (I must have been a bomb, wearing a giant Q-tip on my head) and began making some moves in my direction. I had no idea what to do about it, could barely even speak to him, and I will never forget the bus ride home that night. We sat together in the dark, and he rested his head in my lap. Dizzy with delight, I was beside myself with the buzz of sheer sensual rapture as I felt the softness of his hair and traced the outline of his cheek and ear with my fingers. The intensity of that pleasure was almost more than I could bear, as my whole body bubbled, surged, and melted in a hot stew of steaming hormones. We didn't say much to each other, and I wouldn't go home with him that night.

The next day at school he wanted nothing to do with me, and I asked his friend, the drum major, what was going on. He said his friend had told him, "She's hot, but she doesn't put out."

I had just had the most erotic experience of my life, and it simply didn't register on his radar. Our worlds were far more disparate even than they appeared: I needed something seriously muted, moving in slow motion, just to filter and process the noise, while he was running in a blaze of thunder, seeking to amplify the reverb.

That kind of arousal that I remember feeling in my fingertips, though, igniting the circuits of electric vitality and the wonder of discovery, that is what I think of as pure virginity, something that is merely *virginal*—new and fresh in every way, unadulterated and unobstructed. But the modern cultural notion of sexual virginity, and all its attendant fuss, is a monstrous load of drivel that our minds have been marinating in for quite some time.

Sweet Cherry Pie

Etymologically, the original Latin word *virgin* meant "maiden" or "unmarried woman." Historically, the translation of *unmarried woman* into "one who has not had sexual intercourse" would not have been a great leap. As patriarchal civilization settled and advanced, virginity of the penis-in-vagina kind had to be preserved in women for marriage so that there could be no mistaking whose property she was and whose children she would soon be having. This had tremendous value to males as a means of measuring ownership for the passing down of lineage and wealth, and it still holds great meaning—both literally and symbolically—in most regions throughout the world.

Female virginity is so important in many Asian, Arab, and Latino cultures that hymen reconstruction is a common medical procedure allowing women to fake virginity at the moment of consummation. Hymen reconstruction, hymen repair, hymenoplasty, and revirgination are all synonymous in the virginity industry. The "Hymen Shop" advertises the sale of "artificial hymen repair kits," or "artificial virginity kits,"[20] containing elastic products filled with fake

---

[20] These kits are also known as Chinese hymens due to the location of leading manufacturers. In China, in order to protect their "virginity" and its symbolic seal of freshness, most women will not use tampons. In fact, until just very recently, tampons were not even available for purchase.

As an aside, the 2016 Olympic games became something of an exposé on this issue when China's competing swimmer, Fu Yuanhui, spoke to the media

blood that can be fitted into the vaginal canal. *"Restore your virginity in five minutes,"* they say, *"with this new technologically advanced product! Kiss your deep dark secret goodbye and marry in confidence!"*[21]

The cultural tradition of spilling the virgin bride's blood onto the sheets on the couple's wedding night is so deeply engrained that many Muslim women will consider suicide before revealing that they have had (*dirty, rotten, filthy, stinkin'*)[22] premarital coitus. "It may be the 21st Century but the issue of virginity in Arab culture can still be a matter of life and death," say the authors of an article on the topic. Sex outside marriage is a taboo that, if discovered, may cause a woman to be "ostracized by her community, or even murdered."[23] What I would like to know is what happens to the 44% of women who will naturally lose no blood at all during their first vaginal penetration (a biological statistic, which includes myself)?[24]

Even in the modern United States, deeply identified as we are with proprietorship in general and infused with the proud Christian ethos, the notion of virginity holds sway. Currently, the importance of virginity vigorously promulgated primarily by ultra-right-wing ideological groups in the US receives copious attention, funding[25] and propaganda. These programs, in their attempt to circumvent the controversial problem of comprehensive sex education, push to bring more high school teenagers, by pledging their virginity, into the abstinence-until-marriage commitment. They emphasize that "sexual activity outside of marriage may have harmful psychological

---

    about being on her period the day of her competition, which created quite a sensation, since the public discussion of menstruation is taboo in China (Emily Feng, *New York Times*, Bio, August 16, 2016).

21 www.hymenshop.com.

22 Warrant, "Cherry Pie," Columbia, 1990.

23 Najlaa Abou Mehri and Linda Sills, "The Virginity Industry," BBC Radio 4, Crossing Continents, news.bbc.co.uk/2/hi/middle_east/8641099.stm.

24 Another source claims the number of women who do not bleed at first intercourse is closer to 75% (quoted in "The Straight Dope" by Cecil Adams, San Jose Mercury—News, August 27–September 2, 2014).

25 Since 1996, over $1.5 billion of taxpayer money has been dedicated to abstinence programs used to promote fundamentalist Christianity in public schools. Advocatesforyouth.org, 2014.

and physical effects" while, as I pointed out earlier, ardently striving to actually increase the occurrence *and* the magnitude of those harmful effects just to amplify the fear factor and enhance the scare tactic that they already know doesn't work. All this, at the expense of human welfare, is done in the name of preserving the edicts of a tradition built upon the idea of a loving and merciful god, no less.

Brilliant Disguise

Apart from the brassy vocal minority comprising the fundamentalist factions (data show that the chastity charade *does not* reflect the values of most Americans even though massive programs have been pushed through congress[26]), the idea of preserving one's virginity has morphed within slightly more liberal modern minds. In this context, it becomes simply a precious, emotionally meaningful (rather than religious) thing to be saved, particularly—and significantly—by females, not necessarily for marriage but for the moment when *true love* permits the deed.

For the growing nonfundamentalist populace, woman's libido can still be nicely steered toward convention by teaching her to translate the desire in her loins into the romantic language of the heart—all this being put into place before she's even learned to speak, much less sexually matured. The messages are literally *everywhere* in our culture, so all-pervading that it's difficult *not* to credulously accept the narrative as a true-blue fact of life. And because this education is so deep and thorough, she falls right in without even batting an eyelash. Pretty slick.

I was *all aboard* the Lust-as-Love Boat as I came into my sexually mature condition, and I can't blame my parents for that. They never demonstrated or touted romance as any big fancy deal. In fact, I remember asking my mother about the dawning of her relationship with my father—eagerly anticipating the chronicles of starry-eyed romance—and my crestfallen disappointment at her totally prag-

---

[26] advocatesforyouth.org, 2014.

matic perspective on choosing her mate. No, I'd easily and imperceptibly picked up these ideas from the world at large and taken them directly to heart, now waiting for that perfect soul mate to sweep me off my feet and deflower my cherries, or however that goes, and devoting so much headspace toward developing that delicious daydream of true love and sexual enchantment.

…It was always a crowded room when I saw him. Across a sea of meaningless faces, I watched, powerfully moved by his natural grace and beauty. A diamond in the coal mine. I would watch, riveted, until his deep, warm eyes found my own in a moment filled with irresistible recognition and passionate attraction. With our eyes locked in a gaze that penetrated through to the depths of my being, the immense gravity of our instinctive intimacy would draw our bodies magnetically close, fusing us into a heated embrace that dissolved every cell in sensual pleasure. The End. Uh, rewind. Replay. Repeat. Ad nauseum…

My simple but deeply absorbing fantasies took me far, far, far from the reality at hand, inventing a just-so world of romantic rapture that allowed me to revel in a self-induced stupor of isolated bliss. Some of this is just the nature of pitiful adolescence, I am aware of that, but there is a greater societal daydream that feeds into a much deeper belief system, which inflates it beyond mere entertainment value. Although I did have real-life experiences, there was always that part of me holding out for the *real deal*—that existed only in my mind.

Now this education of females may seem, at first blush, to be relatively benign. Believe me—it most certainly is not.

It has, in fact, manufactured a monster. And this is the monstrous confusion that plagues the majority of us women. By translating lust as love—or sex as emotion—a woman's relationship with her body, *and ultimately reality itself,* is under siege. It's very important to understand this. This is why women are "crazy." It's because we have been taught fantasyland instead of fact, and because of the nature of sexuality, that goes as deep as things can go.

A woman misguided in this way, robbed of her body, robbed of her connection with reality, is robbed of her power, period. Even modern sex therapists, teachers, and authors presuppose women's need for romantic attention and "extras," such as doting gifts showing loving devotion.[27] This is childish, and it not only overlooks the bottom line but also feeds into the whole fantasy rooted in sexual insecurity and disempowerment, thus encouraging the perpetuation of the whole half-baked story.

We'd better heed the Boss, *look hard and look twice*[28] at these ideas, because although it seemed so brilliant in the beginning, I see evidence that this thing is not working out so well—for anyone.

Here Comes My Girl...

Being the late bloomer that I was, it would be several years in the offing before my sappy fantasies could be fleshed out to their naturally limited extent. In the meantime, though, I had a girlfriend, and she had a bathtub. Tomi was a year older but still in my grade. Pretty and voluptuous, self-assured and adventurous, she was more like a big sister than a peer, and I was beneficiary to her wisdom and generosity during our senior year in high school, when her friends had all graduated and left town.

At some point in my demented development, I had sworn myself off masturbation before even trying it. I don't remember exactly when it was on the timeline—somewhere early on in high school—but I remember the moment itself in vivid detail. I was writhing on the floor of my bedroom with intense desire in my gen-

---

[27] Just recently, at an interactive performance-art piece, I was blown away to hear women in the audience claiming that it turns them on when hubby does the dishes or takes out the trash. Come on! Scientific research actually indicates that this is not the kind of eroticism that genuinely fosters vaginal stimulation. This is something fabricated elsewhere! And it indicates how badly out of sorts we are that we need researchers to shed light on an area where every woman ought to be the expert.

[28] Bruce Springteen, "Brilliant Disguise," track 2 on *Tunnel of Love*, Columbia, 1987, 12-inch LP.

itals, a demanding and agonizing heat. I found myself fantasizing about what kinds of objects I could insert into my vagina (thanks to the tampon tribulations, I now knew how to access it) that might provide some degree of satisfaction and relief. My visions wandered into the kitchen (a veritable mecca of utensils) and then toward the refrigerator, locating some attractive phallic objects of the vegetable variety…The more I imagined it, the more my desire began to motivate my limbs to rise in order to manifest the vision…but suddenly I stopped short. A moment of supreme conscience—the kind that would cause the pope to rejoice—overcame me in waves of shame and horror at the offense I was about to commit. I heard the voices of some boys at school echoing in my head, vehement accusations of each other "Masturbating!" as though it were the most mortifying and scathing indictment to be cast upon a fellow human being. God forbid that by my own private actions I should earn such a scorn. And, if it was that dreadful for boys, how much worse for a girl!

This was the milieu that was in place in a small-town public school in the late 1980s, and represents part of that vast and intricate, continually morphing network of societal reinforcement hard at work, ensuring that we have just enough of the right stimuli surrounding and influencing our moral conscience in just the right manner for just the right occasion. What a success story. What a shame.[29]

But Tomi came to my rescue. She took me to her bathroom, instructing me precisely how to recline in the bathtub with my feet up on the ledges so that the water fell from the faucet in just the right spot between my legs. That afternoon I discovered the orgasmic clitoris. How exquisitely I remember that shiny room and that glorious

---

[29] And the enormity of the shame of it cannot be underestimated. I clearly remember one of the boys whose voice, in particular, stood out from the chorus—and I feel obligated to point out, in order to emphasize the magnitude of the tragedy, that he later committed suicide. None of us knew it back then, but he was gay. Now, I cannot say with certainty that his suicide was due *specifically* to being unable to come to terms with his own inauspicious sexuality, but what I will say—with full confidence—is that his inner torment, reflected by the brutal shaming of his peers, must have been dreadfully exacerbated by the hostile environment in which he was forced to sexually mature as a young homosexual.

stream…and my friend, too, who stayed in the room as I requested, being as I was apprehensive about my new adventure.[30]

The time between my freshman-year boyfriend and my rockin' new girlfriend had felt like eons of darkness, and I'd gradually built a near-impenetrable fortress around my sexuality. My only friend had moved away, leaving me painfully and conspicuously isolated, and I drew no attention from any remotely interesting boys. I'd spiraled down into an abysmal self-loathing, fully convinced that, among other things, I was not the least bit sexually appealing. From the depths of this dismal perspective, I generated an ardent disdain and disgust for even my own sexual desires.

As an outlet, I had graduated musically from flute to saxophone through which, when I wasn't dutifully playing in the various school bands, I passionately channeled my pent-up frustrations. In this hot secret life, I was a man fucking the glistening curvaceous lady, filling her with my fevered breath, wetting her inside and making her moan, scream, and shudder, hanging from my neck, until we were both spent—breathless and silent. It was a communion that appeased me sexually and emotionally. I wrote her erotic love poems and played, most preferably, in empty churches, where the acoustics were phenomenal and the profanity of my worship was most gratifying.

But thankfully, with the playful guidance of my new friend, things began to change. I began to tentatively emerge from my shell and channel my sexual energy in a more healthy, less solitary way.

Closely following high school, I spent time with her and her boyfriend, who were both very sensual and inclusive. She was lovely and he, about ten years older than us, was tall and lean and exquisitely muscled. And we danced! Erotic and unrestrained, the dancing was a glimpse and a taste of freedom to come, a raw expression of ourselves and our responses to one another. I was still very reserved but gradually opening to places in my being that I'd shut tightly. The

---

[30] I realized with astonishment, however, that I'd already encountered the mythical orgasm quite some time ago without even knowing it…as the euphoric sensations I'd experienced doing certain fitness exercises in junior high PE classes!

love, the encouragement, the feisty fun, and the music all helped me begin to move more freely.

Train in Vain

Later on, when I was a freshman in college, he came to see me. Tomi, in her juicy magnanimity, had always wanted me to lose my virginity to him, celebrating his tender virtues, skillful experience, and physical endowments. When he arrived, I didn't need cajoling to find myself moving in that direction, as I found him intensely desirable.

At the motel, we soaked in the steamy Jacuzzi. He massaged my feet, legs, and thighs and told me I was sexy. This astounded me to no end. Even though he had said this many times before when the three of us were hanging out, I actually never took him seriously until we were in a setting where the intention behind it was undeniably clear: I wasn't just an auxiliary afterthought tagging along with my beautiful friend. I was *the* object of his attention. This time his statement made an impact, permeating my flesh, and I suddenly *felt* very attractive, which was an entirely new and utterly miraculous sensation.

Back in the room we showered and rolled around in the bed for a very long time. I had never been naked like this with a guy before, and the thrill and the wonder of his body and mine, and the crazy intrigue of the unknown, all swirled intoxicatingly through me. For the first time I experienced myself as an open sexual being—a legitimate and desirable sexual entity.

He handled my body exquisitely, with just the right combination of grace and power, like the skilled dancer that he was, so that having sex actually felt totally natural to me. With his tongue and fingers bringing me to multiple orgasms, we climbed the crescendo of pleasure and then, just before sliding his beautiful cock into my vagina, he hesitated, in honor of my virginity, to ask if I was sure this was what I wanted.

Well, that was unfortunate—supremely selfless and considerate, and exactly what a truly decent person would do—but very unfortunate in the scheme of things. Immediately, my mind began the idiotic chatter about being *in love* and saving my hallowed virginity for that special one, and so it went…In one unutterable instant, I tumbled down the shimmering stairway to heaven, splattering onto the overbaked asphalt of that highway to hell leading straight back into my own personal prison. My entire sumptuous being retreated from its joyful abandon of frolicking through the flesh to inhabit yet again the cramped, squirming confines of my skull. Once there, I was good as gone—just a hapless rat stuck running that same old maze. By god, I stuffed that genie right back into the bottle, and in the wink of an eye, the infinite possibilities of the splendid universe of reality were swallowed by an imaginary toad promising to one day become a prince.

I was blinded, completely blinded, to the special gift of the one before me (or on top of me), and I robbed myself of the opportunity to dispel that burdensome and childish myth with a mature man who was truly capable of honoring the occasion and the sensitivities involved in it. I was too ignorantly distorted, both in my view of myself and in my perspective on sex, to make the appropriate choice. (I could just say I was too young to know any better, but I don't believe that. Youth can be much better equipped and intelligent if properly educated.)

"No," I said. I wasn't in love, so *of course* it couldn't be what I wanted, even though it was absolutely(!) what I wanted in every cell of my body—below my neck. We stopped having sex, held each other the rest of the night, and I left at dawn.

In spite of the blunder of not just doing it like Nike and dispelling the delusion, after that night I felt like I had been set free. And I was—thanks to being initiated into my own erotic existence—although there was so, so much more to come.

Have a Cigar

As it turned out, later that year I fell in love with a musician, the keyboardist in our jazz and wind ensembles. It was "love at first sight" for me. He wasn't an impressively handsome figure, by any stretch (think Dudley Moore in the movie *Arthur*), but I liked the way he carried himself, erect and self-assured, with an animated humor about him. He laughed with his whole being, and his eyes sparkled with lively wit. We became great friends and loved each other intensely…in our own ways, of course. He frequently did not treat me with the greatest respect, mostly out of a lack of maturity and self-worth—and because of my own lack of that good stuff, I allowed for it.

But I was so in love, and we had penis-in-vagina sex on my twentieth birthday. He was a good size for me, not too big or too small. It wasn't painful (and there was no blood to christen the sheets), but I could not handle more than about two penetrations before my vagina felt very exhausted, like a tired aching muscle, so that was it. We subsequently had a lot more intercourse, and I really enjoyed it.

But what, truly, did I get for saving my virgin vagina for him? Well, I guess I never really gave it much intelligent thought after the event itself—but that's the way these things are; you're not really supposed to ask that question. If you continue to buy into the moral fantasy, you can revel in the self-satisfaction of recalling the story over and over again, for years to come, congratulating yourself on the very fact that you saved yourself for *true love* and overlooking the very real yet altogether mundane factual details…which is exactly what I did for a period of time.

But frankly, reflecting on it now, it didn't seem to really mean that much to either of us. Apart from this highly overrated and dramatized idea that had nothing to do with anything in the real world, it was of absolutely no consequence. Besides, eventually we do grow up and realize that a teenager's vision of "true love" has to be the most hysterical distortion known to mankind.

After a year with him, reveling in being in love, his self-destructive habits drove me to distance myself, and I needed to get out. Disillusioned with my love and my major (and staggering fears of burdensome financial debt), I left school and I left him, and I got a job on a tour boat.

Vive L'Amour

I still continued to hold back sexually, however, lingering nostalgically over my first love with cherished notions smothered in romantic attachment. I wasn't the kind of girl who *just had sex*, after all. Even after a good modern girl has lost her virginity (did it fall out in the toilet?), she still has to maintain some modicum of decency by being choosy and sparing in her behavior, which is easy when a woman is trained so well to identify her sexuality with her emotions. Too loose and she is a slut, and everybody knows that's just trash. Generally, women resent and spit on that, and men don't respect or trust it either. Sure, they'll use it and throw it away, but they won't open their arms and welcome it to heart and home, and that's where this is all supposed to be going, ultimately. It still boils down to that same archaic cultural paradigm so deeply embedded in the collective psyche. One man, one woman...that Disney-sparkle bottom line that still defines the powerful undercurrent of the greater world we inhabit.

Besides Tomi's boyfriend, there was another blameless chump burned by the fever of my over-emotionalized sexuality. Bumming on the beaches of Baja California Sur, after working for about a year on the boat, I met the sundog. I had arrived via taxi on the dreamy little beach, Playa Las Palmas, about ten miles south of the small town of Todos Santos, with a disfigured backpack, a cheap sleeping bag, and a sack of groceries.

The first night, stray dogs ate most of my food, and the next day, with no food and no ride to town (1993: no cell phone = no taxi), I wasn't sure exactly what I was going to do. He had watched everything from under the awning of his beachfront living room (this feller had the digs: lawn chairs arranged under a tarp awning in back of his camper, replete with elegant yet utilitarian beach décor—"everything's got a purpose," he would say, adjusting a dried sea fan in front of a candle to disperse the glare).

At forty-two, he was twenty years older than I and a specimen to behold, with a compact, nicely proportioned frame sculpted with well-defined muscles and covered with golden tanned skin. He ambled over—long, curly sun-bleached hair under a straw hat shading his sky-blue laughing-eyed face—and asked me in a strong Cockney-Londoner accent what I intended to do. Well, we solved the problem pretty rapidly right then and there, and I shacked up with him for the rest of my stay.

He spent hours with his head between my legs, and I learned how he liked his hand jobs—with lots of lotion. I found his cock absolutely gorgeous, once I adjusted to the presence of an intact foreskin, and it took both hands to manipulate it fully. I realized in amazement that I really enjoyed my own scent on his face when he kissed me after oral sex, and this was my first acknowledgment that perhaps there was, after all, a reason why men enjoyed going downtown on women!

After Baja, we kept in touch, hanging out together in Oregon and having sex now and then. We only had intercourse a few times, because I had trouble relaxing enough to receive his fulsome length and girth, finding the size of his penis outright overwhelming. The last time we did it, though, I let go. My body relaxed, my vagina opened, and it was truly a rewarding experience for us both. But I was still holding back sexually, and I began to talk to him about not being in love with him (in retrospect, I am sure that was *the* reason I could not let go and literally open to him during intercourse). He said he wasn't in love either but that the sex can be shared and the love can grow over time.

Well, that practical, mature outlook just wasn't quite scintillating enough to keep my dreamy bubble afloat, and I pranced off in search of other things.

In all the time we knew each other, though, he treated me just right. He was an impenitent renegade, a rogue outlaw and—except for a week in the Baja sierra without his cigarettes—a real mensch.

Don't Do Me Like That

It is painful now to reflect on how my confused head (and consequently closed heart) prevented me from fully honoring the sexual experiences that were available to me and giving of myself fully with the people that I should have. I don't know about you, but I feel robbed, looted, swindled and defrauded. And this plundering began way before we even arrived, bequeathing unto us the twisted, wrung-out remains of what should naturally be the most pleasant, innocent, and physically intimate act of joyful abandon on the face of the earth. I think we've all been violated and robbed, and we keep on paying out to the ultimate crime of identity theft perpetrated upon humanity.

Ignorance and a guilty conscience never totally prevent people from having sex; they just ruin the purity and promise of the sex they will eventually and inevitably have. The abstinence-only programs for teenagers have an *88%* failure rate,[31] by the way, neither preventing nor significantly delaying teenage sexual activity and, in addition, negatively impacting the appropriate use of protection. (Although I abstained until age twenty, it did not prevent me from contracting a discrete case of genital warts from my first partner—so much for the assurance of sexual health. Much better to have a comprehensive education, *including how to talk about safe sex*.) For crying out loud, even the church itself can't keep its own devoted clergy in line. Fully *50* percent of Catholic priests are not even practicing celibacy, causing the largest systemic problem of devastating childhood sexual abuse in any institution, worldwide—so much for the assurance of psychological health![32]

Due to the pandemic ignorance about sex caused by the wholesale condemnation of sexuality, kids and adults both just end up doing dumb and dangerous things, and the underlying angst impinges on the mutual honor and respect that are due between partners. (Of course, all the shame, denial, and secrecy around sexually transmitted diseases doesn't help one iota, keeping us from talking about it openly and thus protecting ourselves and one another.) And then,

---

[31] From a Columbia University study of more than 20,000 young virginity pledgers. Klein cites Hannah Bruckner and Peter Bearman, "After the Promise: The STD Consequences of Adolescent Virginity Pledges," *Journal of Adolescent Health* 36, no. 4 (2005): 271–78.

[32] Cited in the 2015 docudrama "Spotlight," directed by Tom McCarthy, about the 2002 exposé of the problem in Boston, Massachusetts.

because the experience itself is degraded a priori, the bad rap against sex is just reinforced and reinvented on a very personal level. And the beat goes on. Under these conditions none of us, not even the sexually uninitiated, remain untouched and undefiled, and therefore who could ever—truly—be *like a virgin*?

As I grew and explored, opened, and learned about sex, I frequently found myself witnessing the situation from the other side, watching my partners flail within themselves, tormented by moral confusion and guilt so much that they couldn't honor the gift that was being offered, or the giver.

From a universal, totally objective perspective, virginity has nothing to do with vaginal intercourse. The definition of it as such, and the supreme "spiritual" significance supposedly behind that definition is a complete fabrication based upon a very particular cultural mind-set. (Some indigenous cultures do not even have an equivalent word for sexual virginity.[33])

Webster's fourth entry for the word *virgin* as an adjective reads, "First or happening for the first time." Sexual virginity, therefore, can actually be found in the bare present moment of contact, almost any contact, if there is enough spaciousness within the being (a.k.a. *innocence*) and attention to the event to allow that quality of freshness to kindle. Virginity isn't just about cherries popped or unpopped, it's about being awake to the discovery of now (like "beginner's mind" in Zen, requiring the absence of all preconceived notions). The moment of now is an eternally breaking wave, always brand spanking new, so "virginity" in this sense is always available. It can be rediscovered, reclaimed, and reborn. It is not lost, just deeply buried, and it often takes radical efforts to recover.

---

[33] Ryan and Jetha, 120.

BORN TO BE WILD

First Flash of Freedom

Some moments in life are forever burnished into my memory in high gloss and technicolor. They tend to be instances when the familiar pattern of life is suddenly scrambled and rearranged, providing a glimpse into the wilderness of possibility.

Scott was my favorite guy at Baker High School. I think he was probably everybody's favorite guy at school, because he was just that kind of guy; he lived life way beyond the confines of the high-school-clique mentality. We became friends our senior year and hung out more intimately after graduation, kissing occasionally, which was always incredibly tender and sweet.

At nineteen, I was still energetically building and ascending the Himalayan heights of garbage in my head about guys and sex, and frankly, his intelligence was intimidating to me. But he was exceptionally kind and receptive to me, and one evening, driving back to Oregon from Boise, Idaho, something about the music on the tape deck reached out of the darkness, grabbing me by the gonads, and I aggressively attacked him in a spontaneous outburst, kissing him passionately.

I'm still not sure how he succeeded in responding so skillfully, managing the sudden surprise, reciprocating a delicious kiss and staying on the road. But fortunately he did so, and when I settled back into my seat, he asked me what had happened. I said I wasn't exactly sure, but for a moment I felt very powerful… and I remember feeling slightly ashamed saying that, afraid he might misinterpret my action as one of manipulation or of toying with him.

But that wasn't at all what was going on for me. The power I was feeling was the result of a moment where the lid of suppression I'd held over my sexual responses and behaviors shifted sideways—thanks to the music, the darkness, and a slurry of other small things—and the force underneath it rushed out directly toward the object of stimulation, allowing me to have a direct expression, unquestioned, undistorted, and unfiltered.

Of course, I had no way of making this interpretation at the time. I just knew it felt pretty amazing, and I was supremely grateful to him for receiving it so well. At the time, it was just a random and momentary glimpse through a window I could not yet understand in a wall I could not yet perceive.

Several years would have to pass before I began, with much discomfort and uncertainty, surprise and delight, to learn about who I actually was sexually versus the story I had learned to tell myself.

Go Ask Alice...

But that time did come, and down the rabbit hole I went. While attending a trade school in my early twenties, I stumbled across a remarkable couple who presented me with a brand-new perspective to consider and the rock-solid support to explore it. The revolutionary approach was simply to look at everything directly and, in so looking, to see clearly and to understand fully by teasing apart fact from fiction, truth from tales.

Simply, however, is the catchword, because when there is so much obstruction in the mind on so many levels, distorting the perception of oneself and reality (as is the case with almost everyone, believe it or not), there must be strenuous work and tremendous courage invoked in order to take things apart just to get a decent look.

It is not an intellectual journey, but one that requires exploration, experimentation, and tremendous risk-taking from the point of view of one's own comfort zone. It means completely setting aside all established beliefs, interrupting the common narrative, and suspending habitual judgments. But the bottom line is extraordinarily and elegantly simple: *just look*. Take off the fuzzy goggles, glasses, blinders, what have you, pick up that looking glass, and look. Then *tell the truth* about what you find. That's not easy. Not easy one bit.

I was terrified at the prospects I was facing in terms of dismantling what was known to me, but I was also very profoundly intrigued. I saw more practicality, more sanity, and far more interesting possibilities in this new approach than I sensed in the direction I was already going with the proverbial herd. So, peeking through my fingers, I cautiously but willingly swallowed the "drink me" tonic and ventured forth to check it out.

For me, this chasing of rabbits would become a complete lifelong personal revolution involving every dimension of my being, tearing my whole world asunder, analyzing all the rubble, healing the damaged parts, locating (and sometimes building) the essential pieces to reconstruct a sound framework to operate within—and throwing out the rest.

Woven throughout this larger picture is the thread of a personal sexual revolution, and that is the story I'm interested in sharing. Let the rumpus begin!

Free Fallin'

A journey begins by putting one foot in front of the other, and regarding the deconstruction of my sexual identity, my first step seemed to be right over the edge. It was 1996; I had gone to a training seminar and had the hots for my instructor. In order to try a radically new way of addressing my attraction, I decided to call him up and simply say that I found him attractive and I'd like to have sex with him.

This bald approach is based upon the admission of the country-fried fact that *sex* is the basis of sexual attraction (rather than romance) and then stripping away all the pork called "beating around the bush" that pads our social interactions. Sure, there are many layered aspects of another person that we find appealing or unappealing. But by looking carefully, instead of with the habitual broad brushstroke that furtively conceals the underlying sexual motive, we can learn to call a spade a spade, rather than continue to enshroud the essential stimulus in the wining-and-dining disguise of romantic courtship.

Now, I'm a modern woman and all, and I wasn't unfamiliar with being forward. I had learned to go after what I wanted with guys, since none of the ones I liked were knocking down my door for such a long period of time in my relatively short life. My relationship with the musician at college actually began with me showing up on his doorstep one evening, saying, essentially, "You and me babe, how about it?" and minutes later, we were making out heavily on his desk. But that was still under the protective umbrella of pursuing a romantic relationship, and that fell comfortably enough within the parameters of my civilized education. (There's a formidably vast expanse of territory between saying "*I'm interested in you*" versus "*I just want your body.*")

This time, I felt like a leaf ripped from the tree, at the mercy of an unfamiliar wind. I was absolutely petrified at the vulnerability of exposing myself solely as a sexual prospect, outside any hint of a relational pursuit. What did this mean about who and what I am? The implications were staggering to my young and naively limited perspective.

I'd begun to slowly acknowledge the possibility that my sexuality might actually be a more separate item from my emotionality, contrary to everything I'd been taught as a female. And that was deeply and wildly disgruntling to my entire being.

The widely accepted (and totally misleading) idea of evolutionary psychology stipulates—among other things—that women, being the party bearing the burden of the physiological consequences of copulation, are, in effect, commanded by their DNA to be persnickety and emotionally motivated. It tells us that feelings of vulnerability, needs for security and comfort, and so on dictate the female's choice of sexual candidates, while men, biologically intent on widely dispersing their spermatozoa, have no such cautionary genes patrolling their behavior.

Seems reasonable enough, right? But really it isn't (later on I'll explain further why); it's just a convenient rationalization of the experience we've invented and perpetuated for ourselves. This line of thinking fits in seamlessly with our social outline for the roles of each gender (as well as the handy double standard), and at this point, probably all Western minds have been impacted by it to some extent. The "science" of evolutionary psychology has gotten a hell of a lot of mileage in the service of social mores rooted in Victorian prudery, but my experiences began to show me that this model is highly inaccurate, as my later studies and forays in this area conclusively proved.

The sensation I experienced at the time, however, around the mere contemplation of an utterly divergent possibility literally made me feel nauseated and vertiginous. It churned my stomach viscerally and reminded me of my first days on the open sea. Now as a matter of fact, in the business of investigating intimately internal affairs, this is the most surefire indication that you're on to something big…

I anchored my ass firmly on the couch in my cozy little one-room cabin dug out of a sagebrush-covered hillside in Medical Springs, Oregon, wrapped myself securely in a blanket, picked up the phone, and carefully and deliberately dialed the number of my instructor. I felt dizzy. When I heard his voice on the other end of the line, I choked out some words of introduction, and the spinning room gathered momentum. I squeezed my eyes tightly shut and told him bluntly why I was calling.

To my astonishment, he responded to me with spectacular grace and openness. He informed me that he was involved in a relationship and unable to accept my proposal but that he greatly appreciated, and respected, my straightforward, honest approach. That's all I remember of our brief conversation.

The next thing I remember after hanging up the phone was very cautiously opening one eye, then the other, and realizing that I, the room, and everything in it were physically just as we were before the call, and that somewhere in my being I had been certain that none of it would be (over the years, I've learned to call this *the hoop of fire*—from one side it looks like you're diving headlong into an abysmal inferno, while once on the other side you see it was just a silly little flaming hoop). At that moment I understood that the world wasn't at all what I thought it was—and that I, in it, probably wasn't either.

(Hello) Yellow Brick Road

Now, emboldened by the friendly flavor of my first venture into the wild unknown regions of naked honesty, I decided to try to reach someone else who had been on my mind for a while and tell him what I had going on about him.

This surly, sexy soul was a steward aboard the MV *Sea Bird* on which I had worked after quitting school. He was lean and muscular with thick brown hair, and everyone thought he was an asshole. He wasn't a warm person; he hated his job and he had a biting, cynical sense of humor that I found absolutely hilarious. I was extremely hot for him. We bonded as friends and enjoyed heated, hidden bursts of passion, wherever we could steal them—ducking into staterooms, alone together on the fantail, below decks in crew quarters, above it all on the lido deck at night...

He was one male who knew how to handle himself sexually, managing to powerfully express his intensity and aggression and throw me around with sexy style. He drove me wild. He quit his job early, cutting short our little affair, and I had retained a sense of incompleteness about it. In our last farewell sexual encounter, under a blanket out beneath the massive sea of stars in Southeast Alaska, we were both naked from the waist down. We made out heavily, and he pressed his cock between my thighs from behind. The desire was hot to have it inside me. His penis delighted me, and how I wanted it! But I held back, since I was still hung up on the musician and the idea that true love must ultimately dictate my vaginal sex life. (Again, it's that overblown inflation of the meaning of the penis-in-vagina moment that keeps us girls on the lady leash.)

But now, with my newly expanding horizons, I realized that I had continued over the last few years to fantasize about fucking him and that I could still ask for it. So I found him in LA and called him up to have a little tête-à-tête. When I told him what I wanted, he seemed pleased. However, when he asked me what had changed for me to allow myself the pleasure, I told him I no longer believed we had to be in love. Suddenly, he turned on me, saying (not with merely a small amount of disgust) that I was not the girl he once knew, and he hung up. I put down the phone, stunned and somewhat hurt.

I contemplated the situation, then stepped outside into the crisp, sweet high-desert air and burned his info and a letter I had begun writing to him. At that moment I understood that there would be casualties along this new path I was traveling. People I knew and even cared for would not share my enthusiasm for the unconventional ideas I was exploring and the choices I would be making.

In fact, the most important thing I came to understand about the way I would now choose to live is that *any path* has its opportunity costs. Knowing this, I realized that making my choices deliberately, willfully, and with awareness would not protect me from pain and loss but would prevent the kind of suffering and misery that comes from trying to be a good girl and doing what you're told and getting the shaft anyway! This is something you can only do when you're willing to hazard the expedition, tear back the curtain, and confront that feeble wizard running the show.

I was not angry, just soberly resolved. No, I was no longer that same girl, and miraculously, I was not in "Kansas" anymore. I was on my way to freedom, and I was not looking back.

Higher Love

Part of my early induction into a dedicated exploration of the great big world of sexual liberation involved taking a "Sex, Love, and Intimacy" workshop with the Human Awareness Institute (HAI). This outstanding organization, founded in 1968 by the late Stan Dale in Northern California, offered me just the right timely environment to catalyze my transition into a more open and flexible sexuality. I cannot speak highly enough of the philosophy and the facilitators at the time, and I would still recommend the courses without hesitation to anyone interested in moving toward a more sexually (and relationally) enlightened perspective based on honesty and personal empowerment.

Shortly after that workshop, still hesitant and unskilled, I found myself forced to utilize one of its fundamental principles in a new relationship that was suffering from the start.

Bob and I grew up in the same small town, so even though he was numerous years ahead of me in school, I'd always known who he was. I had always thought he seemed kind of gay, uptight, and pretentious. He volunteered his time on a nature preserve in the area where I'd found seasonal work, and when he started pursuing me, I still had the same impression. As we spent more time together and became friends, his personality still bored me and at times completely alienated me. My lack of inspiration and, particularly, the moments of total alienation were becoming more and more outstanding to us both as time went on. He was especially bothered by those moments when I shut down to him and he began to ask me what that was about. So I sat down with him on the floor, facing him with our legs intertwined (the HAI "workshop straddle"), and explained plainly but explicitly what the issue was for me.

I told him he frequently came across to me as disingenuous, rehearsed, and repetitious, like a salesman trying to relate through buzzwords and taglines, and that's when I turned off and checked out. I wanted something more authentic, alive, and intimate.

It was intimidating to articulate my response so bluntly, giving this kind of direct negative feedback and not knowing how he would respond to it, but it was also a refreshing relief, which allowed me, of course, to step right into that standard of authenticity and intimacy I was looking for myself. And I absolutely give him all the credit for cornering me in the first place about what I had going on, because who knows how long I would have carried on like that otherwise, avoiding the discomfort of addressing the matter—behavior that is the complete *opposite* of intimacy, by the way.

And, his response was totally outstanding. He was completely receptive, open, and self-reflective, and this moment marked the beginning of our deeply intimate, wildly enlightening, long-term relationship. Because of my emotionalized sexuality, once I opened to him affectionately, I began to realize I also found him sexually appealing, and thus began our sex life together. Neither of us had any idea at the time what a ride that would be!

For almost a year, our relationship manifested pretty much like any other fresh conventional romance. However, due to my newly emerging perspective and approach to things, I was not willing to remain shackled by monogamy. I was interested in keeping the apple rolling in the field of discovery. Although I had warned him about this from the start, when we finally got down to the brass tacks of it, we really didn't see eye-to-eye, and he balked. Non-monogamy was certainly *not* part of his cherished vision of romantic union. Nevertheless, after many long discussions about where we were each going and what we both needed, wanted, and were willing to negotiate, we finally agreed on having an "open" relationship that allowed us each to explore sex with other partners within the context of our "primary" relationship with each other.

We researched and studied about sexually transmitted diseases to educate ourselves on the latest medical insights about transmission, what products were available, and what practices would be the best protection for ourselves and each other, since the two of us were having unprotected sex together. Then we wrote up an agreement that outlined our practices for safe sex with other partners. This outline included a detailed conversation covering sexual history with each of our partners, upon which we were to base, case by case, some of our practical decisions. Some things were preset, such as never having unprotected intercourse with any outside partners. Then, after every encounter, we shared all the pertinent information in order to keep each other abreast on the safe-sex front. If there'd been exposure that made one of us uncomfortable, we had to make adjustments in our practices together. We each got hepatitis B immunizations and went in for regular testing for HIV and other STDs.

For us, the functioning around safe sex turned out to be the most challenging dynamic, due to an imbalance in our standards around the details of our agreement, and resulted in some pretty ugly fights. From my perspective he was an anal control freak; from his perspective I was sloppy. Both were true.

Success in handling all the aspects of this kind of relationship requires a huge amount of alignment between partners, clarity of vision, maturity, discipline, and self-awareness. Difficulty is a given.

Although the logistical drama of juggling multiple sexual relationships could have been a nightmare, this turned out to be a pretty benign aspect for us. Some of our "extracurricular" partners were completely outside our social circle and remained so. Others, having common interests or, in some cases, developing common interests, became introduced, acquainted, and sometimes quite engaged in our circle. (One of his sex partners became relatively deeply involved in our lives as a friend for many years.) Still others were already close, like his best buddy who became a quasiregular sex partner of mine.

We'd been getting to know another couple in our wider circle, had gotten involved with each of them heterosexually one on one, and eventually decided to stir things up by throwing it all in the pot together. That foursome fricassee was one of the hottest dishes I'd ever known you could cook up. It literally felt as though the chemistry—and excitement—magnified geometrically among us.

It was also scaldingly emotional. For both of us it was an opportunity to observe each other having sex with someone else firsthand, leaving nothing to the imagination and bringing the jealousy factor into laser-sharp focus. In that regard, it was one of the most significant moments in my own emotional and sexual development. I saw two attractive bodies fucking right there in the room with me (a big first for my little eyes), and marveled at both the aesthetic beauty and the unexpected ordinariness of it. I felt the sting of emotion, based on my attachment and identification in relationship, and dangled in the space between feeling and observation, ripped in two, crying and laughing at the same time.

Without any doubt, the whole experience of open relationship was worth its weight in gold in terms of an education in sexual psychology, emotional maturity, and intimate relationship. It was a five-year crash course, and the debris from the wreckage flew far and wide! We threw ourselves into the chaos of jealousy, insecurity, anger, and fear. We used our commitment to the primary relationship for stability, as well as the support network of our highly evolved companions.

But foremost as a pillar stood our mutual desire to grow and develop from the experience. We were both interested in utilizing the vulnerability to find out about ourselves, to locate the truth about sex in the midst of all the perceived emotional threats. We used it to examine carefully and study deeply the nature of the internal chaos, to figure out the psychology of why it's so messy, and then to help each other clean up our crap. We learned how to hold space for one another to have and to express the volatile emotional responses that arose. We listened closely to each other, talking through the pain and confusion, and held each other through tearful breakdowns.

Sexual jealousy is often avoided like the plague, as though it is beyond the scope of mere mortals' coping capabilities. This attitude is fostered by a culture fixated on monogamy as an evolutionary directive *and* a moral mandate, the latter of which imparts a sense of righteous entitlement to jealousy's rage. It comes out of the bogus notion that we are *innately wired* to experience jealousy over a sexual mate. There are, however, human cultures (both past and present) organized around very different systems of sexual interaction and mating that throw this notion into question, indicating that jealousy in this realm—its presence *or* its absence—is actually dependent upon cultural and social conditioning.

"So is jealousy *natural?*" asks Christopher Ryan (coauthor of the must-read book *Sex at Dawn: How We Mate, Why We Stray, and What It Means for Modern Relationships*). "It depends," he says. "Fear is certainly natural, and like any other kind of insecurity, jealousy is an expression of fear. But whether or not someone else's sex life provokes fear depends on how sex is defined in a given society, relationship, and individual's personality."[34]

Being thus—and even being, as we are, deeply conditioned along these lines—it *is* possible to navigate through the highly unpleasant morass of jealousy (the authors of *The Ethical Slut* have

––––––––––––––––

[34] Ryan and Jetha, 147–48.

some worthwhile pointers in this area based on their own collective experience[35]). Doing so allows the discovery of a whole new dimension of one's capabilities as a mortal human being, not to mention a whole new dimension of loving in relationship.

Recently, one man explained to me how his passionate jealousy had reached such a fevered pitch that he simply could not take it anymore. At last, being in the military stationed halfway around the globe from his wife, ready to spontaneously combust and recognizing the lack of any other reasonable option, he said to himself, "Fuck it."

And that was *that.*

In one mighty instant, with a determination born of the necessity to spare his own sanity, he broke free of what had hold of him. He let go of that jealous construct so completely within his being that it never returned. And that is a case in point of actually how superfluous the construct really is. (As time went by, he even discovered what had been hidden behind it: *the idea of his wife with another man actually turned him on.*)

For me, the emotional struggles in open relationship were also a magnificent instruction in compassion. When you play both sides of the drama, you get to recognize very clearly where the hang-ups are both in yourself and in the other person. You get to see distinctly where your stuff begins and ends, and vice versa. The wrenching rawness you've just experienced on one side of it helps you feel more acutely that of your partner when he's on that side the next time. The fear and insecurity you felt last week when he had sex with some hotbody, you can witness this week in your partner and recognize the foolishness of it, which helps you modulate your own similar drama when it arises again next week. The constant contrast of subjective and objective experience, in an atmosphere of openness, quickly accumulates a deep reservoir of compassionate wisdom and insight.

---

[35] Dossie Easton and Janet W. Hardy, *The Ethical Slut: A Practical Guide to Polyamory, Open Relationships & Other Adventures*, 2nd ed., 2009 (Hardy co-authored under pseudonym Catherine A. Liszt in the 1st edition subtitled *A Guide to Infinite Sexual Possibilities*, 1997).

Goodbye, Stranger

The foolishness is not that there is no insecurity involved. It is just the opposite. Your partner may fall in love with someone else and pack their bags tomorrow. Truly, the foolishness is that *there is no security*, period, no matter where you choose to bury your head. Even if you are monogamously and legally bound in matrimony, your partner may fall in love with someone else, pack their bags, and hit the road. Even if your partner remains devotedly committed, people die, accidents happen, unforeseen events change the course of every life. There simply is no security. Anywhere. The "open" relationship just shoves that reality into your face right now so that you gotta deal with it!

When relationship is treated as a lifeboat so we can merrily float along pretending we are not alone and vulnerable, that is foolishness. If we dive headfirst into the water, learn to swim among the sharks and jellyfishes, currents and riptides, we can swim alongside one another and offer encouragement and support in the richest ways. But to offer refuge in the promise of security is to offer delusion, which undermines the immense empowerment that comes with surrendering to the truth: that we are each alone and there is no security.

We come into the world alone and we leave it alone, and everything in between is something somewhere on the spectrum of chaos—controlled chaos, if you're lucky. On the road of uncertainty, with entropy at the wheel, we go rattling around in the old jalopy of existence. Birth and death are profoundly personal events, and life is an individual journey that no two people can share on the deepest subjective level.

Because of the way he and I grew together, through five years of intense, intimate work in open relationship, both living together and living apart, I was completely and deeply in love with this man. I loved being with him. I enjoyed his spontaneous sense of humor that would burst out as ad-lib narratives in singsong rhyme (usually following the outrageous antics of our crazy neurotic mutt, Kola), which invariably reduced me to a helpless heap of belly-busting laughter, doubled over on my face on the ground. I loved his patience and his generosity, his capacity and his devotion, his strength and his tenderness. I loved having a companion who knew me inside and out, through and through, and who demonstrated time and time again that he wasn't going anywhere no matter how difficult things got. I was prepared to grow old with this person.

So it was shocking to realize one day that I had to get out. And I not only had to get out, I had to stop dealing with him, period. I could say I have no idea where it came from, but that's not exactly true, even though it felt like it arrived entirely out of the blue. It made not one bit of emotional sense from where I was standing at the time (nor much logical sense), but it was undoubtedly clear to me that I had no business questioning it. I'd have to call it intuitive instruction, and I knew by the way it spoke to me that it wasn't a choice I got to ponder. It just had to be done.

So I did it. I told him what I'd gotten, and it broke both of our hearts. It was the hardest thing I'd ever done.

When we made the split, I was a basket case. I cried nearly constantly. I dragged my ass around in such a miserable state I could barely function. And after two full weeks of this blithering indisposition, it was a simple but searing visual one evening that forcibly yanked up on my bootstraps. Across the room I saw my poor little motley pooch cowering and whimpering by the door, nose stuffed into the deepest corner of the room, unable any longer to endure her keen canine sense of my distress.

The next morning I drove myself up the mountain to the ski slopes, closed that day, and sat in the middle of the empty snow-packed parking lot to have a discussion with myself. Draped over the steering wheel and wailing clouds of condensation onto my windshield, it dawned on me that I was the one wholly responsible for the state of affairs I was so wrecked up about, and I said, "Look here—if you're going to be this miserable, just change your mind, you dope. There's no point in living like this. You're not a victim of anything here, so just go back to him. It's up to you, but this has got to come to an end."

That line of reasoning was starkly sobering, and it stopped me in my tracks. Hmmm...just go back to the guy and stop this stupidity, or don't go back to him and just stop this stupidity. That was an interesting concept. So I seriously pondered it, and I knew very clearly, without much deliberation, that I could not choose the former; the latter was my only viable option (and it was actually what I wanted, somewhere inside me), so I took it, and that was that. I straightened up, wiped away my tears, took a deep breath, and drove back down the mountain to start my life over.

Dirty Laundry

What followed was an astonishing opening in my life and my being. I suddenly felt as free as a bird, and I began to realize that in spite of our liberal sexual practices and our depth of love and intimacy, our relationship had some deep problems and had ultimately been very confining. Absorbed within it, I'd been unable to perceive the underlying dynamic, subtle but highly pervasive, of his dominance and control and my acquiescence. While I had, in effect, dictated the overarching parameters from the start by standing firmly in my disinterest in monogamy, he had modulated his position by controlling, to varying degrees, everything else. Our social circle was his; our recreational activities were his; our plans and daily orchestrations, from elaborate to mundane, were mostly his; for all intents and purposes, *I* was his—in spite of his concession to the wider sexual parameters we had laid out—and I had, quite imperceptibly, come to view myself as his property. He made sure all our practical needs were met, arranging and planning everything, and he was very good at it and very nurturing and devoted. But the confinement was tightly constricting and, like a boa squeezing the life out of its prey, had squeezed out much of my individuality and independence, as I only realized once I'd released myself.

Years later, after having had no contact with each other, we reunited in friendship. Reflecting on the whole thing, he said to me, with tears in his eyes, that he could see why I felt set free upon ending our relationship. He also confessed that following our breakup, he had hacked into my e-mail, broken into my home, and helped himself to my personal diary. By now the darker aspect of our dynamic was vividly clear to both of us.

I said earlier that alignment between partners, clarity of vision, maturity, discipline, and self-awareness are the keys to success, and this is actually true for the success of any kind of truly intimate, committed, long-term relationship (an education I would get much further down the road). The truth is, everything eventually comes out in the wash, one way or another, and this problem between us, with which we were out of touch (through lack of clarity and self-awareness), ultimately brought about the end of our partnership. I'm just grateful my intuition was ahead of the rest of me and that I honored it, as painful as it was.

Most serious relationships, once a negative pattern has been established, require a severe course of action to correct that, or it will simply become more and more deeply entrenched over time. I have watched many an aging couple exemplify the growing magnification of relational malfunction culminating in the infliction of deeply damaging abuses of one another and profound suffering. Mere separation will not cure the negative pattern, as it will likely either be continued in some permutation within the context of another relationship, or slipped into again once reunited with the same person. Only a significant increase in self-awareness, self-discipline, and emotional health will cure such a disease, and that takes very hard work both inside and outside the relationship itself.

Now outside that relationship and its configuration, I was free to explore on my own terms, without answering to anyone but myself, and to discover what those terms actually were. What were my own true personal boundaries around sex and my own standards for safe sex? Toward whom, when, and where did my desires lead me, and how far would I go to manifest them and how frequently? What emotional responses tugged at me? Which ones didn't?

Most importantly, *who was I* as an unattached, untethered, highly motivated sexual creature?

SUCH A WOMAN...

Well, now I've come to the part where I get to elaborate on the reality of the modern witch: that nasty free agent who defies categorization, bucking convention and stirring up so much dust.

At this point, I should give some context. What I'm going to go into is actually relevant to varying degrees everywhere in the US, although certain environments provide more insulation than others. Social networks that foster alternative lifestyles (such as polyamory groups, swingers clubs, gay communities, liberal colleges, etc.) are probably the best for that. Large cities, with greater anonymity and diversity, can offer shelter by modulating the gossip-and-reputation effect that occurs in smaller community settings.

But the reality that permeates much of American culture is pretty darn puritanical, and an individual female choosing to march to the beat of her own drum or, more accurately, the throbbing of her own vagina, represents "such a woman" as I describe.

If you care to notice, you will even see the familiar theme in Hollywood movies: sexually promiscuous woman is "acting out" from psychoemotional dysfunction; her redemption, if found, lies in recognizing and healing somehow from said dysfunction which, naturally (of course), brings her back in line with the low-key, romantically defined, sexually conservative paradigm (the equivalent of our collective definition of female sexual-emotional health)…audience now sighs and sits more comfortably in seats.

Oh, but a woman who is wholly conscious and responsible—sanely, soberly, and unapologetically grounded in her sexually ample volition—she is an entity that discordantly inspires intense discomfort, morbid fascination, secret admiration, silent resentment, and outright hostility. And make no mistake about it, this multiheaded creature is still directly connected, by a tenacious umbilicus, to the dark Middle Ages of the witch craze. Don't think for a moment that we are completely out of the woods here on that topic.

During my "coming out" years, I happened to be functioning in a rural small-town community, so my experience would show me the amplified version of what such a woman is up against. And I'm grateful for the grand edification that came from that. There can be no rosy illusions about the "evolving enlightenment of humanity" when you're not cushioned within a snuggly sphere of like-minded people.

Into the Great Wide Open

By the time I got out of my relationship, I was pretty well seasoned at canvassing for sex partners, so this was no longer a big fly in the ointment. I still felt the butterflies in my stomach when I had to approach someone new but had learned to understand that for what it is—excitement and anticipation rather than terror and dread (there's fear, but similar to the giddy feeling just before a crazy carnival ride). I had spent a long time just practicing the act of approach itself, in order to bring about change in my sexual self-identification through honesty and vulnerability. Whenever I noticed an interest, my standing policy was that I had to go up to that person and at least tell them I found them sexually attractive.

Doing this helped turn a mere mental note into a deeper acquaintance with socialization, giving me the chance to interact with other people more openly and to watch both my own and others' responses around the issue of sex and sexual attraction. Whether or not I actually asked the person to have sex was based on some other more flexible parameters, but since my parameters *were* pretty flexible, it happened a lot…And since I'm heterosexually motivated and men are relatively (as opposed to women approached by men) receptive to this kind of forward approach, I had sex with a lot of different men.

I actually began to get a kick out of the approach itself, savoring the stimulation that came along with exposure to possibilities unknown and the thrill of taking a walk on the wild side of danger and intrigue that can only be known in an atmosphere of repression. I liked the shock factor. And I relished the fact that even if I met with bald-faced rejection (which I sometimes did), I'd performed an act of power, which contrasted dramatically with my mousy self-identification. And I enjoyed knowing that whether or not I got lucky, I had undoubtedly made an impression. There was a sense of validation in it that could have inflated the hinterlands of my head, but with my feet grounded in perspective this remained well within the bounds of healthy data input. Most important was the surge of empowerment (the *internal* validation) that comes from taking the simple but courageous action of asking for what you want (and being ready for the answer).

I Shall Be Released

Now, at this point in my life, I was running a thriving business as a licensed massage therapist and had way more than a little worry about a wanton sexual reputation emerging and discoloring my professional career, which I held in supremely high regard. Embarking on my career in the early nineties, I had already been confronted with skepticism about the shadiness of choosing to be a "masseuse," reflected from a mainstream generation that still associated massage with red lights and prostitution. I had fielded numerous queries and quelled many qualms by offering up my own freshly educated diatribe as well as published information on the emerging legitimacy of therapeutic massage from such prominent sources as *Time* magazine and the *New York Times*. (Ultimately, in a remarkably advanced gesture of love and confidence, my own conventionally conservative grandparents even fronted me the money for the schooling.)

I was acutely aware of the growing, yet tenuous, acceptance of massage into the mainstream professional culture as well as my responsibility as a representative of the industry at this delicate juncture, so I handled my personal affairs with that much more dutiful discretion. I kept my work impeccably professional, and I kept my mouth tightly shut about my intimate adventures. For the *most* part, otherwise, I was conscientious regarding with whom I dallied, making a particular effort to avoid approaching men I knew were married or otherwise involved to avoid unnecessary drama and public inflammation.

My guess is that the outlier to that last set is the specimen that resulted in the scorched-earth policy of those who applied themselves to the task of dishing the dirt around my carnal conduct (assuming some sort of real basis to any of it).

This desperado had built me a kickass pair of lug-soled leather boots that blazed my trampy trails all over the rugged backcountry of Baker, Union, Wallowa, and Grant counties. He was a wild-natured man who found himself confined in the trappings of a life he'd outgrown with a wife who did not welcome his midlife metamorphosis. Dissolution and divorce were on the horizon; details were far from figured out. But we were hot to trot, and our numerous readjustments to customize those boots were often infused with a little more chemistry than the job required.

Eventually, I found myself hanging from his lanky loins on the back of his Harley for a noisy blast of a ride through one dark night on Eastern Oregon's lonely highways. I made the most of that ride, removing as much space between our bodies as physically possible by pressing my crotch tighter and tighter up against his narrow, denim-covered ass. Reaching forward inside his leathers to feel his thighs vibrating with the heavy rumble of the machine, I felt the bulge at his groin swelling to fill every crease in those Levi's. I was deliriously aroused.

After the ride, though, the aggressive combination of his rough, physical force and my growing sense of his untidy family situation sent me hightailing it out of there after a couple of fully clothed minutes of what amounted to more of a frantic wrestling match than anything particularly sexy. I felt like a deer hurtling itself from the clutches of a mountain lion, hardly knowing what I'd walked into, but swiftly taking in the whole picture. Thank God that was all behind me, I thought.

But word gets around in a small town like wildfire on the dry prairie. By the time I actually awoke to the blaze of gossip some time later, it was truly astounding—and oddly captivating—to learn about the untold abundance of bawdy shenanigans I'd been up to. Choking a bit on the smoke, I really couldn't fathom, at the time, the size of the conflagration.[36]

Ultimately, though, catching wind of the rumors myself, while unnerving, was a consummate relief. It was obvious that my randy renown had already been established for some time, entirely unbeknownst to me, and had in no evident manner sabotaged my business. The rap had truly outperformed me, and so, since it was clear that in all reality I could scarcely begin to flesh out the lurid caricature that had already been fashioned and delivered, I realized that any further actions of my own would be laughably trivial. That being the case, I figured I could just beetle on and let go of any unnecessary anxiety over the impending consequences of a potential exposé. Now I could strut and thumb my nose with my gal Joan Jett and not give a damn about my "Bad Reputation!" I kind of liked the new rebel in me. I was beginning to see through the charade, and I felt more alive, more awake, more in charge.

So I continued enthusiastically pursuing my libidinous agenda, becoming more and more comfortable and confident along the way, having lots of fun, and learning a great deal ("the good, the bad, and the ugly") about myself, other people, and the sexual culture within which I was functioning.

---

[36] The bottom line of this intensity is studded with an arrow pointing at sexual repression. Dr. Wilhelm Reich, perhaps the original sex therapist and contemporary of Freud, observed that this kind of fervent fixation and stigmatization of others' sexuality is due to the misdirection of repressed energy (Wilhelm Reich, *The Function of the Orgasm* [New York: The Noonday Press, 1942, 1948, 1961]).

Thorn Tree in the Garden

One of the most theatrical players I encountered on the social scorn set was a psychiatrist who was one of my ex's cronies. This guy was reasonably civil to me throughout the course of my relationship with his friend, but once we split the sheets, whatever reservations he might have harbored quietly about our unseemly relationship transformed into a rabid animosity toward me. The unalloyed contempt seethed out of his pores at every unsavory encounter, as I watched, transfixed, his entire being squirm with the irrepressible compulsion to impugn any available aspect of my character. It seemed at some point he had to let it all fly, and I sensed it was usually shortly after I was out of earshot. I couldn't help thinking it would make an interesting case for psychoanalysis...although he'd already stated unambiguously that peering into *his own* psychology was not a prospect he was willing to entertain.

This character put a rather grotesque face on the witch hunt for me. This was my own personal introduction to the kind of hatred that fuels lynchings, burnings, pogroms, white supremacy... In other eras, in other regions, in fertile environments, these vehement reactions, unleashed, have amassed and mobilized mobs.

A certain local woman put a feminine face on the animus, manifesting in a more duplicitous fashion. Calculating that I was likely at some point to encounter the single stranger sojourning in our cozy little town one summer, she expressly pimped my name out to him as the local slut, nudging him—as a smear—in my dubious direction. Although the tone of intention was clearly more acrid than altruistic, she would later pitch her defense (when I confronted her) as a motherly concern for my sexual health, of all things. I hunted for the logic in her statement, trying to be fair, but came up empty-handed.

"That's a bunch of crap," I told her, and she looked genuinely taken aback, as if she had really thought I would buy it.

At the end of the edgy day, though, she was my inadvertent, unexpected, Lady Luck. Intrigued, the redheaded stranger rode across town and whisked me right up. Winding my fists into the long, kinky strands of his magnificent flaming mane, I threw my leg over the saddle, mounted that rowdy pony, and we had our own little rodeo together that summer as fast friends and fuck buddies. He was a countercultural bisexual punk-rocking wild thing blasting out of New York City and was a breath of brisk air to me in the yonder parts of the state of Oregon that even most Oregonians don't realize exists.

Trailing along on his shirttails, as his luscious visit lingered deep into the fall, I also inhaled some more of the noxious fumes wafting around the neighborhood. At a Halloween party to which I'd have never been invited on my own, I found myself walking through a house of horror I didn't expect. After an indulgent frolic on my living room floor that evening, we arrived at the venue fashionably late. The hostility in the air made my skin prickle and thrust me into putting on a mask I hadn't quite grown into. One man, a medical doctor, grilled me so fiercely for an explanation of our tardiness that, after several attempts at playful suggestiveness for the sake of decorum, I finally looked him in the eye and took him on. "We were fucking," I said, heavily enunciating each syllable.

I have no idea what he was expecting me to say, but it clearly wasn't that. His eyes got wide, his face twitched into a grimace, and he fumbled to overcome speechless stupefication. I, too, was stunned. I was surprised and tickled at my own moxie, and I was flabbergasted at the intensity of the man's belligerent, accusatory aggression (perhaps he'd actually expected me to slither away in shame). I stayed a while longer to give the wingding another whirl, but the air didn't get much better, so I split.

It was my redheaded pony boy who finally gave me *The Teaches of Peaches*[37] about the preeminence of my local stature, and through the smoke things began to become more clear. Plugged directly into Gossip Central via certain family ties, he ended up being the source of my full enlightenment regarding my small-town renown. He gave me the whole salacious scoop. And in a twist of elegant recompense—completely unprompted—he spoke up for me in my

---

[37] *The Teaches of Peaches* is the title of an album released in 2000 by the artist Peaches—part of the "electroclash" (post-punk) genre of which this guy was a fan. Her songs' raunchy lyrics pay tribute to pro-sex, post-feminist attitudes.

absence. In words that were at least unexpected, and certainly out of sync, with the trending gossip, he showed what he was made of.

He told them, "I know a slut when I see one. I've been with plenty. She's not a slut. She's a sexually liberated woman." To him, the implied distinction was that a slut is careless and irresponsible; a liberated woman, just the opposite.

Such a woman is actually much worse than a "slut" in conventional minds, because she cannot just be labeled and discarded out of hand. A slut, so designated, can and will be ripped to shreds by forked tongues, without compunction; but a "sexually liberated woman," a deliberate free radical, really gets the goat. Things start to get really uncomfy around her. (Sure, the shit will still fly all around her wake, but there's a nagging little lump in the throat that festers.)

My dearest female friend, a professional career woman, has encountered more than a fair share of the suspicions and peer pressures from *other women* in her hotsy-totsy California workplace who are disgruntled by her unconventional lifestyle as an unmarried, child-free, un-primped-and-salon-polished yet clearly heterosexual representative of femininity. These peers know no details of her sexual affairs, but it is her mere a-categorical presence that irritates a raw nerve, stimulating all manner of meddling admonitions, suggestive and overt, intended to shepherd an annoying turncoat back into the flock.

In the daily rubbing of shoulders at the office, the nearness and ever-presence of her nonconformity, indistinct from her magnetically attractive personality and humanity, highlights the vexation caused by someone who cannot be disregarded. She has become such a woman, of whom others (in this case other women) must be wary—keep an eye on your man; the devil wears a business suit!

A "slut" has no *dignity* by the popular definition, and it is a woman of credible dignity that really bothers those who disapprove. That credibility is the ultimate threat, implying a not-so-readily dismissible character, a potentially valid existence, and possibly, even, a viable purpose. (The authors of the popular late-nineties book *The*

Ethical Slut[38] deliberately chose the wording of its title as a contradiction in colloquial terms to challenge and upend the prevailing mind-set with a similar suggestion.) These suggestions grate on the touchy nerve endings around a deeply buried truth disgruntling to acknowledge: that something is very ill-conceived within our moral structure.

Think back to my incident with the Harley dude and ponder for a moment why it might have been *me* who was the object of public castigation rather than him. That's the old double standard, sure enough. Eve and that rotten fucking apple again. Where's Adam's responsibility in the situation? Why is she alone blamed for spoiling the garden for everyone? Wasn't it enough to crucify her luscious erotic humanity without skewering her for every little trifle until the end of time? I was a twenty-four-year-old bimbo discovering sexuality, responding to a mutual attraction taking place between two red-blooded human beings. So while I may have been guilty of some callow myopia, I was not prowling around in the twilight with a mutant clitoris, hunting for marriages to destroy, as the rumors would assert. And although I experienced a moment of rueful conscience that contributed to the aborted sexual encounter, I was never the person involved in making holy or legal promises at any altar to any party concerned in the first place. That moment of conscience was a purely gratuitous gesture on my part, *not* an obligation to anyone. So really, why did the local moral police fixate on me?

Part of the issue is something that was articulated in a recent book called *The Purity Myth*, by Jessica Valenti.[39] She describes how the growing social and political trend favoring virginity and chastity in the US is increasingly reviving the deeply misogynistic habit of equating female morality with sexual chastity. (This attitude establishes the Madonna/whore dichotomy, in which you can only be one or the other, and this outrageously outdated relic still clings tenaciously to our modern sexual paradigm.)

---

[38] Easton and Hardy, 1997.

[39] Jessica Valenti, *The Purity Myth* (Berkeley, CA: Seal Press, 2010), 13.

That means that her sex life defines her humanity, in quite black-and-white terms. Valenti says, "While boys are taught that the things that make them men—good men—are universally accepted ethical ideals, women are led to believe that our moral compass lies somewhere between our legs. Literally." And once that compass points a smidge away from modesty, the rest of her humanity is all but lost.

At this point, she may even weaken some of her civil rights if she happens to find herself in front of a jury as, say, a victim of rape. Innumerable legal cases—in modern times, no less—have turned the sympathies of the jury away from the victim if she has any historical indication of even remotely liberal sexual behavior. This is because a lusty woman is *still* regarded, deep in the popular psyche, as troublingly flawed, bound for ruin, and deserving of punishment.[40] (Remember, I was already on the radar of the roundsmen for speeding fast and loose around the neighborhood, well before any illicit joyrides took place.)

What I've come to realize is that, according to the moral enforcement posse, I'm *supposed* to be making those holy and legal promises, otherwise I'm guilty of flouncing around in the sun waving that fresh, juicy apple under other people's noses. It's my moral obligation to society to get hitched and knocked up as soon as possible so that I do not disrupt the pH of the rank environment under the dark canopy of our cultural inheritance.

Due to the chastity-morality equation, an *ethical slut* becomes such an irreconcilable oxymoron to conventional minds that it simply cannot register in the psyche without registering on the Richter scale. Cognitive dissonance, it is called. Any hint of validity within

---

[40] Signs of this punishing attitude appeared during the age of "courtly love" in the twelfth century (before the Roman Catholic Church condemned it as heretical), when women of the higher classes were, for a time, deemed fully human (yet still inhumanly chaste) and therefore worthy of a man's romantic love. These men, however, were still directed to rape the subhuman lower-class females they encountered out and about, as an expression of their superiority and power. Lower-class standing precluded a woman's angel-Madonna status, so the wretch-whore designation remained, leaving her vulnerable to the treatment such an entity "deserved."

that which is viscerally opposed threatens the sense of infallible security in the cherished counterposition, so finding a way, any way, to dismiss that hint becomes paramount. We love to hate, but hate to fear.

Fear, however, is a potentially wonderful thing. When rightly addressed, fear is deeply instructive. Standing squarely in it, looking directly at it, asking pointed questions of it, and seeking understanding through it lead straight into a goldmine of insights.

Hatred just sucks. I've been on both sides, and it burns like a mother———!

Call Me Super Bad

Meanwhile, my reputation was touring the region and had found fertile ground just over the Wallowa Mountains in what some of us in Eastern Oregon affectionately call "the county." One man there unexpectedly grappled with its tentacles.

I found myself spending the night at his cabin, located at the very base of massive Mt. Joseph, for purely practical purposes: a ski trip into the backcountry of the majestic Wallowas with a small group of local skiers, to convene early the next morning. I'm not sure if it's an indication of my total naivety or if this is just the nature of being kept out of the loop, but all I knew was that a nice guy offered me convenient lodging and I gladly accepted. Evidently, though, the situation from his perspective had a more complex array of implications and overtones.

That night, we spent several cozy hours late into the evening talking. But then as I snuggled into my own sleeping bag across the living room, he was visibly shocked. Why wasn't I making rapacious sexual moves on him? (I can't help wondering if he was rather disappointed by the vapid course of events, if only for the theatrical element.) He began a very studious inquiry, admitting his surprise in light of what he had heard about me. Based upon our conversation, I came to understand that he'd had a whole collection of nervous assumptions about how I would go about conducting myself with him, alone together, for the night. I said that I understood he had a girlfriend.

This astonished him even more, and the rest of our discussion unfolded around the philosophical basis of how I conducted my sex life (based upon honesty and responsibility). It's not, by the way, that I'd decided I would never have sex with a man who had a girlfriend (or wife), but I'm not going to knowingly go out of my way to jump into his business. He'd have to be the instigator, and I'd want to know what the deal was—to understand the situation I was accessorizing. I consider everyone as their own responsible agent, in or out of relationship. And I respect that agency, including my own, beyond conventional morality. (As with everything in life, right and wrong are rarely neatly demarcated, and truly responsible choices are filled with myriad nuances and considerations.)

The problem was that the mountain man's whole prior assessment of me was confined within the strict moral parameters that had defined the rumors themselves: you're either in or you're out, innocent or guilty. In other words, you're either conventionally modest (innocent) or you're completely lacking a respectful human conscience (guilty). *How can a slut be ethical?* I realized that the wind in the whispers was really based on this popular dichotomy and that the whole foolish drama can only be perpetuated by such extremes.

But he was fantastic, asking me directly the questions nobody else was willing to ask, and possessing the openness and flexibility within himself to recognize on a personal level who I really was, what I was actually up to, and then to change his position entirely.

Tougher Than the Rest

That's, unfortunately, more than I can say for another man in "the county" with whom I'd been having a lopsided relationship around that time. He and I met at a dinner party among my sister's eclectic Bohemian community in the Little Alps of Oregon, settled into which is the sleepy little town of Joseph. I gravitated instantly to him—pulled by the invisible force of his quiet, easy gentleness and the depth of his dark eyes—and tumbled into love.

I didn't hold back, pouring everything I had to offer into the relationship, euphorically screaming out my feelings down river gorges, no less. I was in, crazy in. But he never really was, and what I got in return was the equivalent of those faintly receding echoes from the canyon walls. He was always holding back—and I knew he was—but I was so crazy about him and high on living free that I was content with the fact that he was somehow interested in spending his time with me. I wasn't afraid to love unrequitedly. But I was also, admittedly, blinded and rather stupefied by my emotional content.

After hesitating for an unbearable length of time, he finally decided it was sort of okay to try being sexual with me—something that, given my liberal activities (and, even more importantly, my reputation), had gone sharply against his Christian-bred grain and image-oriented self-identification.

I remember very clearly the morning we first got sexy and how astonished I was to realize just how much distortion I'd undergone in the intricate crannies of his mind. We lay side by side, mostly clothed, our faces together, just breathing into each other, barely hinting at kissing and enjoying the hot buzz of excitement. It was a completely full and satisfying experience for me to finally share this sensuality with him. When I expressed that, he couldn't believe my response—I couldn't possibly be satisfied with *that*. Evidently, he had decided that being the crude slut that I was, I could only be satisfied with a hard and heavy fuck straight off the porn shelf (as in Horny-Babes-Want-Your-Beef, faster-harder-balls-to-the-walls squealing crescendo exploding theatrically with the Crystal Geyser money shot).

And this was after many weeks of hanging out together having extensive, deeply exposed personal conversations—getting to know each other, supposedly. To me, in the context of our relationship, sex would just be a natural extension of the adventure, part of a whole spectrum of possibility, neither excluding the porn-worthy wild thing nor *by definition* including it. Truly, it could look any way at all. It just shows the extent to which the firm conviction of a stereotype solidifies in the mind.

Even after this revelation, so to speak, I didn't realize what a tough nut he was until it was all over, many months later. It's clear that he could never fully perceive my humanity through the dark fog he'd created in response to my unabashed sexuality. I was a marked woman. I believe that because my entire relationship with sex was not bounded by the criterion of romantic love, he couldn't come around to see that my having sex with him wasn't an act of cold calculation—something completely disconnected from the rest of my being—regardless of the fact that I was actually in love with him! So that's how he responded to me. In spite of how I wore my heart on my sleeve with him in complete vulnerability, he could never quite recognize that I was a feeling person.

In the end, he treated me with a coarseness that showed me just how closed down he was to me. Because my hooch wasn't directly hitched to my heart, he had me figured as hard and invulnerable. It was a deeply painful blow when he casually told me over the phone that he'd fallen in love with someone and was leaving with her. I knew the emotional risk I'd plunged into headlong, and the pieces were my own to clean up, *totally my own*. I did not blame him for his feelings for someone else, nor for choosing to be with her. I could always see that coming. But I do hold him responsible—after almost a year together—for being so out of touch as to have no idea that I *would* feel it sharply. Even when I told him how I felt, it simply didn't compute—he was completely bewildered.

I have to seriously acknowledge that he did try, though. At least my nonconformity (disgruntling as the sexual aspect was) intrigued him enough to look—and venture, too—into something for a period of time that made him deeply uncomfortable. Even though, when it was over, it was plainly clear that he couldn't get away far enough fast enough, I have to hand it to him for his willingness to explore—given the depth of his moral aversions—anything at all with me. Even if they overcame him in the end, he hung in, for whatever reason, for an entire year, investigating something profoundly agitating. That's more than most people will dare to do in a lifetime.

Oh, Woe Is Me

A slightly different, much more malevolent version of this story involves an Argentine. We met in Santa Cruz at a weekly lecture on the Bhagavad Gita. From a Latin culture of male chauvinist Catholics, this impudent hombre had come to California and found inspiration in mystic Hinduism. He was a remarkable concoction assembled from a smorgasbord of misogynist ingredients—from Edenic fable and Catholic sexual guilt to the Hindu worship of semen and reverence for celibacy—all congealed together with a hearty helping of that notorious Latin machismo. What a tasty piece of work.

(There was this, along with his annoying habit of eating all my bananas, but I'll be magnanimous and put that aside.)

I never had strong feelings for him, but I was exceedingly grateful to have a regular sex partner in the midst of a distressing dry spell. I was in my early thirties, peaking hormonally, and becoming deeply sympathetic with my new appreciation for the experience of teenage boys. Eventually though (I was a little slow on the uptake), my perception clarified, and I realized the whole vibration I was absorbing from him felt like poison. It finally became obvious that what I represented to him was something of a cross between an execrable Eve and a medieval succubus—I was the sinister temptation in his loins, leading him into the evils of sexual intercourse, thirsty to drain him of his vital semen for my own parasitic advantage, and were it not for my very existence, he would certainly find himself within the immaculate holy embrace of a celibate life.

His desperate determination to withhold his semen from my diabolical consumption had nonetheless offered a silver lining. In practice, he developed a phenomenal capacity for maintaining an erection. We had exhilarating intercourse for hours at a time—four hours straight one night (nowadays you're supposed to call a doctor, I think)—highly orgasmic on my part. He would just lie back and let me ride into the sunset.

But even that extravagant recreation didn't slow me down once the whole toxic picture came into focus. Fiercely repelled, it was me this time who couldn't get away fast enough.

Hatred sucks.

Wouldn't It Be Nice

Now even though men are (with some volatile exceptions) comparatively amenable and will frequently take advantage of a sexual opportunity presented to them on a platter, there is nevertheless a lot of sludgy sediment that can get agitated inside them.

Over the years, I have listened to innumerable men lamenting women's sexual inaccessibility and expressing a spirited desire for easier access and a more laissez-faire attitude, wistfully envisioning a world where a woman will embody her sexuality, approach *him*, and entreat purely sexual liaison. The idea of "no strings attached" puts a particularly brilliant sparkle in the eyes of the masculine gender. Oh, how he would relish such a scenario!

But where the rubber meets the road and it manifests before him, well now, the actual response is often quite different, particularly for the younger generations of males raised wholly in the backlash era of post-sexual-revolution recoil. At this point, a deep cultural neurosis peeks its wretched nose out of the woodwork and the revel of his imagination quickly recedes, leaving him grasping for the stronghold.

While so many men are outstandingly open, respectful, and gracious all the way (including many modern young fellas), many a man is not. For the latter, the glee and excitement of having the fantasy handed him are overwhelmed at some point by discomfort and moral indignation, and he begins to feel edgy. He is unsure of how to identify such a woman. And *he* cannot identify as he has been trained to do as a man, upsetting and offending his sense of place in the social order.

Uncertainty creeps in from the deep recesses of his cultured (neurotic) sensibilities, casting foreboding shadows of doubt upon the respectability of such a woman and how that reflects upon him as a man, as an upstanding person, in the common world he inhabits—and up rises contempt. He is torn and tormented with no practical instruction or real-life vocabulary for defining a sexual relationship outside the exclusive proprietary contract (that very thing by which he feels so shackled) and no slot in which to file such a rogue document.

Therefore, it registers as suspect, falling somewhere outside the comfort zone and landing in the vicinity of the circular file, consequently getting the trash treatment, or that sideways-looking, dismissive-yet-wary attitude one reserves for crazies on the street (yet with a deeper, much more personal flavor). The fantasy is short-lived, if ventured at all. "Too good to be true" (like free love in the sixties followed by herpes and the AIDS epidemic in the eighties) becomes a self-fulfilling prophecy: certainly this can't be right; there must be a catch to this kind of opulent freedom embodied in a woman.

Dear Mr. Fantasy

My theory is that this particular male romantic fantasy is not typically reflective of a far-reaching vision of a different and more sexually liberal society. Rather, I believe, it represents a *daydream* that's deeply rooted in the same traditional moral culture, one in which the woman is not so much sexually free and open herself as a general way of being (which demands a respective shift in his own construct), but that she chooses to be so *for him*—as an exception. In this way, having his cake and eating it too, he can continue to view such a woman as decent (in the puritanical sense), getting his kicks while at the same time feeling like somebody special within the parameters of his snug self-identification.

This theory of mine is suggested as a general outline rather than a rigid formula, and it is based on my experiences in which a man is initially pleased as Punch by my straightforward sexual openness until the emotional reality creeps in. He will exuberantly devour the opportunity, until he realizes that he is not the only man enjoying it, at which point he gets turned off—actually affronted—by the implications. He is then forced to view me as "such a woman," and the whole thing loses its magical luster and must be thrown, tarnished, into the trash bin—preferably buried.

Since a considerable concern for males is securing *access* to their sexual outlet, a woman who is playing the field with other men represents a real potential problem: she may be out gallivanting around with someone else at some future date when he wants access to her, a very discomforting reality to be facing at such a moment. In a hypothetical world, where females are commonly accessible, this would not present such a problem: she would not have to become his exclusive property since, in such a world, the abundant commodity of sex is happily shared among all. But in the real world, where such a woman is an exception to the norm, *she* then becomes the villain.

Besides myself, the women I've known who have functioned as free sexual agents have, largely, not been treated with respect. While these women are intrepidly carving out a path, through honesty and personal responsibility, for everyone else to enjoy when they decide to wake up from the collective sexual nightmare, they are often treated by men like "whores," less-than-fully-human objects used to fill in the gaps between dealings with the "real women" in men's lives who jive better with conventional standards. This they do, even though the movement toward traditional relationships with these "real" women does not address the deep-seated foundational desire of wanting unlimited access to an unlimited number of women.

In an article from *Men's Journal* titled "Is Monogamy Insane?"[41] Tim Krieder gives voice to the frustrations of many, if not most, modern American men. I picked up the magazine at the gym, unable to resist finding out what a man, writing for men, had to say on this topic so near and dear to my heart.

He admitted, knowing he'd be received in good company among his readers, to being one of those "creeps" (the lecherous and unethical sex-driven males) bemoaned by his female friends as he nods, reassuring them that he's not. "[But] the Creepy Guys and the Nice Guys are exactly the same guys," he confesses on paper, hoping to enlighten a smattering of curious female readers like myself, adding that it becomes "tiresome and lonely trying to maintain this facade of decency in front of all womankind." With all my empathy, I'm sure it does. It's a waste of time and energy, and relationship, all the way around.

---

41 Tim Kreider, "Is Monogamy Insane?" *Men's Journal*, November 2014.

He wants to be able to be himself with a woman, admitting that monogamy is hard and that agreeing to it is a *sacrifice* that he's willing to make for intimacy with her, but not out of a *desire* to be monogamous. Also, well said (realizing, however, that monogamy is not intimacy—nor is sex, per se—as I will discuss in the next chapter). He admits to experiencing a sense of emasculation within the confines of relationship, of losing that undomesticated edge a man feels when single—"being available, up for anything, faintly dangerous"—in other words, with elevated levels of testosterone. (It has been shown, by the way, that male testosterone levels do indeed tend to drop after marriage and markedly so after the birth of offspring in that marriage.)

After making several enlightened observations, the author wraps it all up by admitting defeat, indicating his utter resignation to playing "the game" with all womankind. I had really hoped he was boldly going somewhere.

Tell the Truth

I can't blame a man for acquiescing to the world he lives in (status quo), particularly when fighting against it may create mayhem in the realm of manifesting what ordinary, normal guys might want regarding sex, relationship, and family. Not everyone is cut out for swimming against the current and all the waves it makes. We all have to pick our battles. And admittedly, going beyond the standard model to manifesting a "free love" ideal is much more dubious, ironically, for a heterosexual man than for a woman at this point in our culture's history.

For contemporary men, *not* playing the game with women can mean you are marked even more damagingly than the female slut, sentencing yourself to a form of desolate sexual exile from the emotional-security-seeking circles of the well-trained feminine gender. At least the female slut knows she can *eat* the cake now and then, even if she is denied *having* the whole thing, while a heterosexual male wandering in this environment may often realistically only expect a slap in the face.

So I have great sympathy for the size of the masculine quandary, and I have no interest whatsoever in depreciating it. Nevertheless, because of my own hassles on this front, I find the lip-service approach very tiresome (having challenged it directly and found it frequently empty), and it makes me squint pretty hard at any man who speaks to me about "how great it would be if…" I mean, if we're going to complain about a serious malady, let's not reject the antidote for fear of needles—or a stubborn, reactive moral indignation.

In the end, Krieder rationalizes his position figuring, "it's mostly not the reality but the tantalizing possibility of sex…that gives life its luster" and that is linked with "a certain self-image" of a single stud kind of guy. The self-reflection is admirable and honest, and I'm grateful for that, in spite of my dismay. I believe it represents one version of the basis of that male romantic fantasy I described above involving a troubled and confused mixture of thought and feeling, desire and fantasy, truth and delusion. Acknowledging that the complaint arises, at least in part, from *fantasy* is an incredibly important thing, especially when the reverberations of that complaint add to the tense friction between the two majority halves of all of humanity. All the disempowered complaining and commiserating, without a courageous plan of action, just fuels the fires of misogyny and misandry by blowing hot air on the issues. The whole truth must be told before anything real can be done about it.

This is what it looks like to begin teasing apart reality and delusion in order to get a clear view of what's really going on. Both sexes are stuck in the same trap, each with different complaints about the same problem, neither one willing to venture into the vulnerable no-man's-land of *changing a fundamental identity*. But this is, in fact, what needs to happen. This is right at the hot nuclear (apple?) core of revamping the tortured sexual construct we're all suffering in. No one has very much ground to stand on anymore and point fingers at the other. Enough of that already.

WHAT'S LOVE GOT
TO DO WITH IT?

So, I think again of the salty steward and his bitterness toward my change in attitude around sex and love. He was happy to get into my pants as long as he could continue to view me as a sufficiently modest creature. As with the tough guy from the county, the idea of a woman who doesn't allow her emotions to dictate her sex life tends to list toward fearsome visions of a heartless hellcat. These two men represent what precipitates from the ominous clouds of fear that boil over any concept of casual, round-heeled, *a*moral sex.

Apart from the terror of disorderly women, the question (besides why is it raining men!) is what exactly is the threat? Sex for the sake of enjoyment alone certainly doesn't preclude any of the profound personal and interpersonal experiences afforded by sex had in the context, or under the guise, of romantic love (usually treated with possessive exclusivity, as monogamy). In fact, the act has the potential of being even more intimate, for various reasons.

Intimacy is not security, and security is not intimacy, although they are badly mistaken, and treated, as synonymous. Again, security is a really foolish notion—especially when all wrapped up in that cozy feeling we usually call "love"—that is used as the common currency buying us the freedom to let down our guard and expose ourselves. Uh, sort of, sometimes. Under such circumstances (the transactional exchange of tit for tat), that willingness to be "vulnerable" is actually an impotent statement, with very little meaning. In other words, where's the vulnerability in eliminating the perceived risk?

Because both men and women have learned such conflicting and confusing messages around sex, and because it has become loaded with so many extraneous and pejorative implications and meanings, beliefs and expectations, *and* because it is such a monumentally significant feature of our lives, there is tremendous guardedness around that aspect of functioning. It's no wonder we have devised ways of protecting ourselves in this arena. It's almost crazy not to, from an instinctual perspective. And so where we find ourselves many times is locked in our own prison of self-preservation.

Waiting for a Miracle

A dear friend of mine was a heartbreaking example of how crippling that reality can actually become. Finding each other kicking around in our hometown after some years away, he and I became close for a period of time. We shared an affectionate and reverent tenderness for each other that was a welcome haven to each of us for different reasons. (I was going through the thick of some painful revelations around my family unit, and he was soon headed off to face the hulking trials of boot camp in the Marines.)

We were clearly interested in each other sexually and tried many times to manifest it, but the burden he carried of guilt, self-consciousness, fear, and insecurity around sex became completely debilitating for him, both emotionally and physically. His performance anxiety became so overwhelming that his anatomy refused to participate, which of course only made matters worse.

With all the love in my heart and all the support I could offer, I remember feeling my own impotence watching this whole thing snowball beyond control. I lacked the skills I might now be more capable of utilizing to help him work through the inner tangle, were he willing. He gradually drifted away from me and eventually got married. I don't know how things panned out for him—a few subsequent conversations revealed things were not a bowl of cherries—but I can still feel the ache of that memory of him.

I can't believe that my affection wasn't palpable enough to him. I was positively overflowing to him in my expression, yet he seemed irresistibly compelled to seek out the refuge of a marriage, possibly to assuage the sense of sexual vulnerability—as well as guilt—in an unconventional liaison. Sometimes that refuge offers the only environment where a person thinks they're safe enough to let go.

But are they? There's that knot that's been ceremonially tied, but then there's that much more at stake, so it's not for free—meaning the higher stakes of a public, legal commitment can now potentially augment the underlying angst. Remember the facts about the dirty laundry.

I need to make it abundantly clear that I am not talking about avoiding the responsibility of commitment, of running away from the requirements involved in deeply intimate long-term relationships with other people. In contrast, I'm pointing to the fact that we cannot run *to* the shelter of such an "institution"—effectively running *away* from ourselves—without dragging along all the other crud that clings to our functional cogs. In fact, we can only really manifest the fullness of such committed involvement if we are going to—pointedly, boldly, seriously—address our issues.

Wild Is the Wind

Setting out into that spartan territory where sex is just sex, stripped of its finery, had made me quiver in my boots and shake like a leaf. This was vulnerability to the max for me, because I actually had to "come as I am," which is a blunt, raw, full-bodied sexual entity versus a carefully packaged collection of shrewd insinuations. And *intimacy* is nothing if not vulnerable! The commonly overlooked truth about intimacy is that it is, by definition, somewhat frightening. Which is why conventional security tends to be its opposite.

Intimacy is the vulnerability of speaking and acting outside the safe envelope of security, exposed to the uncertainty of how others will *actually* respond versus how we *assume* they will respond. These assumptions are based on the convoluted matrix of our own inner processes, upon which we place a ridiculous degree of, as it turns out, purely blind faith. So then the irony about relational security is that the *known* is only *believed* to be known, as we sign our real selves away when we buy into the social contract that says we'll all pretend we know what the other person is thinking and feeling. So we simply act accordingly, using the socially acceptable (and extremely dishonest) language of that contract. But just behind that veil of make-believe awaits an open frontier. Even when you think you know someone very well—and maybe in fact you do—there is still the possibility of an infinite variety of ways they may surprise you at any given time if allowed the opportunity and invited into the adventure.

There's nothing quite like the feeling of dangling in that wildly uncertain space, experiencing the quake and the shiver in the interminable moment between taking that bold risk of honesty and waiting for the reaction. What starts out as holy terror, with practice, develops into a sense of vitality and power. The vitality is the *aliveness* that is born out of unburdening ourselves of the baggage that stands in the way of our direct and unencumbered interaction with other people. The power is stepping into realizing that *all of life* is largely unknown, and making the defining choice to live accordingly rather than in the denial fostered within the social contract. Interacting with another person based on this level of vulnerability actually becomes an expression of intimacy (and a true act of power). Through this act we free ourselves to speak truthfully, and we free the other person, in our own minds, from who we have already decided they are going to be and therefore how we need to carefully phrase our language to disguise the dreadful truth. From this place it really doesn't matter so much how they respond. The significance is in the relational and—no joke—existential expression.

Most people understand, intellectually at least, that love actually requires an open heart. But because we live out our social lives through a string of these contractual relationships, there is little exposure to the kind of intimacy of which I speak, that which requires a truly—wildly, perhaps—authentic openness. This way takes constant attention and effort because the default will almost always be some form of caving in to fear and hiding instead (that's how the ego defends itself). I've been working on this for well over twenty years now, and still, every time I have to say something uncomfortably honest to someone (whether it's a stranger or someone very close to me), I have to muscle my way through all the barriers of inner censorship. It looks as though the experience will always come with those same feelings: Fear. Anxiety. Butterflies. And the endless string of compelling excuses for stuffing a sock in it. But every time I soldier through it, I get stronger in my resolve to never stop fighting my way to the prize: life lived alive.

Rusty Cage

Our biggest popular lie is constantly being told by squeezing our vast and ubiquitous sexuality into the tight little container of social propriety, which includes the ideas of sexual modesty, privacy, discretion, exclusivity, and so forth. We've decided we owe it to one another to keep it hidden and covert, "maintaining the facade of decency." But intimacy is honesty, through and through, and when the most pivotal aspect of our humanity is blatantly concealed across the board, a wholesale lack of intimacy is an absolute given, since it is about as dishonest as we can get with others and ourselves.

An incredibly beefy quote is in order at this juncture. Author Uta Ranke-Heinemann says, "Sexuality is not a simply regional, functional determination, but a peculiar feature of the essence of man that goes back to his absolutely earliest psycho-physical origins, a peculiar feature that helps to shape, each time in a special way, all the definable dimensions of the human being, and is also shaped by each of them. Sexuality is not something that a person simply *has* along with many other things, but a fundamental way of *being* in all things, and hence something without which his or her other existential acts and relations cannot actually be thought and realized"[42] (italics in original).

This exquisitely articulated statement makes it very clear why our cagey dishonesty around sex is going to permeate, discolor, and painfully confine every other aspect of our lives and relationships.

And this is why we have to make the clear delineation between sex and emotion. Not because they must never intersect or overlap (because they certainly do), but because the way we have chosen to *obscure* and *justify* one with the other by morally *enforcing* the overlap has confounded the fundamental feature of our very existence, and

---

[42] Ranke-Heinemann, 53.

it must be corrected in order to undo the damage. Because of the way we have distorted our psychoemotional dimensions, we cannot touch the pure essence of that peculiar feature, sexuality, without breaking out of this cage.

I Want a New Drug

Many people, both men and women, will argue that sex is much better when you're in love. But that, too, is based on the array of ways that we have trained ourselves to inhibit or release our passions, which is very much under the control of the cerebral cortex (though often unconsciously).

Interestingly, nature has seen to it that sex for the sake of physical enjoyment does not preclude the emotional experience of loving affection that we mistakenly believe must be exclusive to that special mate. Orgasm releases a great flood of *oxytocin* in both males and females, and this hormone, if left to its own devices (meaning if the physiological experience is not overridden by the psychological inhibitions), has its own way of generating the rapture. In fact (if left to its own devices), this physiological marvel probably holds the key to more harmonious societal alliances overall.[43] In *Sex at Dawn*, Ryan states, "Sometimes called 'nature's ecstasy,' oxytocin is important in pro-social feelings like compassion, trust, generosity, love, and yes, eroticism."[44] He points out that bonobos, one of our closest primate relatives, appear to enjoy the effects of this phenomenon. With sexual promiscuity as a central feature of their social interactions, it functions exceptionally well to

---

[43] I'd like to include here another angle on the role of oxytocin, to flesh out the scientific complexities that must be acknowledged when we translate the specifics of science into the kind of story I'm utilizing for example. John Bancroft (former director, current research fellow of the Kinsey Institute) writes, "The role of oxytocin in pair-bonding or affiliation, while of apparent relevance in some species studied (Carter, 1998), is of less certain relevance in the human, given its complex role as a central neuromodulator. This has not, however, stopped some from identifying it as 'the love hormone.'" *Human Sexuality and Its Problems* (Churchill Livingstone, 1993, 1998, 2009), 128.

[44] Ryan and Jetha, 72.

promote bonding between all members of the community, facilitating a remarkably peaceful and fluid social organization.

The way most of us humans have arranged our current cultures effectively puts our most pro-social behaviors under lock and key. Semantically, we have even defined intimacy *as* sex and then buried that sexuality so deeply under a vile pile of the most rotten moral rubbish that we'll be damned before we can actually locate it in any pristine condition. And then, of all things, we complain about all the violence and dream about world peace as though that could, and should, simply materialize out of thin air, *in spite of us all!*

It is important to recognize and accept, carte blanche, that the hormones of sex are not at all exclusive to a certain special somebody. They are universal and indifferent to such trivial parameters and actually serve us much better as a species if shared more openly on a much broader scale.

The thing is, due to all the myriad influences, we have simply not learned to appropriately value sex. Because of all the added baggage heaped over it, we don't really understand *what it is*, and as a result, we do not really understand fundamentally *who we are* (in all our definable dimensions). Without a solid understanding of ourselves as sexual entities and a thoroughly healthy working relationship with that understanding, we cannot properly value our sexual partners. If we really open to the depth and expanse of sexuality without fearfully and shamefully cringing away (as we do on so many levels, mostly unknowingly), we can meet, at last, on the precipice of sexual intimacy and enjoy, together—outside any other relational and/or emotional context—the healing harmony of tapping the wellspring of our own biological pharmacy.

In my own experience (and to my pure amazement), I began to recognize, in the very midst of my determined work to distinguish sexuality from emotionality, that I was undeniably "falling in love" in one way or another with almost every one of my sex partners, regardless of any remarkably winning characteristics. Before, I had only known that sensation to arise under very particular circumstances—i.e., how closely he happened to match all my preferences and requirements in a mate. But of course, I hadn't really given it the necessary opportunity, had I? I was only *allowing* myself to have sex with those men for whom I already felt or thought I wanted to feel that kind of emotion!

The revelation I got from this experience was that the sensation *behind* these feelings was a natural and unlimited occurrence; it was happening inside my own person and had little to do with the other individual and how his attributes stacked up against my big, fat romantic fantasy. (This understanding was able to come forth only because I was choosing to function outside the traditional mode, and habit, of hitching the feeling diligently to the whole train of relational implications and sexual commitment that convention narrates for us.) What I ended up experiencing was the increased release of rapturous sexual hormones due to relaxing the artificial parameters I'd previously had in place.

And the most important part—the crux of the entire juicy biscuit—is that the *interpretation* of the blissful sensation as "falling in love" is actually a product of cultural conditioning.

Romantic love itself—certainly the "forever" fantasy we know so well—is an embellishment of Western culture and not something that has always been such a foofaraw in human civilization. The idea, evidently drawn from Ovid's epics, was developed by the troubadours of medieval France, and the theme of "courtly love" gained traction among the social elite. Then, with further developments—the printing press, the growth of literacy among the masses and early pulp fiction—the notion spread like wildfire. Now we are an enormous culture of romantic love, propagating its mythos through all aspects of modern media and entertainment to the extent that we have come to regard it as a fundamental fact of life. We have come to *expect* it out of life and from ourselves, and even to require its validation for the worthiness of our lives. In this regard, we have literally become "emotionally programmed to fall in love."[45]

---

[45] I use the words of freethinker James Leonard Park author of *New Ways of Loving: How Authenticity Transforms Relationships*.

The enduring success of our romantic mythology is due to just this kind of experiential reinforcement: I feel it; therefore, it is real. But the real truth is that it's merely a wedding of convenience, uniting the (separate) experiences of the chemical phenomenon that arises from emotional openness on the one hand and sexual arousal and orgasm on the other. So it's not at all the big deal it's made out to be, and it actually ends up causing much pain and suffering, since we allow these ephemeral feelings to dictate more permanent decisions like marriage and totally irrelevant decisions like having children.

Moreover—and this is very significant—*the enchantment with romantic love gets further inflated in an environment where social intimacy is scarce and sexual activity is constrained*. The only reason this kind of interpersonal intimacy occurs so randomly and ephemerally as to make it seem to be a magical arrow, delivered by the bow of a mythical Cupid, is that we so rarely allow that quality of intimacy to transpire. We are generally too encumbered with whatever distractions, protections, prejudices, personal preferences, self-identifications, et cetera, to actualize the ever-imminent potential of such a thing. (And so many of the most blissful memories of being in love are from when we're young, because, as unadulterated youth, we had not yet accumulated all this excess baggage.) Furthermore, we are enchanted by the mystical magic of it because it prevents us from having to look squarely at who and what we really are *and* at what this hyped-up thing called "love" is all about, including how it does or does not involve sex.

As a culture, we have more or less come to believe in the Hollywood dramatization of romantic love as a mysterious, unique, and otherworldly phenomenon, sweeping down from the fanciful heavens and whisking us off into the enchanted sunset. But in an article called "To Fall in Love with Anyone, Do This,"[46] the author describes how love is "more pliable"—and much more organic—than we have come to think. She makes her point using as an example the design and outcome of a twenty-year-old, ninety-minute exper-

---

[46] Mandy Len Catron, "To Fall in Love with Anyone, Do This," *New York Times*, Sunday, January 11, 2015.

iment by psychologist Arthur Aron. By having a heterosexual man and woman engage in a conversation involving a set of thirty-six increasingly personal questions followed by a four-minute period of silent eye-gazing, Dr. Aron was able to cause these subjects—random strangers to one another at the outset of the experiment—to fall in love. Catron aptly observes that love is really based on the action of getting to know someone and allowing ourselves to be known by another—in other words, an act of interpersonal intimacy.

This is simply a platonic way of stimulating the production of oxytocin, which is known even to occur mutually between dogs and their owners during the activity of prolonged eye contact.[47] (Bonobos, again, also spend extended periods of time gazing into one another's eyes…they've got it down!)

While the pleasant sensation may provide the social advantage of a sense of interpersonal, tribal, or even interspecies connection, it only gets turned into the adamant directive toward exclusivity in a cultural environment that condemns a liberal sexuality, confines expressions of interpersonal intimacy, and values the isolated nuclear family over all else as its moral and economic foundation. It doesn't mean we have to throw out marriage and monogamy altogether, but it does mean—if we are to handle ourselves in the sexual domain with a greater degree of intelligent awareness, satisfaction, and well-being—that we really do have to question the *institution*, to understand how all this works, and to cut ourselves some serious slack in the dogma department.

By and by, as I let myself open up sexually on deeper levels, it began to become distinctly clear to me that the glamor and bling of "making love" with that special someone was really nothing more than a self-fulfilling prophecy. In fact, all that was required was the ability to let go, open up, and allow nature to run free. As a result, it helped foster within me a relatively impartial openness of heart that I hadn't known before. It helped me to further dismantle the clinging

---

[47] Jan Hoffman, "The Look of Love Is in the Dog's Eyes," *New York Times*, Well Pets, April 16, 2015.

attachment—that jealous ownership of one another—that intimate sexual union inspires in us according to the design and expectations of our society.

Ahh, so finally there's the answer I'm looking for, all fleshed out: a good reason for the threat. It's very clear that this kind of information is not what we want good girls (and ultimately boys, too, for that matter) to get their hands on. This is a game changer in the realm of everything our society has striven for regarding the confinement of sexuality within the bounds of propriety defined as *monogamy*. It obliterates that whole slew of theories, assumptions, and doggedly defended articles of faith that support the idea that humans—most certainly women—are innately *designed* for it, whether by the hand of God Almighty himself or by the Darwinian evolution of our DNA.

If we allow women to let themselves go and enjoy the full experience of sexual ecstasy with anyone they desire, well, that's a mighty slippery slope, the most dangerous gateway drug on the black market, because next thing you know, she is back in her power. She is no longer lost in confusion about the "love thing" that keeps her under wraps and out of sorts bodily and psychically. Now she is a force to be reckoned with—*rock and roll, sista!*—and this reckoning runs deep.

Love Stinks

Even though it's bejeweled with ornate decoration and drowning in such sweet perfumes, I smell a rat called love.

Now, love is a lovely emotion—who can argue with that? But it *is* an emotion, and emotional states are constantly in flux within the dynamic biochemical slurry of the multifaceted human organism. They cannot, and should not, be forced and controlled. They must only be observed, expressed, understood, and valued appropriately (which is another book in itself).

There is a redeeming scene in the otherwise cheesy 2004 movie *What the Bleep Do We Know?*, where people dressed in hospital gowns are dancing around exuberantly with their IVs—tubes, bags, poles, and all—delivering the desired formulation of emotional biochemistry. It's choreographed as a statement of how we are individually addicted each to our particular emotional cocktail, which we keep flowing through our veins by behaving in patterns that stimulate the endocrine system's repeated production of such constituents (like *dying* to fall in love!). Poking fun at the ludicrousness of it, the point we can take from the scene is that it is really a form of sickness.

As a society, we are addicted to *love.* This humble little emotion has been singled out to represent the panacea of all ills. But, unfortunately, along the way it's become a very cerebral affair at the societal level, because while being force-fed its endless demands, very few of us ever learn *how* to really love (because we're too busy learning how to effectively lie about who we really are). After expertly eviscerating its living qualities, leaving only the crusty exoskeleton of an idea—dangling from the strings of irrelevant notions manipulated by the hands of a neurotic puppeteer—it doesn't even make us feel good anymore! Love has been taken beyond its living practical status as a capricious emotion to represent the ideal of a universal constant. Because of its socially benign attributes, love has been glorified, deified, canonized, and otherwise exalted among almost all sections of humanitarian, philanthropic, religious, and spiritual circles.

To Christians, Jesus's message—and God himself—is love, so for us to love is to be more holy. To most Buddhists, love in the form of loving-kindness is the goal of practice, so our degree of enlightenment comes to be measured by our loving feelings and inspired gestures of servitude to others. To the New Agers, love is everything, so you better get busy faking it, no matter what.

But the contradictions that arise as a result of how we define love itself and ordain the appropriate manifestations of it are enormous and, often, enormously devastating. The self-righteous claim to the word of God on sexual love has caused the widespread oppression of virtually all forms of human sexual experience that fall outside the narrow guidelines of traditional Judaic, Islamic, and Christian rubric. The missionary dissemination of Good News to the far reaches of the earth has resulted in decidedly bad news for the recipients, as in the "loving to death" of innumerable vibrant and viable human cultures.

The premature insistence upon loving-kindness and service to others within Buddhist instructional circles stands squarely in the way of practitioners sinking into the solitary depths of apprehending the most key fundamentals at the heart of the Buddha's teaching, and therefore stifling the real, genuine spiritual development—which, of course, is what leads to the deep understanding of the human predicament at the very core of enlightenment itself.

The New Age movement, influenced by Westernized Eastern spiritual traditions, belligerently obstructs most other avenues of authentic interpersonal response as everyone clamors to claim and keep up the appearances of love and tolerance at the expense of nearly every other healthy human expression. Just under the surface festers intense animosity and resentment, because love—the simple emotion that it is—has its limits.

Once love is a socially defined entity, and controlled accordingly, it sets up some pretty strong boundaries. Think of the possessiveness of lovers, often manifest as militant monogamy, the ferocious (often homicidal) anger inspired by the love of another god, or the exclusivity of familial love. Just how much violence, subtle or extreme, has resulted from jealous love is immeasurable. The reason is simple: struggling to control the uncontrollable is always going to backfire violently. It is practically a law of nature.

By now, love has been called so many things and infused with so much meaning and import, from chicken soup to world peace, that it has become the unquestioned and unassailable foundation of soapbox and pulpit, from which so many well-meaning—yet frequently self-serving—do-gooders preach to the rest of us about how we ought to be feeling at any given moment. This presumption has become so standardized that to question its validity practically indicates some kind of demonic possession or deranged psychosis in one who would so inquire. Love is expected as proof of our human decency and demanded of us from all angles to ensure our contribution to the common good. And yet *love* is possibly the most ambiguous word in the English language, so it's easy to toss it around in almost any way you can dream up in order to manipulate almost any given situation.

I'm risking it all here in order to point out why it is such a tricky proposition to even suggest that love, to speak the most truly and clearly, has nothing to do with sex. The suggestion puts into the crosshairs one of the most profoundly cherished fundamentals of moral and ethical conviction, making it one of the last ranky places people want you to go sniffing around for the real truth.

Because of the preeminent approbation of "love," it has been used—and abused—for justification, glorification, accommodation, and circumscription of the otherwise "dubious" affairs of the flesh. So to get out, once and for all, from under the dark umbrella of the sex-negative mind-set, that whole reeking construct has to be incinerated.

SUPER FREAK

Now that we've stepped into the really wild frontier, time to turn up the volume, fasten our seat belts—click it or ticket—and enjoy the ride.

(I Can't Get No) Satisfaction

Marilyn Chambers is Insatiable[48]…and the erotic world ate it up. Mmm, I wonder who else might be, and is it really such a menacing threat to find out?

Apparently so…and not surprisingly, in a world that has dedicated so much toward obliterating any manifestations and intimations of that possibility from religious moralists to research scientists. When female sexuality has to be controlled, her sexual *appetite* becomes a foreboding entity that must be beaten into submission from all angles…and truth be told, it has. Think back to the beginning chapter of this book about the demands of patriarchy and religion for maintaining social order by controlling, most urgently, female sexuality. The appetite within must absolutely be denied, lest we flirt with the menace of mayhem. And this brings us around to that story about modern pharmacology.

As companies work on developing drugs to enhance female libido, we see something emerge that we didn't see as they worked

---

[48] *(Marilyn Chambers is) Insatiable* is a classic pornographic movie starring Marilyn Chambers and directed by Stu Segall. Released in 1980 at the end of the 'porn chic' era in the US, it was followed by a 1984 sequel, *Insatiable II*, also directed by Segall.

to formulate Viagra for men—a fear of creating sexually aggressive women and the societal anarchy envisioned as a result. Officials huddle in boardrooms discussing concerns about FDA approval in the event of a wildly successful product. They plan ahead and prepare their strategies for handling the sure-fire requirement to provide assurances that the drug's impact is *selective*—that it works but not *too well*.[49] So round and round we go, wrestling endlessly with that edgy, impossible problem of keeping the ladies right where we want them: willing, receptive and responsive *to the appropriate man* versus ill-behaved, cock-stalking nymphomaniacs (no wonder medicine moves so sluggishly with regard to female sexual health). "Oversexed" women represent a holy terror to the anxious social construct we've built ourselves into.

It's a topic that threatens the warp and woof of our culture's sense of balance just like global warming threatens the fabric of a fossil-fueled economy: we've become deeply embedded, if not inextricably embroiled, in a way of life that we invented ourselves, with big players making deep investments that must be protected at the expense of human welfare. And "the rest of the world" simply enters the fold and buys into the program, just because that's the way it is. It's the world we live in; it's who we are. *Except it really isn't who we are*, and playing along with this putrid pantomime is going nowhere. Therefore, it only makes sense to just keep rolling stones (thanks, Mick) and examine what's underneath…

Indications of this underlying behemoth abound in the popular media and provide some good fodder for making a few fat, highly relevant points.

In a *New York Times* article considering whether or not pornography hurts kids,[50] a research psychologist and faculty member from UCLA was quoted saying one of his major concerns about porn was the fraudulent message "that all women have insatiable sexual

---

[49] Daniel Bergner, *What Do Women Want: Adventures in the Science of Female Desire* (New York: HarperCollins Publishers, 2013), 179–180.

[50] David Segal, "Does Porn Hurt Kids?" *New York Times*, Sunday Review, News Analysis, March 28, 2014.

appetites." I wish he'd given us a bit more about that, but I'm left to speculate…Is this kind of comment a flashback to the prude consternation met by Alfred Kinsey's 1953 publication of *Sexual Behavior in the Human Female*, in the vein of protecting a more angelic Victorian vision of our mothers, sisters, daughters?[51] And why doesn't a look at porn raise such a concern about the male sexual appetite? Because everybody knows the grandiosity of the male sex drive, and we're all comfortable with that. Yet, in *Newsweek* in 1953, Kinsey concluded that the range of sexual behavior in the female far exceeds that of the male.[52] While both of his books raised controversy and consternation at the time of publication due to the cultural context of that era and generation, the revelations about women clearly overstepped a boundary that was beyond what many could stomach.

And yet our continuing enforcement of the insipid notions of the unbridgeable chasm between male voracity and female reserve remains stubbornly in place today, preventing us from moving forward freely into mutual fulfillment. Marty Klein (sex therapist, author, and educator) suggests that the consistent theme in pornography of female lust expresses a male-female mutuality that is a human truth, and one that actually threatens the scarcity-model mind-set about our sexual economy and gender hierarchy. The exposure of certain such truths in pornography, he explains, is what makes porn subversive and threatening to the cultural status quo, which is why it is so ardently opposed by conservatives.[53]

On the other hand, is that author of the *Times* article attempting to protect young men (like his own sons, whom he mentions) from disappointment when their forays into sexual activity present them with a more dismal experience (because, due to their training,

---

[51] Discussing why the publication of the book was such a huge media event, John Bancroft, director of the Kinsey Institute, said, "The lid was taken off, so to speak. Women were more sexual than conventional wisdom and morality would want us to believe." Susan Williams, "Kinsey, the Media and Public Reaction," January 31, 2003, www.indiana.edu/~ocmhptst/013103/text/kinsey.html.

[52] "All About Eve: Kinsey Reports on American Women," *Newsweek*, Medicine, August 24, 1953.

[53] Klein, 153.

young women do not generally allow themselves much in the way of full sexual expression)?

Does it reflect a concern for protecting the safety of women, in that this message could lead to justifications of rape, harassment, even murder? (In the 1970s, antiporn feminists campaigned with the injunction "Pornography is the theory, rape is the practice."[54]) This is not outlandish, as I'll discuss in a moment, but it is yet another limited view that, while certainly well intended, just continues to feed the big scary monster we've constructed in the closet that has crept out and taken over our lives.

Sexual violence is primarily stimulated by abuse and repression, which are prevalent in our society at all levels. It is then further exacerbated by the manufactured imbalance in our sexual culture that historically recognizes men as aggressively libidinous creatures while encouraging the identification of women as sexually elusive, difficult, coy, and demure. (And, thanks to evolutionary psychology, this poppycock is now postured as scientifically based fact.) This is nothing less than a nightmare in the making. And we're living it—the belief and the nightmare—so dutifully and ignorantly, unable to awaken because there is no alarm, literally, as it has blended unremarkably into all the background noise of the general malaise we call normal.

We have to stop running away from the truth about female sexuality.

The reality is that women, hardwired to be highly sexually motivated and active, have, in large part, lost touch with innate sexuality even while obsessing over the erotic appeal of the body. The internal twist tightens as the mixed messages about sex grind and gyrate around inside. The overt attitude all over the ubiquitous media screams out to us about the supreme importance of sex in our lives, making us believe we've actually accomplished some kind of sexual liberation. And yet, when push comes to shove, we all find ourselves ever so tightly confined within a social order defined by a deeply

---

[54] John D'Emilio and Estelle B. Freedman, *Intimate Matters: A History of Sexuality in America,* 2nd ed. (Chicago: University of Chicago Press, 1997), 351.

prudish popular morality. And here we have the living reality of that sexual confusion in our lives—*denial and indulgence, suppression and stimulation, punishment and exploitation, secrecy and display*—fleshing out the brilliant quote at the front of this book, and undermining our precious human dignity every step of the way.

From what I can see, even among the young adults involved in the modern hook-up culture, who appear to be free and easy with sex, there is still a grasping for escape from inhibited confines. More often than not, it seems that some form of intoxicant is utilized as a crutch, which tells me "free and easy" still ain't such, and people are still not at home within their sexual selves.

When Doves Cry

In another article titled "Prisoners of Sex,"[55] the author points out "the tension between our culture's official attitude toward sex on the one hand and our actual patterns of sexual and romantic life on the other" in the context of a discussion about the larger cultural significance of a recent killing rampage by a sexually frustrated young man. This tension of which he speaks is constantly tugging painfully at the gaping rift between the sexes, resulting in the exacerbation of bitter enmity along with endless speculations on it and misguided solutions for it, including those offered in his article, with the deepest problem remaining unaddressed (that the vast chasm between us is our own make-believe, self-perpetuating creation).

He says, "The…killer's pulsing antipathy toward women, his shame and fury over sexual inexperience—these were amplified horribly by mental illness, yes, but visit the angrier corners of the internet, wander in comment threads and chat rooms, and you'll recognize them as extreme versions of an all-too-commonplace misogyny." He comments further, stating, "This tension between sexual expectations and social reality is a potential problem for both sexes, but for a variety of reasons—social, cultural and biological—it's more likely to produce toxic reactions in [males]."

---

[55] Ross Douthat, "Prisoners of Sex," *New York Times*, June 1, 2014.

My own experience has shown me that this tension is not just a potential problem, but actually a very real, live one. I've observed, too, that women also have very toxic reactions to the situation manifesting internally as toxic emotion and illnesses of obscure etiology and externally as passive-aggressive behavior, manipulation, and outright physical aggression. The situation is toxic all the way around. Men are violently angry at women because their balls are physically aching, while women—severed from their bodies, disempowered and suspended in Disneyland—are bitterly disenchanted that men are not living up to the Prince Charming they have been promised since childhood and, therefore, to which they feel entitled. (A visit to the angrier corners of any strip club dressing room reveals the full impact—admittedly a more extreme version—of the toxic misandry harbored among women.) And as it turns out, domestic violence involving women abusing men is much more common than most people realize.

Meanwhile, pick up any men's magazine and notice how the articles, steeped in the now-standard school of evolutionary psychology (EP), strive to help men groping around like gorillas in the mist, eager to understand women—to woo them, to screw them, and to keep them interested. According to the "authoritative" material in circulation, these men must understand the complicated female sexual condition, accept the "hard" evolutionary science behind the reality of it, and then cater to the delicate psychosexual nature of women (playing her needy game) in order to manifest any kind of satisfactory sexual relationship with her. That's the fine kettle of fish being fried—because *that's how women have learned to view themselves* (at the behest of men) and, therefore, how men have figured out how to go about trying to have sex with them. All this cavorting around to finagle an activity that everybody wants so badly to be doing... go figure.

Breakdown

So finally now, let's take this EP bull honky by the horns and wrestle it down into the mud.

Here's the question: Is it a preestablished (hard-wired) psychology expressed through the dictates of genetic evolution over deep evolutionary time, or is it actually a *socialized* psychology that has taken shape—not in the genes, but in the mind—within the highly and intrinsically malleable context of culture (and the brain itself)? And do we even know enough in general about how nature versus nurture[56] shapes real-time human psychology to draw up reliable evolution-based theories pertaining specifically to sexual attitudes?

It may well be the case that gender role socialization itself actually changes the *brains* of boys and girls.[57] In this case, to analyze current male and female sexual behavior and psychology (and even the underlying structure and physiology of the brain) would be highly misleading. Any conclusions drawn from outside the greater cultural context would be not only presumptuous but also downright inane, especially when you consider the massive cultural forces acting directly to distort it, most forcibly in the last two thousand years.

One of the most remarkable features of the brain is its staggering plasticity. This is most astonishingly evident in cases where babies

---

[56] The evolutionary psychologists really hate being pigeonholed in the nature vs. nurture dichotomy, retorting that the "cognitive architecture," or functional design that we now have, "is the joint product of genes and environment" and that *how* the environment affects an organism is critically dependent upon that evolved architecture. But this is not an argument, since what they're giving us, all said, *is* a product of nature, established by natural selection in the environment of early hominid evolution, and remaining essentially unaltered ever since (so that, in their own words, "our modern skulls house a stone-age mind"). Regarding reflexive instincts, like fight or flight, an evolutionary explanation is totally reasonable, but the EPs make many more grand extrapolations that extend well beyond both rationality and science. An example of the highly dubious nature of their stance is found in their EP primer, where they repeatedly attempt to hang flimsy hypothetical suppositions on the hard science of evolutionary biology (often using utterly preposterous arguments). Please check it out and see for yourself (*Evolutionary Psychology: A Primer*, by Leda Cosmides and John Tooby, http://www.cep.ucsb.edu/primer.html).

[57] David P. Schmitt, "Are Women More Emotional Than Men?" *Psychology Today*, April 10, 2015. Schmitt acknowledges that "finding sex differences in emotionality would not mean the differences evolved, even if the sex differences have neurological substrates."

born with literally *half* of the anatomical structure of a brain grow into normal, healthy, intelligent adults, indistinguishable from their peers. And it is evident to anyone witnessing the recovery of determined stroke patients (as I did with my grandmother).

Understanding the implications of possessing such a remarkable organ, we should all strive to be in a state of heightened awareness of how we are shaping its circuitry moment to moment! Any change in our habits of thought and behavior has immediate effects on the brain and body chemistry. Electromagnetic brain imaging can observe this, biochemical analysis can measure it, and in my experience, an attentive person can actually feel the biochemical effects physically. The human brain/mind is a flexible, responsive, ever-remodeling tool—and this, I believe, is the closest we can reasonably characterize any "universal, species-typical architecture," as sought in evolutionary psychology.

It is much more evolutionarily feasible that our genes evolved in favor of a biologically plastic brain organ with a complex cerebral intelligence as a functional tool, as well as a high degree of social malleability[58] that would have favored survival within the necessary context of tribal community. (From what I can see, evolutionary psychology has done—and is doing—us all an enormous disservice by convincing us of fallacies that cloud the truth of who we are with mistaken ideas of what we are made of, particularly in the realm of sex where further confusion is so destructive and problematic to our social existence.)

I propose that the sexual "imbalance" suffered between men and women is not inherent in our biology, but an invention of our culture, and because it's the source of so much strife, the sooner we get to excavating this megalith the better off we'll be.

---

[58] Julian Jaynes, author and Princeton University psychology professor, suggested that *consciousness itself,* or that rich subjective experience of our inner selves, is a social construct "learned at the mercy of a collective cognitive imperative," or group belief system, and at a *recent time* in our history (*The Origin of Consciousness in the Breakdown of the Bicameral Mind* [Boston: Houghton Mifflin Company, 1976], 340).

She's Not There

Because this cultural invention has been such a ghastly success, too many women now believe and function accordingly, as sexually reticent creatures motivated by their hearts instead of their hormones. What nobody wants to admit, however, is that this idea is completely at odds with the reality of sexual nature in all known living creatures. And then everyone is so terribly frustrated, of course, as the dirty laundry agitates in the wash.

In 1966, Mary Jane Sherfey wrote in *The Nature and Evolution of Female Sexuality* that "our myth of the female's relative asexuality is a biological absurdity," and even that "to all intents and purposes, the human female is sexually insatiable."[59] How could any respectable scientist hold such a position in the midst of the swarms of undeniable evidence to the contrary that surround us everywhere in our world? If this has any validity, why don't we see it manifesting around us, within us?

Well—in addition to the reasons just stated—somewhere someone is beginning to get some scientific insight into this conundrum, penetrating through the thick, sun-blocking, truth-devouring locust clouds, and pointing in a very telling direction. Daniel Bergner, in his outstanding book *What Do Women Want*, highlights the current research (much of it conducted by women) into the nature of female desire. One study investigates visual responsiveness by inventing a way, using a keyboard and a vaginal sensor, "to get past the obfuscations of the mind, the interference of the brain's repressive upper regions, and to find out, at a primitive level, what turns women on."[60]

This approach successfully demonstrated that women actually respond immediately with significant physiological arousal *to a much wider array of sexual imagery than do men*. Women, equipped with vaginally inserted detectors (plethysmographs), respond with increased blood flow and lubrication to the vaginal walls, in varying

---

[59] Sherfey made these comments based on extensive scientific studies of the anatomy and physiology of women actually having sex (data from Masters and Johnson). *The Nature and Evolution of Female Sexuality* (New York: Vintage Books, 1996, 1973), 112, 113.

[60] Daniel Bergner, *What Do Women Want: Adventures in the Science of Female Desire* (New York: HarperCollins Publishers, 2013), 4.

intensities, to images ranging from homo to hetero, human to non-human sexual activity, and naked men alone, with and without erections, all indicating surefire sexual stimulation of an "omnivorous" nature regardless of their stated orientation. (Flashback to Kinsey's statement about the greater variety found in female sexual behavior.) In contrast, the men in the study responded much more selectively.

This data should run like a Mack truck straight through the delusion we've all bought into that men are the animals who respond visually, while women—the emotionally wired, modest-by-nature ones—do not (once again, a theory vigorously promulgated by those evolutionary psychologists). And do you know what all these women said using their keyboards to capture the same moment? They said, oh no, no response to that, no arousal, not me…The cognitive surveys were completely incongruous with the actual physiological responses taking place in their bodies. The men's subjective reports, on the other hand, were completely in line with the objective data from their genitals.

That is the power of social and cultural training. Make no mistake about it.

One of the researchers considers an anatomical explanation for the incongruence,[61] and Ryan and Jetha,[62] referencing this same experiment in their book, suggest that a woman's difficulty in knowing what she's feeling may have its cause in her "erotic plasticity" (the innate lifelong versatility and malleability of a woman's sexual proclivities as opposed, ostensibly, to that of a man's). However, both of these ideas collapse under the weight of two things: (1) the overwhelming force of the heavy-handed history of psychological conditioning that has constrained female sexual expression, and (2) the provable fact that with training and practice of a mindful and accepting nature, women *can and do* learn to recognize when their bodies

---

[61] Meredith Chivers considers the possibility that the female's "more covert architecture might make the messages less clear, easier to miss" (Bergner, 15).
[62] Ryan and Jetha, 274.

are sexually aroused, something which I will address at length later on. There is no innate obfuscation of, or anatomical barrier to, a woman's sensation and cognizance of her own body's sexual stimulation, only a psychoemotional one.

The evidence from studies like the plethysmograph experiment—that the female DNA is, in fact, ready to rock and roll—is screaming in neon to anyone who cares to know. Bergner sums it up, saying, "Women's desire—its inherent range and innate power—is an underestimated and constrained force, even in our times, when all can seem so sexually inundated, so far beyond restriction."[63]

So really, don't we all wish women would find their freak and let it out? Ah, true liberation for women! I think maybe we do, once we look a little more honestly at everything. But let's take a peek at some other things...

Janie's Got a Gun

Reading Bergner's book, where he presents the accounts of several modern women's fantasies, an interesting phenomenon shows up.

One woman's rape fantasy allows her imaginary self to receive pleasure without guilt—since she is helplessly being raped against her will, it is not her fault for enjoying pleasure. She is not responsible and therefore does not have to explain herself to Jesus or to her parents. (What kind of a world—and its god—have we created where a longing for violation, powerlessness, and utter irresponsibility becomes someone's only viable outlet for our God-given eros?)[64]

On the other hand, many of the other fantasies also involved rape, bondage, and aggression, yet several of these women articulated a profound, uneasy guilt about desiring scenarios of domination that

---

[63] Bergner, 7.

[64] This problem is not reserved to the female realm. A male friend of mine, formerly a devout Protestant Christian, described his own youthful rape fantasies (sex-crazed women with box knives!) and recalled how it was based upon this same model of irresponsibility. Again, this exemplifies the infinitely (so often unhealthy) creative power of repressed sexuality.

didn't jive well with their education in women's liberation and gender equality.

This is a fascinating juxtaposition: One woman conjures a rape fantasy to *escape* from the imposed guilt of a conservative morality; the others *take on* guilt for their rape-like fantasies from a "liberal" morality. Besides the tragic consequences of a religious belief system shown by the first account, the latter exemplifies the unfortunate reality that women's liberation has had a double edge to it that is in some ways damaging to those it is actually intended to liberate.

Interestingly, and not altogether surprisingly, these two sides found common ground and even political alliance in the 1980s. During the Reagan administration, the New Right had coalesced into purity crusades with a special commission on pornography established by Attorney General Ed Meese. At the same time, certain radical antiporn feminists were also pushing for the censorship of obscenity, convinced that "pornography is the propaganda of sexual terrorism"[65] waged against women and encouraging violence like rape. So it became a very handy moment to reach across the aisle.

Other feminists at the time, however, recognized the danger in censorship to limit "women's exploration of the erotic." Ellen Willis, for example, said a woman's enjoyment of pornography can be a defiance rather than an endorsement of her oppression, celebrating the expression of a "radical impulse" defined as the domain of men. She wisely worried about how the "good girl, bad girl" polarity propagated by the censorial mind-set would impact many women's access to and exploration of the erotic[66]—*and it does to this day*.

Women in every aspect of the sex industry are stigmatized as "bad girls" from both conservative and liberal sides, whether they are workers in or consumers of. And as the resulting admonitions arrive from both the outside world and within any ordinary woman's

---

[65] Quoted here is Andrea Dworkin, theorist of the cause, who teamed up in the early eighties with feminist lawyer Catharine MacKinnon to draft up their own obscenity bill (John D'Emilio and Estelle B. Freedman, *Intimate Matters: A History of Sexuality in America,* 2nd ed. [Chicago/London: University of Chicago Press, 1997], 351).

[66] D'Emilio and Freedman, 351–2.

own socialized conscience, so her process of expressing her "radical impulse" is, indeed, thwarted.

Personally, I find myself constantly batting away this annoying pall that hovers between my inner censor (good girl) and my inner freak (bad girl). It most certainly smothers, in its furtively muted manner, my spontaneous capacity for sexual abandon so that often I really have to fight in order to access it.

The libbers against pornography focused on the wrong aspect of the issue, rallying their efforts on entirely the wrong level. Pornography tantalizing and stimulating male desire is only problematic in the environment where sex is made into such a limited commodity, where men and women are scandalously brainwashed to *be* at odds sexually from a vastly and deeply distorted background of out-and-out manipulation. These feminists knew there was a flammable problem at hand, but their mistaken approach, revealing a shallow understanding about the nature of the fire, ended up just throwing fuel onto it rather than acting as an effective retardant.

Regardless of how it is packaged and presented, any indiscriminately imposed social agenda that denies the underlying reality of natural desire—keeping large aspects of it under wraps—manifests as a form of oppression, regardless of who is constructing it and why.

In the name of social equilibrium, we have done ourselves a huge disservice by all but eradicating the most important aspects of heterosexual desire. A reactive hodgepodge approach of pasting Band-Aids over broken bones promotes fictitious division (i.e., the Mars and Venus quandary, evolutionary psychology, etc.) where there is none, and enforces homogeneity (as I'll describe in a moment) where it doesn't belong.

Because of the heavy burden of constraints coming in every conceivable form and from all directions, it is therefore necessary to tap into the indomitable freak coiled tightly into the core of our female chromosomes. And to tap it triumphantly requires a level of abandon that can only be achieved when the hang-ups are unhung and we let ourselves completely off the hook in order to experience the body's unedited version of raw sexuality.

That means we eradicate from our psyche all the perpetrators, beneficent and well-meaning as some of them may be, that have trespassed upon our innocent erotic impulse. We gotta let go of all the inhibiting admonitions of Jesus and Mary, mom and dad, misguided feminists (and the presumptuous postulates of EP) for a moment of total redemption and thorough liberation of the primal kind.

Trust me, the rest of the universe will stay in place (we will not be sending the planets out of their intended orbits) and through the obliteration of all the unnecessary crap, progress will inevitably result.

Equality of civil rights is essential to the health of our modern democracy, but it need not level the scintillating terrain that allows us to thrive sexually. The truth is, we ultimately thrive on *both* our differences and our similarities.

Little Red Corvette

The most significant similarity we can thrive on, if we allow it, is that we're all horny as fuck. We have only come to espouse the deep-seated belief in an inherent male-female discrepancy as a result of all the ways we have trained the genders around sexuality. We then simply rationalized the annoying results with superfluous theories about planetary origins and evolutionary causation.

We're all driven from the groin primarily by testosterone, and the levels of this androgen in the blood affect that drive. But this does *not* mean that because women naturally have lower levels of it in the system that we are that much less sexually driven than men (as Rollo Tomassi, spearhead of the "manosphere" and author of *The Rational Male*, proclaims), because, physiologically, women's testosterone receptors are much more sensitive to the hormone.[67] Therefore, there is no clear statement to be made about equivalences at this level.[68]

---

[67] Mark E. Richards, "Treatment Process for Women," myhormonetherapy.com.

[68] In fact, women are much more highly sensitive to all the sex hormones (androgens and estrogens) than are men. This stems biologically from the fact that all human fetuses are innately female, embryologically. For a female to develop requires only the basic blueprint, without relying on sexual "differentiating" hormones from the gonads; for a male fetus to differentiate from its female

Furthermore, and highly pertinent to the issue of social-sexual balance, with lower levels of testosterone *and* greater sensitivity to it, women will be much more vulnerable to even slightly altered levels of it in the system. This stresses *all the more* why it's so urgent to get ourselves out from under the thumb of the heavy hand on the long arm of the medieval body politic!

It is well-known that psychology and emotion are biochemically based phenomena, causing effect—and vice versa—measurably in the body. Because of this, *sexual repression*, being a psycho-emotional process—essentially, a negative feedback loop—naturally affects the what and the how of the relevant hormonal constituents in the body (and, of course, the way women overemotionalize sexuality probably adds to this). It would follow, then, that the *very act* must inevitably have both an instant and cumulative effect of dampening what would otherwise be more vibrant fluctuations of testosterone—sexual drive—in the system. Therefore, when a person is not censoring from the inside out, the endocrine and nervous systems are free to function like the tachometer of a well-tuned race car, with instant facility and response.

To sum it up, repression functions like condensation, clogging the fuel lines and interfering with combustion, and that's what women tend to suffer from sexually, both because we bear a proportionately larger share of the repressive societal burden and because our systems are more sensitive to its biochemical impacts. The unveiling of the radical sexual impulse, then, through the rejection of repression and self-censorship, liberates the sleek, aerodynamic forces of biochemistry that enhance a woman's own fluctuating sexual hormones, allowing her to tap into, once again, the power of her drive, thus

---

blueprint requires gonads producing androgens in copious quantity (initiated by the instructions on the Y chromosome at the appropriate time in male fetal development). Since the males' development is hormonally determined, he must develop "resistance" to the estrogens in his mother's bloodstream, whereas "the female's relative lack of differentiating hormones during embryonic life renders her more sensitive to hormonal conditioning later in life, especially to androgens," suggests Sherfey (Sherfey, 142).

equalizing the natural sexual compatibility with males that actually exists underneath.

Boys and Girls

The scintillating differences, upon which we thrive heterosexually, lie within the anatomical, hormonal, and energetic manifestations of femininity and masculinity, and these need enhancement, not modulation.

The women's lib movement, as extraordinary a force as it has been for empowering all our lives as women living in this country, has largely overlooked the celebration of femininity. There was, at first (and perhaps necessarily), a tendency toward masculinizing women as a way to muscle our way into the male-dominated world. Furthermore, in a world where a woman often feels like hunted prey[69] it can be a stretch to fully bask in the qualities that have made us so exploitable. Therefore, it can be even harder to admit to having a sexual interest in masculine aggression. But, nevertheless, it's a turn-on *because* it's masculine. It is an expression of his levels of testosterone, and our aroused response to it heightens our own levels, which enhances the intensity of our excitement.

So, as you can see, the inability to celebrate *femininity* partly rests upon the refusal to celebrate *masculinity*, due to the fact that the latter too easily represents the oppressive problem we've fought so hard to overcome. Admitting to pleasure in the feeling of being ravished by that manly beast, however, is *not* equivalent to accepting or condoning a culture of violent rape. It is merely indicative of one of many aspects of sexual desire. Remember, the definition of actual rape pivots upon the *lack of consent* on the part of the victim, male or female. Admitting to an appreciation of aggressive domination is not *consenting* to rape, a literal oxymoron. (As an aside, to help illustrate my point, serious participants in BDSM have a sober, mature

---

[69] Having traveled solo in third-world countries as well as in remote regions of the US, I've had a vividly personal experience of this reality that has greatly impacted my perspective.

understanding of the incredible levels of consent and responsibility necessary for taking part in extreme activities with another person in a vulnerable position. They have thus devised skillful methods for communicating and manifesting potentially dangerous stunts together. It's not such a complex thing, and it should offer some reassurance that we can loosen up and trust ourselves to handle things just fine in a less limited environment, if we set ourselves to the task.)

We do ourselves a mighty favor by looking directly at the reasons behind our resistance to letting ourselves go. Part of our aversion to wholeheartedly stepping into this is based on the disturbing issue of sexual violence, suffered by victims at the hands of aggressors. But, while our concerns are rational and deeply meaningful from an objective societal perspective, they can become irrational and even destructive when filtered down into the deeply *subjective* levels of the subconscious mind. The thing is, when we internalize a cultural fear of sexuality it tends to become repression—which, collectively, ends up creating just the kind of environment where rape and violence are more likely to be problems! So, as usual, shining a little light of intelligent awareness into the crannies where we stuff these things brings freedom and possibility instead of the mindless limitations that lurk about more subversively.

Now, while the New Age movement following on the heels of women's liberation has offered us all a bone by providing an emphasis on celebration of the feminine—with yoni healing, goddess worship, and the like—it has simultaneously denied men the full, natural expression (celebration) of their masculinity. Men are indeed being trained in cultivating the feminine quality of receptivity, which by itself is actually very positive, since it is an important piece in a man's ability to benefit fully from sexual exchange with a female. Yet, although the "jewel of the lingam" is honored ceremoniously, it is not given its due power. The reality is that the *fucking* essence of it is awash in a sea of wishy-washy sop as he floats about, penis semi-flaccid, on the waves of the New Age emotional ecstasy. I've become deeply troubled by the movement, calling itself enlightenment, that encourages men to convert the masculine manner into feminine expressions and ultimately steers them into fearing their own masculinity. It's hurting people.

In order to successfully celebrate and cultivate something, either masculine or feminine, we need to understand truly what it is, *and* we have to give ourselves the room and the permission to do so. But…the male phobia (of female power being equivalent to a world of chaos overrun by mannish dominatrices), driving them into petrified obstinance, certainly doesn't meet either requirement. And… the New Age stuff emphasizes a platform of emotional lovey-dovey romanticism because—surprise, surprise—that's our habitual warped view of the feminine. But that doesn't work either, since that's not at all what *feminity* truly is (in fact, it's the impotent, spayed version, that spawns so many other problems), nor does it reflect what *sex* truly is, so it's a totally inappropriate thing to put forth as the basis for ideal erotic union. And then…with both men and women shying away from powerful *masculine* expression, we're not doing any better (not to mention the fact that men are often taught that "respect" for their female partner/girlfriend/wife means restraining the aggressive animal within). As a result, both male and female are becoming stranded in fantasyland—out of body, out of mind—with both creatures disempowered by the evisceration of their carnal essence. All of this amounts to, again, misguided thinking and diminished levels of hormonal oomph.

We've got to get with the program! We've got to steer this beast away from the Bermuda Triangle of mass androgyny, which may serve us in some spheres of cooperation, but certainly *not* in the sack. No wonder so many couples are terminally bored. We've lost our bearings and we're missing the mark. It's time to recalibrate.

Take It to the Limit

Recalibration involves a swinging of the pendulum to the far side of center, opposite the status quo, before the happy middle can become a genuine reality. The far side of restraint is excess. Unless and until that zone is tasted, the gravity of habitual repression will pull that pendulum right back over to the first side, where it will surely stick again.

Anyone who has actually seen the movie *Insatiable* can probably picture the closing scenes where Marilyn goes on and on repeating, "I want more, I want more, *I want more!*" And maybe witnessing this greed is not only a little distasteful but kind of scary as well…what becomes of someone caught in that bottomless quicksand? Well, there are certainly those who are at risk of losing contact with reality, becoming vulnerable to delusion and addictive excess whether the object is sex, drugs, or—seriously—religion. That's always going to be the case. But the fear of the loss of control that grips a wider population, particularly regarding sex, is based on the wide-ranging propaganda of fear selling sexual morality like "Reefer Madness" for the soul[70] (think utter apocalypse for Orthodox Jews, dishonor punishable by death for Muslims, eternal damnation for most Christians) and is practically irrelevant to most people.

The bottom line for most of us is, keep your head on and your eyes open, heal your heart, and clean up the trash that litters your loins.[71] This is part of bluntly facing the facts of life and boldly wrangling out the working reality of living with those facts. This is called assuming full responsibility for one's own needs and actions. It is also called maturity. And this maturity is sorely lacking, particularly among people too afraid to roll up their sleeves for fear of getting their hands dirty. Well, what actually happens to such people is that not only do their hands get dirty (because, well, "shit happens"[72]), but then the sleeves, too, are such a mess!

---

[70] This is no exaggeration. For instance, if you read some of the print that comes straight out of the Catholic Church via the publisher Our Sunday Visitor (www.osv.com), you will find exactly what I'm talking about: catastrophic-proportioned hysteria about the unimaginable dangers of unauthorized sex (masturbation, pornography, promiscuity, etc.) designed, literally, to put the fear of God's merciless wrath into the hearts of his beloved people. Be afraid, it says, *be very* afraid!

[71] For victims of sexual abuse, this may involve a deeply rigorous therapeutic process, because the psychoemotional consequences of such abuse can be extensive.

[72] Think of the endless list of examples, like President Bill Clinton, Governor Eliot Spitzer, Catholic priests, and any one of the other gazillion anonymous

By doing the job of conscientiously unhooking the scads of hang-ups, I've tasted my own insatiability and it has not reduced my life to ruin and wreckage, sucking me into an endless abyss of darkness, disease, and devil worship (much to my dear old landlady's astonishment!). Instead, it's given me a radically clearer view of the vast horizon of sexual appetite and capacity (and even how that intersects with enlightened awareness, as I will discuss in a later chapter). I have also met, and known intimately (and biblically), others who have happily stepped over, and survived, that frightful horizon, all of which has given me great reason to seriously question, then dismiss, the trepidation around the topic.

The idea itself may come across as obvious and elementary to those who identify as liberal and have allowed themselves a fair bit of sexual exposure, but it is often the case that this position is actually quite superficial. We should not ever underestimate the impact of all we have internalized from the ubiquitous sexual pessimism pervading the world all around us. The resulting presence of underlying hang-ups, conscious or subconscious, most assuredly will affect our ability to experience that abandon of which I speak. A boldly deepened exploration is full of surprises—and rewards—for people from all walks of life.

Having the (direct, awake, aware) experience of insatiability offers a very unique perspective that is possibly the most important part of developing a rudimentary understanding of the nature, not only of sexuality—male or female—but of our lives. As a large part of the taproot of our living existence, sex pervades the very essence of survival and our will to live, both functions of an innate physical desire structure. Therefore, getting the full unattenuated picture of this desire structure is actually the key that opens all secret doors to the understanding of self.

---

infidelities or instances of sexual "misconduct" that trash people's dreams and lives. These things happen because our sexual nature is generally too confined (and thus squeezing out of the seams), and it makes such an awful mess because we are too afraid to confront this reality in a mature, responsible manner.

Homo sapiens are evolved to have a sexuality vastly unlimited in scope as evidenced by the lack of an estrous cycle. Furthermore, the evolution of our biology away from the confines of an estrous cycle inherently allows us the opportunity to have a perpetually more balanced state of affairs on the gender front, although we have historically insisted on, and succeeded in, removing that advantage.[73] The *biology* is in place for an unlimited natural appetite, and being in touch with this reality is part of a healthy understanding of who we are. It is the *psychology* that causes the pervasive dysfunction. But the psychology, once freed from its culturally concocted confusion (misunderstanding based on misinformation) and set back upright, can help lead the way into far more healthy frontiers.

What are the implications of realizing that the female sexual capacity and appetite is, indeed, rather insatiable? What if her sexual hunger and copulatory capacity actually exceed that of the male, as Mary Jane Sherfey has also been quoted saying? This fear—that men will find themselves incapable of sexually satisfying women—drives the controlling ego to extravagant extremes. What if we do consider for a moment the possibility of the scales actually being skewed in the *opposite* direction from what we've decided?[74]

Certainly, in the one-man-one-woman cultural ideal, that's a pretty intimidating (you might even say terrifying) prospect for any man faced with the task of satisfying a woman enough to keep her around for himself. I would say that would surely be enough for

---

[73] One author suggests that the absence of an estrous "heat" in human females results in the tendency for women to require prolonged foreplay in the majority of situations, since her tissues are not "pre-primed" by the hormonal intensity of estrous. She emphasizes, however, that this idea is culturally enhanced to cater to gender-role behaviors and cautions her readers to realize that sexual aggression and passivity are behaviors determined culturally rather than biologically (Sherfey, 104).

[74] In fact, evidence that we've already been confronted with this possibility so extensively permeates our midst that it's almost absurd to pose this question. Numerous Old Testament stories reveal a view of women as subversively erotic creatures (Eve, if you read it that way, Ruth, Tamar...); there is the Muslim tradition of keeping their women in birkas, literally under wraps; there is the myth of the succubus, the terror of the vagina dentata, and on and on.

him, in the name of procuring what has been demanded of him—socially, economically, and biblically—to go about looking for ways to "handle" the situation. Then, of course, it is much safer to try making everyone (especially her) believe she isn't so strongly sexually motivated. Christopher Ryan bluntly points out the irony in the contrast between the ideological insistence upon females' relatively passive sexual nature and all the extreme measures taken the world over to control and constrain women sexually.[75] Sherfey stated very aptly decades ago, "The strength of the sex drive determines the force required to suppress it,"[76] and modern sex researcher Meredith Chivers says of all the "prohibitions and restrictive perspectives on female sexuality," that all these "barriers are a pretty incredible testament to the power of the drive itself."[77] Obviously something perverse is going on here!

Nowadays, around here, we raise her with the proper training, saddle her with children (within the limited context of the nuclear family, which concentrates the stress of childrearing) before her peak sexual years so she's too busy (and too exhausted) to pay attention to it and simply call it a wholesome, productive life. But then…sooner or later somebody will generally admit that the couple's sex life is suffering. And then everyone is completely bewildered about what the problem is because it just isn't anything like what we had been led to expect while fixating romantically on the "white picket fence." There are little bugs inside gnawing away at the woodwork.

Let's say that when a woman is allowed to develop sexually according to her true nature, free of oppressive and repressive forces,

---

[75] Ryan says, "Despite repeated assurances that women aren't particularly sexual creatures, in cultures around the world men have gone to extraordinary lengths to control female libido: female genital mutilation, head-to-toe chadors, medieval witch burnings, chastity belts, suffocating corsets, muttered insults about 'insatiable' whores, pathologizing, paternalistic medical diagnoses of nymphomania or hysteria, the debilitating scorn heaped on any female who chooses to be generous with her sexuality…all parts of a worldwide campaign to keep the supposedly low-key female libido under control. Why the electrified high-security razor-wire fence to contain a kitty-cat?" (Ryan and Jetha, 39).

[76] Sherfey, 139.

[77] Bergner, 65.

she is then able to function with full abandon, which allows access to an insatiable sexual appetite. This is that "Mr. Fantasy" daydream of many men that I mentioned earlier. And this, also as I said, is where the rubber meets the road, specifically because this means she will require some kind of serious performance from one male or…egads, fresh horses when she rides this one out. Well, we've set ourselves up to condemn the despicable obscenity and utter unacceptability of the latter, so that leaves one man to do the job. So what's he got to do? He's either got to develop *his own* sexual control to maximize his performance, or he's got to subdue the forces inside *her*.

Even if female appetite and capacity does not exceed that of the males, but simply meets it toe to toe, that can still be extremely intimidating. The one thing a man can't do sexually is fake it (in terms of a natural erection), so that puts him in a position of vulnerability, especially when we define the man's ejaculation as end of story. The knee-jerk, human-nature reaction to vulnerability is fear, and for whatever additional reasons—politics, religion, random chaos—man has focused more upon subduing woman. And so here we are (balls-deep in rotten apples), with male performance often lacking and female abandon hard to come by, arguably the two most important ingredients required for sex between men and women (outside of an orgy, God forbid) to be mutually fulfilling, fully compatible, and ultimately successful.

So many men complain of their female partner's lack of sexual interest. So many women wonder what happened to their own desire. Sometimes it's a reason for extramarital affairs and dishonesty, sometimes the basis of eventual divorce, sometimes just accepted as the way it is and quietly suffered. This is how it all comes out in the wash. And maybe, one by one, it doesn't have to be this way.

Personally, I have no reason to proclaim that women are more sexually insatiable creatures, with a copulatory capacity beyond the reach of mortal men. What it looks like to me, based upon experience, observation, and study, is that we are naturally very similarly libidinous, with the greatest discrepancy to be found primarily within a given encounter rather than across the board. In other words, most men just blow out before the (fat) lady sings; most women haven't developed their operatic vocal capacities (yet sense there's something missing). The bottom line is that we are both, in different ways, functioning way below par. Male lack of ejaculatory control leaves female copulatory desire unsatisfied. Female inhibition leaves males craving more sex. This is actually something that can be straightforwardly resolved. It will be addressed by way of training males to value and develop their own sexual control—once and for all, completely shifting the deep-seated, longstanding, counterproductive, and devastating emphasis upon controlling women. And it will be addressed by radically unburdening females' sexual psychology to open themselves to the fullness of what is available as a result.

Another very important piece will be redefining the "end of story" line about male ejaculation. Defining male ejaculation as the end of the encounter eliminates nearly limitless possibilities for mutual satisfaction. Altering the endpoint mind-set can offset the immense difficulty involved in learning ejaculatory control.[78] If he can train his mojo to rally himself, and wholeheartedly participate with her post-ejaculation, he can succeed in satisfying her by offering oral, manual, or other forms of stimulation, for her to reach the peak of her squealing pitches beyond his own climactic blow-out. Learning to effectively stave off the ejaculation will give the man a more heightened full-body experience of sexual stimulation throughout and may ultimately result in a more fulfilling encounter for him; however, he loses nothing (and gains much) from uncoupling the ejaculation-endpoint mentality.

In part, we must consider the possibility that most women (not to mention most men) would be much more healthy, happy, and balanced if they had not necessarily all the customary essentials of the American dream hemmed within the whitewashed fence of social sanction, but a larger sexual playground in which to frolic. With ownership and control of one another as the law of the land, expan-

---

[78] In my current and long-term sexual relationship, I have personally witnessed the enormity of what is demanded of a man mentally and physically in developing ejaculatory control. I have a firsthand appreciation of the fact that it is an incredibly arduous undertaking involving, at times, abysmal failure, so any tool available to offset this result should be accepted and utilized!

sion of this dimension is highly limited, even between two monogamous people, because how much honest exploration can there be within a police state?

In a nutshell, women must take full ownership of the truth of their natural sexuality, and men must take control not of women, which only backfires on them anyway, but of *themselves* so that we can all achieve mutual satisfaction. We have to loosen the jealous grip enough to graciously welcome honest communication with each other about what really, truly turns us on. And, mostly, that domain is not limited to one special individual.

I believe the implications are most promising for everyone involved, once we forge through the stages of fearful resistance to fundamental change. This fundamental change involves, again, attitudes—the attitudes that shape our deepest identity as sexual beings. Males and females both are plagued by the most excessively burdensome attitudes about sex and sexual relationship that simply have to be excavated and purged so that we can function optimally and get the most out of it together.

LET'S GET IT ON

I've been laboring to make the point that men and women are really equipped to coexist in much greater sexual harmony than what we're currently manifesting. The biology presents no inherent discrepancy between the interest and the drive of the separate genders. Everything is available to enable us to share in reciprocally satisfying sex throughout our lives together on this planet. It just requires that both parties are able to tap into the depth of instinctual desire, run it through a healthy and mature sexuality, and allow real fullness of expression. The world we live in has just made that simple thing inordinately obscure.

It is obscured by an atmosphere where women are led to believe that strong sexual desire and enjoyment are abnormal and even shameful, and both sexes are exposed to either direct or indirect indoctrination around the "sinful" and inappropriate nature of sex. It is obscured by an environment where men may fear accusations of rape from legitimately confused and unstable women suffering from postcoital regret (since women are *trained* to attach so much destructively irrational meaning to it, who can blame them for this?). This environment leads to inventions of further cumbersome ritual, such as elaborate romantic overtures designed to camouflage the underlying sexual motive and the detailed codes of conduct laying out the rules of consensual sex every step of the way for adolescents in college. When it comes to sex, Rube Goldberg 'R Us! It's no wonder the pure instinct—although always undeniably poking its nose out of the underbrush—becomes unrecognizably distorted. Moving irresistibly toward one another in attraction, then shying away to varying degrees from the bare-naked truth of sex, who knows whether they're coming or going in the unfolding chaos?

As Marvin says, let's just *stop beatin' 'round the bush*![79] Part of the recalibration of the gender roles involves, again, recognizing that *both* men and women have aggressive, powerful sexual desire and motivation. This involves putting aside all the illogical fears, rationalizations, and misguided beliefs about men and women, masculine and feminine, and sex in general. Then we can go forth and discover our capacity to co-create whatever kind of sexual encounter we would like, satisfying the sexy thrill-seeking adventurer inside, fostering real intimacy, and simultaneously honoring mutual power, responsibility, and consent. This is where having a *healthy* and *mature* sexuality comes in.

The healthy part is about tapping into instinctual desire and realizing that there is nothing wrong with having powerful sexual urges of any inclination, top or bottom, to borrow from the vocabulary of B&D. (I will dare venture to say that any modern American woman—conventional or alternative, gay or straight—if she looks closely enough, will locate within herself beliefs and judgments about the "inappropriateness" of her sexuality, in various forms. And men, too, for that matter.)

In addition to the traditional right-wing propaganda, women should not take on the same damn doctrine of guilt—only rewritten by their own pens and rephrased as liberation—that squeezes them into yet another model of the ideal female. Women should not feel guilty pressure from either extreme: the conservative extreme that says they should be passively asexual or the liberal extreme telling them they should always be in command. And men should not be confined to either identifying as brutes or castrati. They should not have to *feign* emasculated tender submissiveness in order to join the progressive era of gender neutrality, nor even the New Age of neo-Tantrism and spiritual sexuality. For sexually active people,[80] sexual health involves discovery, acceptance, reclamation, and ulti-

---

[79] Marvin Gaye, "Let's Get it On," Tamla Motown, 1973.

[80] As opposed to those actively practicing celibacy as a spiritual discipline.

mately, some form of expression of who and what we really are as sexual beings.

The mature part is about discovering the ways to manifest the potent urges responsibly and respectfully. Sexual maturity involves truth-telling (first to oneself and then to others) and responsibility (safe sex practices, psychoemotional independence, accountability, and self-determination). Really, most of us can be voraciously carnal, multifaceted, and even perverse human beings together and still function as intelligent and responsible adults.

One of the keys to manifesting this together is communication, something we have learned *not* to do around sex. The fantasy is that the perfect mate knows exactly what you want and how to get it done. But that just isn't so.

Speak to Me

One of the obstacles to communication lies in the fact that communication is work. The popular belief is that if things are all going well, then everything flows effortlessly without any "work," which is synonymous with drudgery for many people. The idea is that we only have to "work" if something needs to be fixed.

Generally, when it does, sex tends to flow in this effortless way in the early phases of a highly charged sexual relationship, when the hot-factor is so stoked up on the tinder of all the fresh new sensation that all potential glitches can go easily unnoticed. The truth is that at some point, a few pointers, suggestions, and requests would be most productive if everyone's egos weren't in the way, getting worried about the implications involved in having to actually bat around something that we've decided should automatically look and feel like Hollywood, fully edited and produced. (I even remember one poor guy who couldn't function without the soundtrack. That was bothersome—I like to *rock*, but not when it upstages a good *roll*, if you know what I'm saying.)

I happened to read two articles that, together, point to a hefty source of our social-sexual headache.

The first one, titled "Good Lovers Lie,"[81] touted the virtues of dishonesty in order to "celebrate the intoxicating illusions of love," quoting Shakespeare to emphasize the significance of smug flattery between lovers and admitting that in times of more honesty, there is more intimacy, but "in a sickening way." He concludes that to have love in your life, you must sacrifice honesty and intimacy, and lie. (What then "love" is to such a person is a pretty heartless prospect, and why anyone felt an article needed to be written, and published, *at all* to promote the kind of childish, run-of-the-mill functioning that every socialized creature figures out early on in a hard-knocks fashion at a nonthinking level evades me.) Even though this stance is admittedly a little over-the-top, the underlying sentiment still reflects the all-too prevalent notion that it's best to leave each other in the dark about the unpleasant or edgy aspects of the truth—because, conveniently, it's the "kind" thing to do (instead of just the cowardly thing).

The second article, called "Searching for Sex,"[82] analyzed big internet data, drawing the conclusions that (1) everyone, male and female, is totally confused by sex, and (2) one of the significant reasons this is so is because we lack reliable data. Why? Because people lie. To friends. To lovers. To doctors. To surveys. And to themselves. Consequently, for one example, men obsess about insecurities based on the belief that an adequate penis must rival the dimensions of porn icon John Holmes's inordinate appendage, while women are far more frequently troubled by penises that are too large rather than too small. Wouldn't it be a far more loving and compassionate act to let each other in on the facts?

Talking needs to start happening immediately between sex partners, then practiced and cultivated until it is as natural as the body itself. It's the shame we've picked up around sex and the resulting bashfulness that keep us from talking about it so openly. At the root of that shame is often that idea of sex as a base "animalistic" urge.

---

[81] Clancy Martin, "Good Lovers Lie," *New York Times*, Opinion, Sunday, February 8, 2015.

[82] Seth Stephens-Davidowitz, "Searching for Sex," *New York Times*, Opinion, January 24, 2015.

However, at the same time, if the shame prevents us from utilizing our most highly evolved capacity, language, it is itself responsible for *lowering* the act to a shallow, less-than-intimate activity, less human, and less humane. Without communication, we are not engaging as whole people. We are instead compartmentalizing body, mind, and heart (our bodies, our hells!).

Good communication requires practice, and like any practiced skill, the ratio of effort-in to quality-out decreases over time. The work gets easier and more enjoyable, and the product becomes more refined.

Recently, I ran into a sexual liaison from the very early days of my exploration. Very curiously, I asked him what his experience was of me twenty-some-odd years ago. He paused thoughtfully and then said, "Very clinical." I laughed and reflected on my rudimentary attempts at navigating through the peculiar passages of communicating about sex, how awkward it felt, and yes indeed, clinical.

Now, after numerous years of intensive practice within an ongoing partnership, imagining sex without a serious level of communication involved leaves me feeling pretty cold and incomplete. And yet…I *still* have to push through nagging concerns about offending my partner, hurting his feelings, or even my own uncertainties about what I need and want at times. The work continues because the habit of reticence—and the fear of exposure—cannot be reversed in a day!

The Thrill Is Gone

What about the inevitable…the boredom…that eventual issue of sexual dullness and disquietude within a long-term relationship that has been famously called "the itch"?

"Familiarity breeds indifference," says writer Sonja Lyubomirsky,[83] going on to explain how evolutionary biology (not evolutionary *psychology*) indicates that seeking sexual variety is an

---

[83] Sonja Lyubomirsky, "New Love: A Short Shelf Life," *New York Times*, Opinion, December 1, 2012.

adaptation that evolved to prevent the genetic disasters of incest and inbreeding. She says, "It doesn't take a scientist to observe that because the sex in a long-term committed monogamous relationship involves the same partner day after day after day, no one who is truly human (or mammalian) can maintain the same level of lust and ardor that he or she experienced when that love was uncharted and new."

Woody Allen, as per his aptitude, humorously captures this annoying fact of life in the movie *Play It Again, Sam*. As the main character's wife is walking away (permanently), she says that things were different when they were dating, that he was more aggressive. Just before she squeals off in her VW bug, he pleads, "*Everybody is during courtship… You can't expect me to keep up that level of charm— I'd have a heart attack!*"

Lyubomirsky says studies show that women actually crave sexual novelty even more than men and that in long-term relationships, they are the ones who will lose their interest in sex, and lose it sooner. I will add that because women are generally less attuned to their sexual bodies, trained to fixate instead on their emotionality, they will more often attribute this growing indifference to an underlying disinterest in *sex* in general (and perhaps even to a deep personal flaw) rather than a need for something new, fresh, and different.

Most of us have picked up the notion somewhere along the way that sexual dissatisfaction within an established relationship and/or the desire for extracurricular sex is an indication that something is wrong with the relationship. This is because we have been indoctrinated with the idea of the perfect mate who is "our everything" and the belief that when that person is located, sexuality can and should fall contentedly into its natural container of blissful monogamy. In many cases, these desires (or lack thereof, or desires for unconventional or kinky sex even within that relationship) seem to tell us there is something seriously wrong with us personally. So, when the issue arises, in whatever form, it is swiftly and furtively swept under the rug with zippered lips, most certainly *not* something to disclose to or discuss with one's partner but instead something to be guarded at all costs. A discussion of this nature has come to be seen as a morbid threat and probably a mark of the beginning of the end—of the complete unraveling of the sense of comfort and trust within an intimate bond. So it is kept quiet in the dark recesses of the psyche.

Isolated and insulated from the rest of daily reality, it can take on a life of its own, with growing feelings of guilt, doom, and remorse surrounding its very existence. Disconnected from the rest of our selves, shaded from the sunlight of ordinary sanity, and fueled by the ever-burning fire of our commanding sexuality, it either becomes the center of gravity for a growing array of fixations, clouded judgments, misguided and deceitful actions, or a dead zone, like a black hole that slowly consumes the flames of sexual vitality altogether. This, of course, ultimately results in an expanding alienation not only from the person with whom we had intended to share our life most intimately but even from ourselves.

Walking on Broken Glass

The truth is that over the course of time, boredom is going to arise at some point or another—that glass is already broken. The nervous system grows less excited by familiar stimuli. Even if I'm married to *People*'s "sexiest man alive," I'm going at some point to yawn when he climbs into bed with me (I am woman; hear me snore!). Boredom is basic biology. The nature of the beast. Get used to it. Talk about it. Use it to go deeper into monogamous intimacy and creativity, or draft another plan, one with expanded parameters. But don't run from it, because you cannot hide.

There's a system of range management called holistic resource management, or HRM, designed by a dynamic Zimbabwean named Allan Savory. Although originally devised for managing grazing in the context of arid southern Africa, the system presents useful strategies for appropriately managing resources in any environment. As conscientious custodians of their own acreage, my parents became rigorously involved in the study and practice of this model.

The essential feature of HRM is a set of principles that guide the management process, and these principles, ultimately boil down to the decision-making processes of people. The bottom line in HRM is human values. Savory says that invariably, successful management breaks down at this level when the people managing do not share the same values and therefore cannot come to consensus. The most diffi-cult thing, it seems, for people to come to terms with when they have common interests and investments, is a discrepancy in values, because this means some fundamental adjustments need to be made—a "par-adigm shift" involving a divergence from prevailing beliefs or tradi-tion. When people care for one another *and* about their common investment, they often have trouble talking frankly about things at this level because it is so businesslike. There is hallowed ground of highly emotional attachment that people are unwilling to tread upon so pragmatically. And if we can't talk about something pragmatically, we surely cannot begin to resolve any problems.

I watched as my parents' practice of HRM broke down, essen-tially for this reason. For them, fully addressing the discrepancy in certain values would have meant a radical reinvention of the oper-ation they were running, and there was already simply too much investment (blood, sweat, tears) and inertia to approach something like this. So they continued, for the most part, as they had always done, not really seeing eye-to-eye, not fully agreeing on things or coming to consensus around decisions, but carrying on piecing it together with no radical progress in the management style.

Like our *values* define the bottom line in HRM, sexual rela-tionship boils down to the issue of our *needs and desires.* When it comes down to matters of sex, discussing frankly these things and the practical ways to deal with them, we come up against the same obsta-cle where the decision-making process is blocked by the emotional barriers of attachment and defense. Because there is so much other unspoken, mixed-up stuff in the mire, it is all too highly emotionally charged for a subject of rational discussion.

But it doesn't have to be so, and in fact, it must *not* be so if we intend to have a truly fulfilling sex life together. The fact that emo-tional sensitivities feel violated by the harsh light of logical pragma-tism is a problem that must be addressed. This requires a bold shift out of defending that vulnerability—a momentary quantum leap of courageous faith—that can feel as threatening as death yet gives in an instant the breath of new life. It is life-affirming because it renders quite practical this enormous aspect of our lives that we have enshrouded in a romantic myth governed by intangible forces of the universe. A frank discussion of sexual needs and desires between intimate companions is about as empowering as it gets for everybody, because this is real emotional maturity and personal responsibility. Getting directly in touch with ourselves in this way is about no longer leaving the meeting of our needs and desires to chance or placing the burden of unspoken expectations onto someone else.

Therefore, a shift in values—a *paradigm shift*, emphasizing honesty and vulnerability around sexual needs and desires rather than an unassailable haven of protective (make-believe, in my opinion) security—would come in handy and save many a relationship as well as prevent and heal much undue suffering in this heavily afflicted realm of our lives.[84] We've simply got to get down to the brass tacks of business in order to allow the real magic of intimacy to unfold.

Sexuality is such a vastly varied and wildly colorful thing with so many avenues of possibility it is truly a kaleidoscope of crazy pieces waiting to be strewn about. Therefore, *the bell curve of normal* in this arena, as a very astute friend of mine pointed out, *is a straight line*. Because there are so many possible expressions of this dimension of ourselves—hetero-, homo-, bi-, metro-…human, animal, vegetable…organic, inert, electric, inflatable…missionary, doggie, cowgirl, sixty-nine…seated, standing, lying, driving, hanging, flying…oral, anal, vaginal, manual…twosome, threesome, foursome, then some and more some…masochistic, voyeuristic, hermaphroditic, exhibitionist, flamboyant, simplistic…aggressive, submissive, familiar, strange, incestuous…one-nighters, lifers, rebounders…young,

---

[84] HBO's *Silicon Valley* star Thomas Middleditch describes his nontraditional relationship, saying, "To be honest, swinging has saved our marriage… It's better than feeling unheard and alone and that you have to scurry in the shadows… I'm sexual. I'd always thought I was a romantic and that when I fall in love, that stuff fades away… But it's part of me. If that's part of your being and it feels important to you, find a way to explore it, because repression sucks."

old, dead, and so on—and because we have ordained such a tightly restricted framework in which to express it, that glass is, again, already broken. (There's a whole world of untapped, even wholly unconsidered, possibility for bringing variety into even a monogamous arrangement. It remains unconsidered because it has been so successfully tucked away by the unconscious censorship apparatus in the psyche.)

In the monasteries of Buddha's day, there were so many ways the monks found, and invented, to circumvent the rules of sexual austerity that the Buddha had to continually attach (some truly fascinating) addenda! To those of us far beyond the monastery, to demand—as much of the world has done—that satisfaction must reside contentedly within the bounds of a single heterosexual, monogamous relationship manifested primarily in the missionary position, ideally for the sole purpose of procreation, until death do us part, is to force far too many things under that ragged rug of denial destined decidedly for damnation and destruction. We simply were not meant to be so sexually restricted for our entire lives.

Ryan and Jetha expound in detail on the copious evolutionary evidence that casual, promiscuous sexuality is likely the most natural thing for us humans. The modest degree of our body-size dimorphism (males are on average about 10 to 20 percent larger than females) corresponds best to our primate relatives who are neither monogamous nor polygynous but bilaterally promiscuous (meaning both genders are fast and easy). Penis size and design, ejaculatory patterns, seminal fluid composition, predictable fluctuations in sperm production, testicular volume and location, even statistical pornography preferences (i.e., "gang bang" and "money shot"), as well as female copulatory vocalization, orgasm, and vaginal biochemistry, all point strongly to a history where sperm competition between males took place after copulation with the same female.

They conclude, "The assertion that human beings are naturally monogamous is not just a lie, it's a lie most Western societies insist we keep telling each other."[85] And, honestly, just reading the book

---

[85] Ryan and Jetha, 270.

exhausts—very deeply and agonizingly—my patience with the fact that such correct proponents of the facts have to go to such inordinate lengths to convince everyone that the emperor is not actually wearing any clothes. In a *Ted Talks* video discussing the proposition, Ryan said, "Evolved sexuality is in direct conflict with much of the modern world. Contradictions between what we *ought to* feel and what we *do* feel generates [*sic*] a huge amount of unnecessary suffering."[86]

In other words: broken glass.

Only once we understand and accept the full reality of the nature and scope of our human sexuality can we hope to incorporate real sanity into our sexual existence, so we can finally just get on with gettin' it on! This involves recognizing the fact that sexuality as we know it is unduly encumbered with baggage that can and must be removed from the premises. Then we can happily tootle across those shards of scattered glass without getting cut and unwittingly bleeding out those relationships that ought to be vibrantly alive, respectful, and sustaining.

So again, that means we have to learn to talk about sex. But in order to really talk about it, we have to get back in touch with all those things that have been hidden under the carpet.

---

[86] "Christopher Ryan: Are We Designed to Be Sexual Omnivores?" ted.com, February 2013.

SEXUAL HEALING

As a result of the violent clashing over the millennia between society's progress (involving its various "movements" and associated stipulations) and the inextinguishable demands of horny human biology, we are the products of an elaborate, near-global morass of sexual confusion that has achieved epidemic proportions.

We have swung wildly between eras that produced the likes of the Kama Sutra, sexual tantra, sacred prostitution, hedonism, wedding orgies, Dionysia, Bacchanalia, flappers and free love, and those that brought the world Stoicism, ascetic austerity, Victorian prudery, orthodox antisex dogma, pious abstinence, chastity belts, witch hunts, and genital mutilation. And now here we are, dangling from the limbs of a gnarly old snag, deformed by the harsh elements of history and the fickle winds of human fancy—confused as ever—among the tattered and uber-fortified remnants of our sexual schizophrenia.

The world we live in today is particularly intricate. With the global population expanding to and beyond every border and technology facilitating ever more interface, with so many layers of race and culture each carrying its own moral customs and convictions constantly colliding, intermixing, and overlapping, who can sort out the debris burying the naked truth of who we are and who we really can be sexually?

Sex is given a different brand everywhere you turn: change the channel, get a different message. We are taught that sex is crude, shameful, vile, and mortally sinful while simultaneously learning that it is absolutely vital to physical and mental health, relationships, and general wholesome well-being. Sex is either *everything* or worse than nothing; our egos are aggrandized, then assaulted. As we struggle to hold it all at once, it tears us limb from limb. Most people, when asked their views and beliefs, will present a pretty disjointed and randomly conglomerated response, plucked from the general social milieu and slightly molded by their own personal history, perhaps even by the immediate context and the way they happen to be feeling at that moment.

Somewhere in the midst of this imposing heap of refuse, there must be a way to wholeness and health, and it really may only be possible one individual at a time.

My Generation (Won't Get Fooled Again?)

If I've learned anything of any certainty through studying the history of human sexuality, it is that every era is filled with multitudes of contradiction[87] and every movement is infused with the belief that it holds the moral high ground.

If I want to find the truth, I have to take all the examples I have before me and recognize that the moral high ground is high only because it has won the popularity contest that determines which ideas survive at all—and the judges of this contest are mostly none other than the random chaotic conditions of sociopolitical happenstance. (For example, Christianity may have remained an eccentric cult had not the emperor Constantine around 325 CE happened to favor it enough to instate it as the "official" religion.) The winner writes the book and the rest of us just carry on ad-libbing the best we can to keep up with the story! And much of that ad-libbing ends up looking like trendy frivolity. (Reflecting back to the discussion about the sixties revolution, it vanished because, to so many people, it was merely in vogue.)

As Townshend says, *"Meet the new boss, same as the old boss."*[88]

---

[87] For examples of this, check out *The Pearl: A Journal of Voluptuous Reading (The Underground Magazine of Victorian England)* (New York: Grove Press Inc., 1968) and *Walter: The English Casanova* by Drs. Phyllis and Eberhard Kronhausen (New York: Ballantyne Books, 1966).

[88] The Who, "Won't Get Fooled Again," Track (UK), Decca (US), 1971.

In my early thirties, living in Santa Cruz, at the peak of my estrogen levels and explorational development, I read an article that really sobered my views on the prospects of deep, enduring social transformation of any kind, including sexual. I no longer remember the source of that article, except that it was mainstream, but its contents—the white-hot facts—scorched me.

I had been reveling merrily in my own liberating personal discoveries with the added sense that there was an ongoing parallel movement burgeoning vivaciously above ground in the public realm. Sex workers like Annie Sprinkle and Veronica Monet were touring the public circuit, extolling the virtues of their trades in porn and prostitution. Literature in various forms was provokingly and unabashedly risqué. Kids on campus at UCSC were celebrating regularly scheduled "sexcapades," a liberated and informed venue of sexual exploration and responsibility of their own design. Sex workers were unionizing, and erotic dance classes were being offered in San Francisco. I felt as though I was riding on a wave, an epic Santa-Cruz-style wave that would never break until it brought you all the way in to the smooth, sandy shore. And then that article came along, like a nasty little reef under the glassy surface: People are bored with risqué, it was declared. Prude is back as the new cool! I felt momentarily disoriented, like the discombobulation of being tumbled in the surf, and then I began to froth. It hadn't occurred to me that risqué was *cool.* I had thought it was just about speaking more openly and that the truth was finally coming into its self-evident own. Rise and shine, little schoolgirl.

I was so aghast at the trivialization of something so deeply meaningful that I could barely see straight. It was hard to accept that something so important, with such vast repercussions on every level of our human experience, could be at the wobbly whim of passing fashion.

But it is. And this is also why those of us on the perimeter diverging from the paradigm end up going it alone for stretches, because, after all, the ebb and flow of these changing tides don't stop the Annie Sprinkles of the world. The ones jumping in for shits and giggles will drop out and the hoopla will settle down for a while, but the serious characters at the heart of the issue will prevail regardless of the fluctuating conditions. Instead of the tidal wave of sensation carrying along with it all the flotsam of fanfare, they will sink beneath the surface as an undercurrent to be discovered by more earnest seekers in search of the undisclosed esoteric truth.

Those seekers will be the ones who realize that something is desperately out of whack and have become profoundly sick and tired of being pointlessly tossed about on that frenzied, if fashionable, surface.

Lost in the Supermarket

The inconvenient reality of truly actualizing a real modicum of progress in the arena of sexual healing is that it requires dedicated work over an extended period of time. This is the part (that drudgery!) that hinders most endeavors.

There are innumerable avenues available to people who are looking for something different: books, workshops, retreats, seminars, psychedelics, encounter groups, raves, Burning Man, erotic festivals—you name it; it's probably out there somewhere. And many people achieve catharsis in these various situations. But how many then settle back into business as usual after the giggly jiggles dissipate, as they naturally do? Then it's on to the hunt for the next euphoric high.

Cathartic experiences, like tender sprouts, need fertile ground that is well worked and weeded to take hold and flourish. It's the working and the weeding part that is uninteresting to people who tend to prefer a stroll through the supermarket to a vocation in farming. Only if I'm dissatisfied enough with what's at hand, when I realize that the bright, shiny produce at the market isn't really nourishing and sustaining my deeper freak, will I venture stoutheartedly into the fields to do the work myself. And indeed, comrades, sturdy we must be...

The Boxer

In the real world, we cannot simply adopt progressive affirmations and expect them to painlessly pull us through into a sexual rebirth. Because of all the rose-tinted, gooey-eyed, and emotionally airbrushed ideas about opening to sexual fulfillment and the typical emphasis on safety and comfort, it can feel abrupt to hit the bedrock of the real tough stuff that has to be addressed on the deeper levels. Hitting that layer, and venturing into it, is going to feel really sincerely out of sorts, and like I said earlier, that's your indication (if you're not being reckless and stupid about it) that you're probably right on target.

It *should* rattle your cage and knock you around. But like a boxer, you learn how to take the punches and stay in the fight. Once you know what it feels like to be hit in the nose, it ain't such a big deal, and maybe you'll even kind of like the invigorating, life-affirming part of joining the fight club, in the name of radical sexual transformation! And, those of us who are in it to win it—although we certainly experience the pain, discomfort, and outright fatigue that's involved in pushing envelopes—simply don't view all the work as drudgery. We call it, once again, life lived *alive*.

Louder than Words

A couple of acquaintances of mine were recently involved in the production of the local Erotic Exotic Ball and urged me to go and party down as it was "right up my alley," they'd decided. In spite of my reservations—I envisioned a rave-like scene with everyone sky high on ecstasy and other substances, pulsing to the music and the reptilian brain with nary a synaptic connection to ordinary awareness—I acquiesced, if only to observe the mayhem for my ongoing study.

I rallied my partner (not a small accomplishment) to accompany me as anchor to my vessel amid the unleashed erotic storm I expected to encounter. We journeyed downtown, walked up the sidewalk to the heavily policed building, up the concrete steps to the entrance, and gave each other a wry "well, here goes" glance as we slipped in between the heavy doors.

People inside on the dance floor were costumed up for action in a near-full spectrum of dress and undress: go-go vixens in matching outfits writhed inside the barred walls of the "spanking station"; shadow dancing, and a buffing, bondage and whipping stall graced the stage with a live DJ, bare-chested with a faux fur vest and skin-tight leather pants. A seclusive tent called the Temple of Sacred Touch was lushly strewn with Kama-Sutra-esque pillows, tapestries, candles, and other decor intended to inspire an ambiance of lavish luxury.

The environment was a bounty of seductive suggestion and overt sexual proclamation, and yet, resounding over and above the music and all the trappings at the ball was a palpably buttoned-down and surprisingly self-conscious atmosphere. People seemed to feel fairly awkward and tentative, keeping rather stiffly among themselves. The spankings and whippings I witnessed—diffident pats that could scarcely stun an innocent bug caught between the board and the buttock—summarily encapsulated the scenario.

Nevertheless, this apprehension and uneasiness had a moving quality because it indicated that people had put themselves in a setting that was obviously a wee bit vulnerable, and they hadn't just obliterated their senses with drugs and alcohol in order to do it. There was enough consciousness for *self*-consciousness to arise, which is worth something…if you're paying attention. By listening, we can hear what is being said by the body's psychoemotional bio-chemistry (in this case, uneasiness), and there is a very important message contained within the bodily sensations that is trying to tell us a truer story of who we are.

BURNING DOWN THE HOUSE

Over time, I've learned to recognize the annoying discomfort that tags along with vulnerability as the bitter taste of good medicine. That squirming sensation of self-consciousness can point us in just the right direction to start studying our own inner workings in order to bring about a higher form of "self consciousness" in the Delphic-maxim sense "Know thyself." And this involves some demolition and pyromania.

So here's where we separate the men from the boys, the women from the girls, the freedom fighters from the lily-livered candy-asses. Here is where it really gets real, because now we're moving dead ahead on the idea of venturing into that no-man's-land of *changing a fundamental identity* in order to forge that new path toward genuine sexual freedom.

I Need to Know

Now, if I'm really getting started on my search for the naked truth, I have to know—in no vague and amorphous terms but in great depth and detail—where I'm standing right now. That means, as a first glance, I need to scan through my psychological files and jot down what I've got logged in there. Literally make a written list. And then contemplate each item. Where have they all come from—family, friends, school, community, church, books, media, specific personal experiences, ambiguous impressions, unknown etiology? I must dissect it and study every angle of it. What thoughts, ideas, opinions, and beliefs float around, and which ones are firmly lodged?

Which ones cause the squirm, and which ones scream out, "Don't fuck with me!"?

And I question everything…is any of this stuff I've collected truly my own, and either way, how is it founded? I think of the bumper sticker that says "Don't Believe Everything You Think," and I expand it to implore you not to believe everything you feel, as well (this means going from "I feel it, therefore it's real," to "*I feel it, therefore I feel it*," which is the truest reality of emotion). As it turns out, *everything we think we know* about our sexuality, because of the endless ways it has been manipulated by the world around us—from day one of our lives and for millennia—is suspect and should be treated as such. Our deepest thoughts and feelings have come to *conform* to our training and socialization, so get out the microscope and prepare for some major analysis and revelation.

If I'm approaching the subject of sexual morality, for instance, even a simple thought experiment is chock-full of revelation about its subjective nature.

Take the example of homosexuality. Currently, as we find ourselves in the early phases of emergence from an era of intolerance, we all have front-row seats to witness the pliability of societal conscience, that thing that creeps slowly through the layers of private and public life in the world influencing, first, individual attitudes, then gradually expanding into relationships, the media, politics, and public policy. So we should pay very serious attention, because we're talking about the things we call *right* and *wrong*, for god sakes.[89]

Obviously, some people are still convinced enough of the absolute wickedness of homosexuality that they were, as of 2015, drafting up a ballot initiative in California calling for nothing less than the *execution* of the guilty! Enough signatures collected and you'd have

---

[89] Author Hanna Blank points out that it has only been possible to *be* "homosexual" (or "heterosexual," for that matter) since 1869, since that is when the term was invented. These dichotomous (and misleading) terms correspond with the recognition of only two distinct sexes, while many biologists have asserted, on the basis of chromosomal genetics, that humans have at least *five major* sexes and, therefore, an array of natural sexual orientations (*Straight: The Surprisingly Short History of Heterosexuality* [Boston: Beacon Press, 2012], xiii–xv).

seen this one on your California voter's ballot. How tenuously the course of history unfolds.

Drawing more historical data into the thought experiment on homosexuality, I can call up the context of ancient Greece, where those (males) who did not publicly participate in "gay" relations, sodomy in particular, were scorned and ostracized. Anyone unwilling to dedicate every inch of his manhood to the custom of male bonding and initiation was guilty of shirking his civic duties.

Jonathan Margolis describes in *O: The Intimate History of the Orgasm*, "Homosexuality was seen straightforwardly as morality in action, the unquestioned proper way to bring up a boy to be an upstanding citizen. A man was not really considered to be upholding community standards unless he practiced sodomy. Lycurgus, the Spartan legislator, refused to consider any citizen to be a worthy man if he did not have a male lover. And any parental squeamishness about anal intercourse would damage the boy's education. The best teaching was conducted through the love between teacher and student, called *paiderastia*, and there was a common feeling that virtue could literally be implanted in a boy by receiving the anal ministrations of his teacher."[90]

It's important to note that we're not referring to some obscure cult here—we're talking about the most advanced civilization of its time, the civilization that ultimately gave rise to the Western world we inhabit today, its thinking minds generating the basis of our most fundamental ideas of philosophy and democracy. If morals such as these (in my example, both homosexuality *and* pedophilia), generally assumed to be universally unquestionable, are indeed showing such contortionistic flexibility, then what to make of my own collection of values and beliefs? How to hold them? How to regard them? (We should start by holding them at a healthy arm's length and regarding them all as open to question!)

Just a perfunctory glance at this kind of information doesn't really do much. This stuff is always floating around somewhere in the

---

[90] Jonathan Margolis, *O: The Intimate History of the Orgasm* (New York: Grove Press, 2004), 160–61.

periphery, in the amply seeded clouds of our information-inundated existence. But doing a serious contemplative and pointedly reflective meditation on this set of data to make it hauntingly personal and immediately relevant should cause some healthy turbulence in the deeper waters of the psyche. And this is what is called for. The point is not to assure myself that I am a tolerant, open, and flexible individual, but to reveal to myself that I, too, absolutely have places where I hide and ideas to which I stubbornly cling.

Many—if not most—things can only be revealed by putting ourselves through the motions of real-life, hands-on R&D. Therefore, after dissecting my position, and identifying a few outstanding issues that I'm ready to dig further into, I then get to move on to trial and experimentation. What actions am I going to take to actually put it to a test? I am doing an experiment to find out for myself, personally, if I can validate or invalidate the standard lines I've bought into.

One of My Kind

It's hard to take a serious look at one's own sexuality without coming face-to-face with a very personal consideration of the question of sexual orientation and its sometimes-perplexing ambiguity. Alfred Kinsey noted, in order to explain the biological reality behind his seven-point heterosexual-homosexual rating scale, "The world is not to be divided into sheep and goats. Not all things black nor all things white. It is a fundamental of taxonomy that nature rarely deals with discrete categories....The living world is a continuum in each and every one of its aspects."[91]

As for myself, I always manifested as strongly heterosexual with some bi-curiosity arising situationally. But my hypothesis is that the overwhelming and enduring power of my heterosexual responses is grounded in the fact that I always viewed and utilized males as my sexual outlet. Many years ago I came up with an experiment that I

---

[91] Alfred C. Kinsey, Wardell B. Pomeroy, and Clyde E. Martin, *Sexual Behavior in the Human Male* (Bloomington, IN: Indiana University Press, 1948, 1998), 639.

wanted to run on myself and never did—or haven't yet. The idea is that maybe if, for a long enough period of time, I only allowed myself to access females as an outlet, that I would begin to see them differently—more sexually arousing in that vagina-tingling way—and experience a stronger sexual oomph toward women. In other words, I wonder if my heterosexual bias represents *magnetic north*, aligning itself with massive underlying social conditioning and if, perhaps, by modifying that influence, I may discover *true north*, or what is more innate about my sexual orientation.

Some say women maintain more fluidity in their sexual orientation (that "erotic plasticity" mentioned earlier), able to transmute their tastes according to what's available, while men's sexual proclivities tend to become established as more of a fixed topic, usually at some earlier point in their pubescent maturation process. Maybe that helps to explain why a number of lesbians are "converts," while you rarely come across this story with gay men.

Indeed, this fluidity came in handy during the feminist revolution when heterosexuality "was removed from the realm of the 'natural,' and reinterpreted as an ideology and an institution that kept women bound to men and blocked their struggle for full liberation," ultimately presenting lesbianism as the *sine qua non* of political rebellion.[92]

Although men sequestered together in the absence of women (in prisons, monasteries, etc.) will utilize other males as sexual outlets, the environment would not be likely (according to this notion) to influence their original set of preferences, and their activities would not likely represent a viable reflection of genuine erotic interest. (In my opinion, however, this too could very well be another example of cultural biases and social training hard at work, so we have to watch out for these kinds of theories.)

My own indiscriminate responses caused me acute agitation as a teenager early in high school. As my sexuality grew inside me, I felt more and more self-conscious about having physical touch and

---

[92] D'Emilio and Freedman, 317.

affection with other girls. I noticed a distinctly sexual undercurrent present with any sort of physical intimacy, which I found confusing and unnerving. I had no idea how to relate to its nose poking in outside the authorized heterosexual context. Consequently (and with sorrowful long-term reverberations), I channeled the physical expression of my affectionate behavior toward males almost exclusively.

I knew I was being manipulated by forces I didn't fully understand—namely, sexuality and socialization—that I was missing out on a significant component in my female relationships that I truly craved, and that something was amiss with the whole thing. But these forces nevertheless continued to govern my behavior as I watched and wondered.

It's obvious to me why I find men to be such a turn-on: I love masculinity, in its *differentness*. All the stereotypical masculine differences in their bodies from my own—the flat, muscular male chest, the broad shoulders, the narrow hips, the definition of lean muscle, facial and body hair (yes, please), and the hardness and coarseness—all rev up my engines. The penis, that throbbing tower of power, is an architectural marvel, and the testicles are a sensational wonder (to be able to hold his gonads in the palm of your hand, and tune into what wriggles within, is almost otherworldly).

Conversely, with more sexual maturity and a greater volume of varied experiences, I've realized that the *sameness* of the physicality of a woman offers exhilarating sensations that cannot be duplicated any other way. I have even wondered if a man can possibly experience a woman's softness to the same degree that another woman can, due to the relative coarseness and hairiness of male skin. That, unlike mythical Tiresias, I cannot ever know (although, technically, these days I guess I could, but I'm having too much fun being a woman this time around).

As a young woman, there were a handful of females for whom, if I hadn't been so narrow-minded and afraid of sex in general, I would have admitted I'd fallen head over heels—the way I would typically expect (and wholeheartedly *allow* myself) to fall for a man.

My first big girl-crush, my senior year in high school, was a slightly boyish yet exquisitely elegant German girl with a gentle poise and grace that enchanted me. I could not take my eyes off her. I could hardly believe she showed an interest in me as well, and we had a tender connection of a timeless quality that was partly the result of the language barrier and partly of our adolescent vulnerability both within ourselves at the time and with one another. We were exchange students placed on separate islands in New Zealand, so our encounters were very limited—we never progressed beyond managing to communicate an intensely felt response toward each other. But I remember vividly how simply being in her proximity felt just like the shy, tingly buzz of my freshman encounter with the drummer on the school bus. Saying goodbye to her felt like ripping off my flesh. We remained pen pals for a while after returning to our homelands, but somehow, that eventually dissolved. My romantic love for her never did.

Three years later came the biologist who traveled aboard our tour boat as part of the natural history educational staff. Same thing: I was enthralled with her physical beauty—with her thick waist-length flaxen hair, glacier-blue eyes, slender, athletic build—as well as her softly understated yet exuberant personality, in a way that moved me through and through. The respectful and gentle intimacy that we shared as friends was unparalleled in my experience, and her graceful strength and open vulnerability poetically inspired me. I was just smitten, and I wanted to be with her. As her work took her traveling around the world, we kept in touch through the mail. Again, time weakened the long-distance connection, but not my feeling or my memory of her.

Both of these women I could have happily pursued sexually, but I was far too timid and ignorant of that aspect of life and of myself. Instead, I translated everything coursing through my being into romantic hues of emotional rapture, as I was prone to do. And I believe that the incompleteness within me that resulted from my inability to express the fullness of my response to both of them, because of the way my sexuality was inaccessibly compartmentalized, has left a gaping hole that still feels somewhat painful.

Finally, there was the woman who taught one of my classes at massage school, and I was, again, mesmerized. I didn't want to let her out of my sight, so when the course ended, I enrolled in her yoga class, grasping to maintain contact without having to reveal my motives. Eventually, she ended up becoming a central feature of my life (the female counterpart of that "remarkable couple" I mentioned in an earlier chapter), initiating me into the great big world of reality, holding my hand through the rough and tumble of confronting things as they actually are, and pushing me firmly to step into my own strength and grace. Because of the world of risky honesty they opened for me, I was able to realize that beneath my enchantment was the heaving sea of sexual desire. So I was able to speak this to her, and although we never had sex, that expression was a big moment for me in bringing my sexuality into alignment with the real world and, therefore, with the totality of myself.

My fleshly adventures with women are summed up rather shortly but, nonetheless, sweetly.

I remember vividly the first time I hugged a woman completely naked. It was a nonsexual interaction, yet it was extremely sensual. The peculiar unfamiliarity of fleshy softness, with our breasts pressed together, made my head slightly woozy, my legs a little wobbly, and brought up bubbly laughter through my body. It was wonderful— so dramatically different than the feeling of a man. And this was another moment of recognizing what it might be about women that could drive a man crazy. Femininity is sexy; estrogen rocks!

As a freshman in college in 1991, hanging with the thespian crowd gave me access to a juicy collection of multisexual guys and gals. At our parties, we drank wine and cocktails and made out indiscriminately with one another, which was deliciously intoxicating all by itself. One particularly bacchanalian evening, when we all returned from a night out clubbing, where my first deeply passionate kiss with a casual girlfriend rocked my world, I partook in a little bisexual orgy involving a pile of six, four gals and two guys. I focused on the women and all but ignored the boys that night, completely absorbed in the soft novel delight of making out and feeling each other up.

Years later, in my latter twenties, I'd begun having sex with a woman I really enjoyed. Damn that woman knew how to kiss! And for the first time I had the experience of sinking into full-on, sober sex with another woman. I remember how I had to throw some switches in my being in order for me to give myself to the experience of genuine erotic excitation. There was a deliberate shift I had to make in order to overcome an ingrained resistance to responding sexually to her. I had to break down that barrier I'd built within myself back in high school! But once that was done, it was sex, just like it was with a man. I was ecstatic with the discovery and intoxicated by the fresh exploration of sexual femininity. But there was something else I had to hurdle. I had a squeamishness resulting from my own deeply rooted prejudice against the vulgar vagina and I was literally terrified to go down on her. So, with her sweet presence and participation, I ventured facially, yea, down through the valley of the shadow of the vagina…and I came out alive, very much alive! The smell and initial taste was not off-putting, just unsettling and unfamiliar. Then after a while, it reminded me of the surprising pleasure I had discovered with my partner in Baja, kissing him after he'd given me head. It was musky and sexy as hell.

Around that same time, I also tried this (a bit more clinically) with a circle of women, when we all traded the favor as a sisterly gesture of supportive sexual empowerment. Through both situations, I realized that my biggest fears stemmed all the way back from my pubescent development, with the visceral terror and disgust I felt toward my body's changing shape and function, and the substances and smells that came along with that generally traumatic evolution. Being able to share these sexual and explorational experiences with other women had an overwhelmingly powerful impact on me psychologically and emotionally.

Recently, I watched a beautifully made video of an orgy among innocent, playful, erotic young women.[93] In addition to being aroused, I was deeply moved and found myself crying tears of both happiness and sorrow. Watching these young women play together and enjoy one another's bodies both tenderly and passionately, I knew that this experience would never allow them to harbor the fear and disgust toward their own bodies that I have known. I felt sad know-

---

[93] *The Fall (Original Sin)*, directed by Vex Ashley, Four Chambers, 2016.

ing that so very few women have had or will have this experience among open, loving, sexually powerful sisters. To be honest, I could still use much further intimate acquaintance, involvement, and acclimation to the female body to address my homophobia rooted within me as a woman deeply conditioned in repugnance toward her own anatomy. I promise myself that one day I shall again walk through the valley of the vagina, and fear no evil!

Across the Universe

One of the most valuable and far-reaching experiments I've done was an ongoing exploration of my own sexual standards. The deep space and dark matter of this aspect of sexuality usually go unquestioned and therefore unexamined.

The issue of standards is very deeply personal and usually outrageously complex and overinflated—especially for women, who have been conditioned to wrap up so much of their own identity as a person in their choice and capture of a man. Because we, as women, have learned we must tightly bind together the emotional and the sexual, and because our sexual forays bring in tow all manner of implications and expectations of permanence and commitment, it follows that *every* sexual prospect is subject to an inordinately stringent list of specifications.

It's only in reflection that I can clearly see how utterly pickled I was as a young woman within this psychosexual brine...and how crippling it was to the exploration of my sexuality—which is, of course, precisely what it's designed to do! (It is another way we are surreptitiously guided down the narrow chute of chastity, as very few sexual prospects, of course, can really measure up to those comprehensive emotional and material requirements.)

In the very beginning of this whole sexual exploration of mine, there were a few men in my constellation of friends with whom I was just becoming acquainted, and we began to talk about the prospect of having sex. None of them, not one, was particularly my cup of celestial seasonings. There were bald and balding heads, somewhat bulging guts, underdeveloped chests and shoulders, and damn, no outdoor enthusiasts. The thought of rolling around naked with any of them was something that made me feel a whole bunch of things, but not sexy. And hidden in plain sight among all my disgruntled feelings was a fierce hostility.

It's not that any of these men were actually repugnant, but nevertheless, when it came to the idea of sex with them, what I felt was disgust—hot, angry disgust. So when I looked more carefully at the venomous intensity of my aversion, it was pretty evident that something was seriously out of kilter, and as much as I wanted to reject it out of hand, I had to admit that. The anger, I realized, was a stern defense. The question, however, is begged by the presence of any defense: what's to defend? Every one of these men was open and receptive, clean, honest, good-natured, straightforward, and thoroughly respectful—and I was running out of good reasons for not giving it a whirl in the name of "science." So, eventually, I had sex with every one of them…and not just once. There were some really intimate, worthwhile, and—shocking!—hot experiences shared as a result, and the walls of my ignorant little cell came crumbling apart. I began to recognize that each one of these men was appealing enough to me in one way or another, each in his own way, to turn the motor on.

This was the beginning of breaking down the fortress in which I had sheltered myself from so many sexual possibilities and opportunities, in the name of…self-respect? That seems to be what it boils down to, that and control. I actually felt safer within the bounds of my restrictive standards. (As a woman in this world, I think there can be comfort and a distinct sense of safety in *self-control*, which can come to represent—within the mind, at least—a modicum of control over the circumstances.) Of course, this mind-set can only continue to exist in a milieu where we are taught that our untamed sexual nature and uninhibited expression are *not* respectable (outside those very narrow parameters), are actually *unsafe* (regardless of the presence or absence of any real danger), and must therefore be kept under wraps.

For me, the initial prospect of stepping outside the deeply fur-rowed delineations representing my sexual "standards" made me feel a bitter sense of vulnerable disempowerment, although I couldn't artic-ulate or even clearly discern it at the time. It unearthed a fully buried meteorite of subconscious distrust of the opportunistic, exploitative sexual agenda of men.

Even back then, that distrust was light-years removed from my conscious awareness. Having grown up with a gentle, loving father and a genuine lifelong gravitation to male company, I certainly never felt, as genders, we were creatures from different planets at odds with one another. Quite the contrary, I tended to feel a more natural and easy rapport with the opposite gender than with my own. I always felt more like one of the boys than anything else. But nevertheless, in the maelstrom of sexual development, I had somehow managed to absorb into my oyster a fleck of that nasty cosmic debris that would form the seed, not of a luminous pearl but of a very particular sort of guarded bitterness that could only ever be revealed under very partic-ular circumstances. And here they were. Relinquishing that scrupu-lously constructed envelope of restrictive sexual criteria felt nothing like arousal at first but instead called up feelings of uneasiness, expo-sure, and—as a defense—hostility.

The searing anger I initially felt reflects, in part, the natu-ral response of the ego to having its staunch positions challenged. (Remember what I said about not believing everything we feel? In this case, the feeling represents something very real happening inside, but the *interpretation* of that feeling—that I'm actually pissed at these guys—is way, way off base.) But even beyond feeling provoked and exposed, the extreme temperature of my reaction ultimately reflects the hemmed-in repression of a very hot fire—sexuality itself.

Originally, I would have never thought that such a thing as "my own standards" could be so self-limiting and confining, and that penetrating the fortress could be such a welcome relief. But, I delight to say, *it changed my world!* They never were, in fact, my own true sexual standards, because they had been fashioned by someone who knew nothing of her own true sexuality. The doors flung wide-open as I likewise spread open my arms, my heart, and my legs to embrace more fully the spectrum of sexual response, acquiescing to my body's *own* inherent opportunistic agenda equal to that of any man.

We all know too well the eye-rolling refrains about *men*—in fact, we know them so well that all a woman needs do is roll the eyes and state the syllable, because we all know what that means about what they want (!). Only in recognizing that this quality of appetite is what is going on sexually for *humans*—not one lousy gender to the exclusion of the other—can we begin to meet on the level.

It's also very important for me to point out here how those men with whom I tore down my self-justified walls, and by whom I viscerally and irrationally feared exploitation, were more honoring toward me as a woman and as a sexual liaison than many of the men who actually measured up on my fantasy yardstick. And this is important as a lesson in reality versus make-believe in a realm where so many of us find ourselves embroiled in situations that are far less than ideal, far less than healthy. This is because our standard measures (a.k.a. romantic fantasy) and their made-up mandates have largely been taken on from outside ourselves. We end up in unhealthy relationships because our whole sense of ourselves (rooted, as it is, firmly in sexuality) has been so severely bent out of shape by that mixed-up external environment that has done everything in its power to call a spade *anything* but a spade when it comes to sex.

In order to stop living out this interminable nightmare, we have to resurrect the reality of who we are as vibrant sexual entities rather than mummified madonnas pinched into modern masks. That means calling sexual interest *sex* and then handling it accordingly, as *separate* from relational involvement—at least as separate as it needs to be to honor every other element of relational truth on a case-by-case basis. Calling a spade by name, we become free to act on purely sexual impulses and attractions without confusing sex with love and commitment and every other made-up synonym for sexual fulfillment, while keeping a clean perspective on the rest of what makes up a healthy and fulfilling life.

What this brings us to is nothing less than a deeply radical liberation for women and, consequently, relief for the men who no longer really understand or even enjoy the position into which they have put themselves. The time has come to get ourselves out of the old-fashioned model, fully and completely. Only when women can reclaim the power of knowing our own bodies and taking action accordingly—meaning, beyond all imposed constraints and with full awareness of the implications (or lack thereof!)—and men begin to recognize the significance of the *mutual* benefits of that course of events will we as fellow humans begin to function happily together.

So what was I defending? I was defending the mandate—and my right—to be choosy as an expression of *who I am*, adamantly in my ignorance. I was defending my right to hide behind the story I had chosen to believe that there were truly only a small number of individuals who could turn me on sufficiently and that there was absolutely no justification for accommodating anything outside my narrow band of preferences when it came to simply having sex. On an emotional level, my sexual standards had represented and defined *me* in a meaningful and reassuring way. On a realistic level, however, they only succeeded in defining *my emotionality*—and, of course, severely limiting my sexual exploration. They did not accurately reflect my real sexuality.

Everywhere it is pounded into our skulls that "simply having sex" for the sake of having sex is that lowly animalistic act that is below our hallowed humanity and therefore empty, worthless, and ultimately destructive to character. (I love how Christopher Ryan points out that the capacity to indulge in sex for sex at our leisure, rather than according to a biological program, is actually a crowning evolutionary glory that sets humans apart from most other animals!) I had to overcome this obstacle as I embarked on my experiment of deliberately having sex for sex rather than for some other inflated imaginary reason.

I was defending a myth—no, a *lie*. That lie is defining *who* we are by a completely fabricated distortion of *what* we are. It is serving us a universe of misinformation about how our bodies function by design as well as the nature and meaning of our desires. And then, for the fluffy whipped topping on that cosmic pie, that lie capitalizes on the resulting confusion by fabricating and disseminating a moral code of conduct (fobbed off as divine law) by way of which to channel our lustful wayward impulses.

Come Together

Now, burning down the structure of standards does not mean that we have none. It just means that we destroy the make-believe ones to discover the real ones. For a woman, there is so much extraneous clutter in the head composed of all that superfluous criteria for a "mate" (such as social and economic status, intellectual and recreational interests, personality particulars, etc.) that it's easy to lose sight of the actual *sexual* criteria she responds to in a man (as in what increases the blood flow to her vagina). And often, in addition to the confusion in her mind, there's so little real experience sexually that she couldn't possibly even know the range of her own body's responses.

It is experience, and only experience, that allows us to discover our true standards. (But—and this is of utmost importance—this experience must be amassed from a healthy platform, one that is informed in a very particular way, disentangled from preconceptions and distanced from whatever neuroses dictate our relations. It must be done with the highest levels of objectivity and responsibility holding us to superlative standards of honesty and humility within ourselves, putting our own chubby feet to the fire, and burning away all the fat that insulates us from the truth. Otherwise, our experiences will be shaped by the inner demons of our own ignorance simply driving us deeper into our habitual delusion.) It is this kind of raw experience that shows us, truly, how we *really* respond sexually to all that body hair or that extra flesh or that muscle-bound bodybuilder or that coiffed and cologned *GQ* type.

Women, the so-called emotionally driven ones, who have been trained (counter to our nature) to superimpose onto sex the value of attributes beyond the physical, have in turn trained men that a fixation on the physical is disgustingly—downright offensively—superficial. So while women are busy focusing on the things that represent comfort and security in its various dimensions, men are busy pretending they're *not* focusing on the babe's lady lumps…and everyone is fumbling around in a mixed-up fashion causing further obfuscation of the real data.

It was pointed out to me very early on that we all have our *minimum standards*, at and below which it is really not feasible to get the engines going enough to engage in what we can call worthwhile sex, involving stimulation and responsiveness. It was also explained that these minimum standards are actually quite low. *That* I found hard to swallow. I was still holding pretty firmly to my identity bound up in my standards—and when this is the case, a lowering of standards translates directly to a devaluation of self. This is such a messed-up model that I can hardly begin to articulate the problems involved. But…as I experimented and explored over many years, I eventually had enough background to validate for myself that that statement about minimum standards was, indeed, so very accurate. So onto the pyre with all the other nonsense went my glorified standards, reduced to ashes, while I basked in the red-hot glow of my sexual revival.

What I have found for myself is that the bottom line is chemistry and that determining whether or not I have good chemistry with someone takes me beyond almost every other typical criterion of preference, such as height, hair, facial features, clothing, personality, and body type. If you can't get beyond these kinds of things, you'll never chance discovering that chemistry hidden in "unlikely" places that will blow your mind and all its fancy ideas to bits just 'cuz you least expected it.

Case in point: one of my most mundane sexual experiences was with a man that ranked a perfect 10 on my pop charts. He had the looks, man, as well as the suave! I was beside myself jumping out of my pants for him. But the sex—what a letdown. No chemistry. I barely remember anything about it anymore, except the kind of disappointing surprise it was. I was young enough, too, that it was a real eye-opener for me in terms of bursting apart that dream-guy fantasy-bubble we are taught to inflate, ooh and ahh over, and worship like a god.

On the other hand, if the chemistry isn't there, and your partner is near the lower threshold of pure physical appeal, you've got nothing to fall back on. So that's the end of the encounter. No harm, no foul. Hey, nothing ventured, nothing gained—and nothing lost either by venturing into infertile territory. As long as the communication is honest and respectful, it's simply honoring a matter of fact. But it all requires maturity—sexual and emotional maturity.

It is really, quite simply, an attitude of openness, and ease within one's own sexual and physical being that shows the true scope of sexual responsiveness. It is the mind with all its multifarious hang-ups that gets in the way of it. The only way to achieve real sexual understanding and self-knowledge is to dismantle the mind-sets that stand between us and that ease of being by preventing adequate freedom of exploration. And—I'll be frank—it's a bumpy road getting there. It doesn't come together (*right now!*[94]) all on its own. Nothing of real value typically does.

It is as Don Juan explains to young Carlos Castaneda: "Every time a man sets himself to learn, he has to labor as hard as anyone can....Fear of knowledge is natural; all of us experience it, and there is nothing we can do about it. But no matter how frightening learning is, it is more terrible to think of a man without knowledge."[95]

The terror lies in all the piss-poor choices we make in life—in the case I'm making, due to a profound depth of culturally fostered sexual ignorance and misinformation—that cause so much suffering if only we dare to look a thin sheet deeper than the tottering appearances being touted.

Fortunately, in the case of sex, waiting for us beyond the laboring itself—the edgy part of stretching our self-identifications to allow it—is a field of frolicking fun. Through the process of torching the limiting mind-sets, we find within ourselves a spaciousness of being in which the flames of pure sensation, usually smothered by the hang-ups in the head, flutter freely with spontaneous abandon, as they are naturally given to do.

---

94 The Beatles, "Come Together," Apple, 1969.
95 Carlos Castaneda, *The Teachings of Don Juan: A Yaqui Way of Knowledge* (New York: Simon and Schuster, 1973; Berkeley and Los Angeles: University of California Press, 1968), 61.

FREEDOM

Christopher Ryan is fond of saying "Men are from Africa, women are from Africa" as an answer to the Mars and Venus conundrum. He's saying this to bring the conversation, both literally and figuratively, back down to earth. Beyond the evolutionary context within that statement, there is also a historical one that can be expressed allegorically.

We have all been, in a sexual sense, abducted from our native domain and forced, coerced, and transformed into servitude to a master demanding obedience to a domesticated way of life that is completely out of sync with our wild roots and nature. We are now entangled in the disgruntled confusion of finding ourselves a *long, long way from home.*[96]

The struggles and drama around sex and sexuality that we constantly encounter are symptoms of the existential crisis arising from being disconnected from those roots. We have, so to speak, found ourselves suffering from a crisis of "identity."

Who Are You?

Self-identifications, as it turns out, are the whole kit and kaboodle when it comes to psychological obstacles in the way of sex.

Because sexuality *is* the essential feature of our humanity, stripping away these self-identifications one at a time can take us all the way down to the birthday suit to rediscover that sexual innocence we

---

[96] Paraphrase of the lyrics of "Freedom" sung by Richie Havens at Woodstock in 1969.

possessed upon our unadorned arrival into this world. From that vulnerable moment onward, looking to the world to help us form our functional identity—with which we will carry out all of our "existential acts and relations" throughout our lives—we have been donning layer after layer of tawdry identifications to clothe all our "definable dimensions," each one shaped by, and shaping, our sexuality.

Part of the ease in training us as biddable slaves to such a carnally oppressive master involves our titanic human weakness, that irrepressible hunger to *be somebody* (which, for us social human animals, gets taken care of at all levels of society and culture, through acknowledgment and approval or shaming and shunning). We are raised on a diet designed for the constant nourishment of self-importance, and we thrive on it—except that past a certain point, we really don't.

Developmentally, for figuring out (physically, mentally, emotionally) that we are an entity unto ourselves and working out the particulars of survival, defining the self is of utmost importance in navigating through our existence. But the continued pursuit of (and heavy investment in) our identities begins to become an incredible burden, and we just keep feeding the behemoth without realizing that we have reached the point where we have outgrown it, in spirit, and it is time to move on to nourishing more grown-up ways of being. Instead, we turn a blind eye to the incredible suffering underneath the fun and games of the masquerade ball. Caught up in the ostensibly gratifying but incredibly myopic condition of being somebodies, we reject the pains of growing *in spirit*, from emaciation to emancipation.

Unfortunately, a bombastic obsession with identity has exploded among young people. Now, with the latest PC movement around sex and gender, these kids have a whole new gospel of identity imposing upon themselves the injunction to choose a sexual identity before they even know anything about sex! The trouble is that identifying just generates additional baggage that actually restricts a person's sexuality, which is and ought to remain a spectrum of possibility. Sex and sexuality should be fluid, particularly at younger ages when we're just beginning exploration. By identifying, we confine ourselves to a particular role, forcing us to step over vast fields of sexual discovery. When the mind fixes on a defined idea of who it is we think we are, sexual exploration loses a vital level of flexibility. Sexuality is about *responding*; identifying is just a needless obstacle standing in its way (not to mention how it adds into the whole "us and them" ordeal). The irony lies in inventing distinctions in order to fit in. The more distinct and special we are, the better we play into the whole charade while entirely missing the point of the whole thing to begin with!

Highlighting the insanity of our collective dementia, as the Supreme Court ruled in June 2016 in favor of gay marriage—an epic victory for homosexuals—what showed up in the media immediately following was a vociferous contingent already expressing discontent, lamenting about losing the sense of "specialness," community, and common purpose that comes along with being an oppressed group.[97] Similarly, in the early nineties, I encountered a few former East Germans, members of the underground liberal movement, who shared these same sentiments after the deconstruction of the Berlin Wall. In these cases, the addiction to an abstract identity actually holds more value than the living reality of a more open and liberated society (precisely *the* thing these people were supposedly fighting for—and, if you recall, this is basically the same beef I chewed out with "Mr. Fantasy" in chapter 5).

Recent studies in neuroscience have begun to reveal the anatomy of our self-centered existence. Images of the brain both in meditation and on hallucinogens converge on the same region (the default mode network) recognized as the seat of the ego. Both meditating and tripping can bring about radio silence in this part of the brain, linked to experiences of loss of self. But most fascinating is the fact that when this region goes quiet, the rest of the brain lights up, opening a whole new world of inner possibilities (or freedom from habits of mind associated with who we think we are). Both groups tend to describe overwhelming feelings of peace, love, understanding (what's so funny 'bout that?), and universal connectedness (I'll bet you any-

---

[97] Jodi Kantor, "Historic Day for Gays, but Twinge of Loss for an Outsider Culture," *New York Times*, June 26, 2016.

thing if they took blood from these people they'd find bumper levels of oxytocin).

Besides the most important piece about inner freedom and heightened awareness, this shows how our obsession with ourselves (defining, distinguishing, and inflating the value of it all) crowds our capacity to just be simple fellow humans and either really love one another or leave each other well enough alone.

Like those East Germans, I can relate to the invigorating (and validating) rush of defying tradition and authority, but again, we have to be very honest with ourselves about what it is we *really* want and if we really value the endpoint toward which we struggle. Though few of us can sustain the state of total egolessness, dialing back our obsession with ourselves is a must in order to tolerate one another and get along better. So if I want to opt out of the futile fighting (and get on with fighting the really good fight), I must tell myself the truth. I'm not special. I'm not a beautiful and unique snowflake (nor am I, alone, the disgusting rotten apple of the bunch). We're all on this compost heap together—*the all singing, all dancing crap of the world* (sorry I couldn't come up with something a little sexier).[98]

Back on the sexual front, we have invented the showy courtship ritual to cater to our needy little inner peacocks! This ritual gives us the whole luscious experience of the movie-star ego, acting out our favorite leading roles, displaying ourselves before the two-way mirror of the game, and relishing the riveting reflections of reciprocated interest. So sexy.

Sure, it's fun. Yes, it feels good. But because we have come to believe on so many levels that this is the ultimate avocation of life, we've forgotten it's just kids playing house. We seem to think that the experience of *falling in love* represents nothing less than the jewels of heaven, while it is actually just one of those cathartic moments, not altogether unreal, yet completely ephemeral. People spend lifetimes daydreaming about, and chasing, this fleeting dream through imagination, pulp fiction, and the tabloids on the magazine rack.

---

[98] Paraphrased from the script of *Fight Club*, directed by Mike Fincher, 1999.

But this whole affair does not serve our deeper, more innate biological needs. It is, instead, a superfluous cultural construct built to serve the faulty notion of the monogamous ideal that emphasizes the emotional glory of romantic love over and above the genuine underlying biology of sexual appetite. (Now, remember this about the fascination with *romantic love*: it gets grossly overinflated in an environment of *inhibited social intimacy* and *constrained sexual activity*. The highly exalted—yet ultimately meager—morsel baits our deprived innate craving for intimate social connection while we're bursting at the seams with sexual repression, dying for a certified outlet. And this is how we, as fundamentally social-sexual creatures, are held so firmly by the shortest of the short hairs!) In reality, the *excitement* of falling in love is merely the socially acceptable mask disguising our sexual penchant for novelty. It is we, obediently doing as we're told, who attach to it the fiat of forever that leads us formally by the nose down the aisle toward the altar of promises and grand expectations.

The experience of courtship and lust is so exquisitely scrumptious and so richly validating, specifically *because* it is overflowing with the infusion of sexual appetite, like molten lava oozing at last from the very core of being where it has been boiling beneath the confining crust of culture. But then, because all that elaborate attention has been poured into the extravagant *affair* (and because of the added dysfunction around sex), so much energy has been expended on pursuit alone, that the moment of truth—sex itself—is drained of its vitality and often ends up being a letdown.

This is precisely what the author from *Men's Journal*[99] articulated when he said, "It's mostly not the reality but the tantalizing possibility of sex…that gives life its luster," with the emphasis falling upon the enjoyment of his own self-identification. What kind of a life is that? And is this really who we want to be—perpetually hungry people chasing after carrots that exist only in the mind?

This phenomenon (let's call it carrot versus apple) is a direct result of the early training of which I spoke in the beginning of this book, teaching us pumped-up, future-oriented notions about

---

[99] Kreider, 2014.

romantic conjugal union right alongside fear of sex and the squelching of now-oriented adolescent sexuality. So, instead of being taught how to gracefully mount and skillfully ride the powerful steed of growing sexuality, we end up (as adults) being sexual adolescents deprived of an understanding of how to have great sex and healthy sexual relationships. So, carrot or apple? Chasing after illusions and empty promises, or eating of the fruit that brings self-knowledge and a rockin' good time? Emaciation or emancipation? I know which one I would choose!

In the movie *Don Jon*,[100] Julianne Moore ends up teaching young Gordon-Levitt—disillusioned from chasing the perfect "dime" into his bed and still finding porn more satisfying—the art of being fully present in open communion during sex. It's a beautiful story of dropping out of the game and discovering a much more deeply rewarding reality.

Through our self-identifications, we have made the *idea* of sex—the big-screen daydream and the self-validating acquisition—so much more than it really is, and we have simultaneously made the *act* so much less. A friend of mine told me that now that he has an established relationship with a delightful woman (a friends-with-benefits arrangement), they choose to have sex much less frequently. For him, he says, it's lost the thrilling ingredient of "trying to make her my woman…" In other words, the performance-and-acquisition piece is lacking, and now we're down to the mundane reality of who we actually are versus how we want to package and present ourselves. (When I recently examined the boredom within my own long-term monogamous relationship, I saw in myself a craving for the external validation coming from the amorous attentions of new and exciting men.[101] This craving, I found, besides its portions of genuine and legitimate erotic desire, can also be a sneaky distraction from dealing with some of the deeper layers of sexual insecurity, which I'll discuss in depth in a later chapter.)

---

[100] *Don Jon*, directed by Joseph Gordon-Levitt, 2013.

[101] The theories of sexologist M. Meana on the narcissistic element of female desire are discussed in Bergner, ch. 5.

Once we pierce through the glossy veneer of ego posturing that we've coated over sex to hide reality (which is what happens anyway as soon as we get bored), then it's down to the nuts and bolts, which, at first, feels disturbingly mechanical and decidedly unglamorous. We can feel we've lost that juicy, edgy, exciting part of ourselves, and so our minds begin to wander, either nostalgically toward those fleeting magical moments bygone or wistfully toward greener pastures. But pushing through that level of annoying discomfort (these are actually growing pains) and continuing to do the labor of hoeing the clods and winnowing out the chaff, we may finally begin to unearth the bounty of subtle energies we've been missing all along while we've been too busy playing giddily in adolescent frivolities.

Ironically, the pains of growing into this kind of maturity are about shedding the inordinate attire of the ego, acquired by way of our excessive juvenile bent on *being somebody* (or, as is often the case, being *somebody else*), in order to manifest again the capacity for simply *being*.

Who we are. As we are. What we are. (And here, at last, we discover real intimacy.)

It has been famously stated, "Lest ye become again like little children ye shall not enter the kingdom of heaven," and as T. Rex (less famously) said, *"Heaven is hot![102]"*

---

[102] T. Rex, "Main Man," T. Rex (UK), Reprise (US), 1972.

MAIN MAN

After roughly a decade of freestyling it solo in the grand erotic arena, sowing the wild oats, seeking out the skeletons, and gathering the forbidden data, I got an offer I couldn't refuse—although it took some major adjustments.

The person who had become the most important feature of my life, profoundly supporting every aspect of my ongoing path of personal and spiritual growth, initiated a conversation exploring a radically new topic between us that lasted over a year. Now, if there *is* a sane man anywhere, this is the chap. But the prospect we were beginning to entertain—of embarking on a serious, committed sexual affair—felt, at first, completely bananas.

First of all, Steve had been strictly celibate for over twenty years. That means, since I had met him roughly ten years before, he was 100 percent opted out of that sector for the entire time I'd known him, so I had to make a jarring recalibration of my orientation toward him.

The initial emphasis of our conversation pressed upon the question of whether there was a strong enough sexual attraction toward each other to embark upon such an endeavor. He had spent a lengthy time himself tuning into this prior to bringing up the idea with me and would not have ventured to do so, potentially disrupting the equilibrium of a longstanding, deeply intimate relationship had he not felt certain enough of his own level of interest. Plus, of course, he had to make sure for himself that he was absolutely ready to dramatically and radically alter the parameters of his own sexual existence.

For me, though, it came right out of the blue, and I honestly had no idea exactly where I was at with it. Out of respect for his discipline of celibacy, I had always maintained within myself an asexual attitude toward him in his presence. Even though at moments I couldn't help noticing that he was a pretty damn attractive man, I simply never paid any attention to my sexual responses to him. I would say that I had, unconsciously, fostered a bodily disconnect in that regard. Inaugurating this brand-new line of thinking took a bit of handiwork to reassemble because I actually had no solid sense of whether or not I was really hot for him at all. So I had to locate and fit together some scattered pieces in order to shape that picture.

In spite of all this, however, in the very first dialogue we had about it, with my head and body spinning into a new dimension, I could feel the power surge in a sense of rightness about it. Again, and aggressively, that nauseating feeling—of knowing an absolute in the gut, while the dizzying chaos in the head and heart swirls about coming to grips with it—had its way with me. It was as though all the sexual content that had been dutifully checked over the last decade came unglued and began to tumble around inside my body.

Additionally, the whole panorama—where our relationship had begun, from me as a wide-eyed, wavering novice in the field of audacious inquiry, to the higher plateaus of development with expansive vistas of personal and relational possibility—came into view, and with it came the crisp realization that this was the man I needed to be having sex with, and seriously, at this juncture. It was one of those weirdly solid yet ethereal moments that suddenly organizes sensibly the scattered fragments collected from years of navigating through quasi-darkness, where the nebulous and the undefined come shockingly into focus. It was clear that he had what I was ready for in a man and in my sexual life—respectively, lots of yang and lots of vision.

Jump!

Nevertheless, in addition to the excitement and joyful incredulity I felt about the bright new prospect on the horizon, there were a lot of other less sparkly emotions that came along with making the decision in general. This should not have surprised me, but it did anyway. I felt scared about committing to what we were laying out—a monogamous arrangement that would dive as deeply as we could manage into sex and relationship as a spiritual practice.

I felt a mournful sentimentality over the impending loss of the adventurous freedom involved in my sexually nomadic existence. That piece, including the time in open relationship, represented a massive and (mostly) merry chunk of my life up to this point (about half of my entire life and almost all of my sexually active life).

Because we both agreed that either of us holding down a full-time job would interfere with our overall objective and since he was the one with the resources on which we would mostly be living—I felt discomfort in giving up my financial independence. This was extremely disconcerting to a certain part of my liberated-woman self-identification, not to mention my deeply engrained farmer's-daughter work ethic.

I recognized, in spite of all his spectacular qualities, the unquestionable level of my sexual attraction and interest (once I sorted that out), and the rightness of the overall affair, that he was decidedly *not* my romantic fantasy. My preferences clearly yearned for a much younger version of him. I wanted his formerly thick black lion's mane more intact and someone on my arm who appeared more in line with what remained of my youthful, thirtysomething self-image.

And, finally, I felt unrest about letting go of my plans to continue directly on to graduate studies after my upcoming college graduation. This decision represented a distinct fork in my road between worldly and more spiritual aspirations: my life was absolutely going to look completely different depending on this very choice.

In light of all this, I had to do a thorough, and fairly impromptu, inventory of my values, priorities, goals, and ambitions. What surfaced was the vivid sense that I had to jump, and now. This was not something to be passed by or postponed. Beyond all else, my deepest feeling was that to do so would be impertinent to the grand providence of timing, not to mention the unseen mechanisms of providence itself…and so I did.

I and I

Now, in order for me to segue from my free-flying MO into a whole new mind-set and way of life, we agreed that a period of celibacy was an important step along my way. I was just finishing up my undergraduate degree (at thirty-five, being a "nontrad" student was either on par with a generally nontraditional life or a continuation of the late-bloomer syndrome), and so I committed the last six months of this time to observing that practice, with the guidance of a consummate expert.

At this time of my life, the practice of celibacy both aided the focus and aggravated the nervous condition involved in wrapping up finals and graduation requirements. And it was stuffed with an education of its own.

I learned first and foremost that practicing celibacy is not simply about abstaining from sexual relations. If it is done fully, it is an up-close-and-personal, cut-to-the-chase, multidimensional, full-time, in-depth study of sexuality at every level of your being at every moment of your existence, waking or sleeping. This takes you spelunking in regions that never see the light of day. I made an effort to do it fully.

I policed my attentions and behaviors both internally and out in the world at large, day and night. I saw an astonishing shift in my interactions with people, mostly with men, as a result of recognizing my own sexual posturing (based on a very fundamental sexual self-identification possibly linked to gender-role socialization). This should not have surprised me—but it did anyway, given that my sexual agenda had been so deliberately overt and my motives straightforwardly *non*-ulterior. It allowed me to see distinctly the subtleties involved in how sexuality shapes our social existence.

My primping routine—involving clothing selection and its assorted adjustments, hair presentation, and so forth—although not elaborate to begin with, all but entirely dissolved since all that image stuff, when you look straight at it, represents, largely (if not always completely), a form of sexual posturing, as in the desire to look attractive. If you're absolutely off the market, the contradiction and outright counterproductivity of such behavior becomes dazzlingly self-evident. After rudely confronting deeper layers of the equation of self-worth with physical appearance, I appreciated the freedom from these habits and especially enjoyed the extra energy that resulted from such "not-doings."

My dreams became graphically and obsessively sexual, frequently culminating in full-blown physical orgasm. That meant I had to spend time before bed setting my intention to maintain the restraint while sleeping by consciously pressing that objective toward the deeper layers of my subconscious mind. There were occasional successes in that area, but mostly my inner nymphomaniac went maniacal.

Overall, celibacy showed me how sex nuanced so much more of my functioning than I ever imagined, and I'd already allowed my "imagination" to run wild, so to speak. I'd been studying sex from a practical perspective for many years. However, no such study of sex is fully complete without some form of serious foray into the realm of celibacy.

Just as one cannot truly give up something with which they have no real experience (thus, knowing exactly *what* is being given up), the opposite is also true—utterly giving something up reveals hidden aspects that cannot be seen while you're actually involved in it. Therefore, a person can't really have the deepest knowledge of sex without having earnestly practiced abstinence…and six months is not nearly enough to approach what I'm talking about, but it certainly helps.

A couple of months into the celibacy, an enlightening episode took place in the university gym. It was so astonishingly trenchant that it literally made me laugh out loud. There I was, minding my own business as I pumped my triceps on the universal, fixing a restrained gaze straight ahead so as to avoid appreciating the fit young bodies around me, when, suddenly, a neck—a *neck*—passed directly through my cautiously framed field of vision. In an instant I transformed from Snow White into Count Dracula as every visceral particle and quantum of sensation within me performed a virtual lunge upon that luscious cross section of male flesh. That moment packed such a wallop I realized instantly that I was sparring with Ali, and it's just simply time to wake up and smell the coffee. This opponent could obliterate me in the blink of an eye. No kidding.

This revealing moment itself, riding upon the massive landslide of all the other data I'd collected, annihilated within me any remaining traces of those conservative presumptions about female sexuality. Sometimes only when we are backed into a tight little corner are we privileged to observe the reality of our own sexual nature: that we indeed are the same equally hot-blooded creatures as men, moved by the same set of stimuli, even—contrary to the deeply engrained popular theory—the visual. And if the temptation is to write it off as one woman's isolated anomaly, I invite others to—in addition to reading Daniel Bergner's book—well, *"check it and see"*[103] for themselves.

Stuck with You

So why would I possibly go back to monogamy ("monotamy," as Christopher Ryan has offered, combining the words *monotony* and *monogamy*), after reveling in the voluptuous glory of sexual autonomy? For me it was about the whole process of, first, widening the parameters by breaking down the various known and unknown taboos and self-limitations, allowing myself a full radius to discover and freely function according to my true proclivities, and then—in response to what the circumstances presented—choosing to narrow down the focus to sink into the even deeper unknown regions within. In other words, it's about exploring the uncharted wild frontier to map out a sense of the broad reaches of the territory and its topography, locating a specific site in which to drill a mine shaft, then digging as deep as it goes to get to what's down there—the trash and the treasure—so that ultimately there's both a horizontal and vertical axis to the scope of study.

The latter must be done together with a partner equally committed to the kind of focus and attention that that involves, but only after the hinterlands have been boldly explored and adequately addressed. You can't find the exact spot for the mine until you've tra-

---

[103] Foreigner, "Hot Blooded," Atlantic, 1978.

versed the entire domain, and you don't know what the domain has to fully offer until you've drilled deep into its interior.

Besides the outward appearance of our monogamous situation, nothing about our arrangement was orthodox. The whole reason for bringing our lives so closely together was about facilitation rather than romance; the whole basis for monogamy was about focus rather than security or convention. Our primary objective with one another, sexual and otherwise, was to utilize one another's qualities each to our own ends, as long as those ends were intimately aligned—in other words, as long as we shared the same goal, which we spelled out very precisely.

This is where having a partner with an exquisitely clear vision of things was worth the world. He heroically led the way, and I can see, in hindsight (with awe and gratitude), that one of the most important parts of this vision involved how to initiate and carry out the activities in a thoughtful, systematic fashion. After extensive discussion, we drafted up a very detailed agreement delineating both of our obligations and intentions sexually, relationally, and spiritually, as well as financially and materially. We agreed to a four-year renewable contract, which accommodated both of our needs for the stability of a commitment while having a determinate option—allowing for an honorable discharge, so to speak—if either of us wanted out.

Having all the logistics painstakingly outlined and established helped us both address and put aside all potential glitches of that nature—to the best of our ability—and plunge headlong into the embrace of our mutual endeavor. This whole process required ruthless honesty about each of our fears and uncertainties both about each other and about ourselves. We each had our own qualms about committing to life with one another at this level of intensity (having had more than ten years of observing each other's, let's say, idiosyncrasies), as well as doubts about our own abilities.

For me, since my only other committed long-term sexual partner was in the context of an open relationship, I had not experienced the challenges of finding long-term sexual satisfaction in one person. Furthermore, I had, in that relationship, experienced a great deal of frustration and anguish around a muddled issue of desire with my partner. It got to the point that I could not tell within myself if I desired sex with him or not. I couldn't tell whether I was having sex because *I* wanted to or because *he* wanted to, and now I felt a squirming trepidation arising at the prospect of possibly coming face-to-face with that problem again. I never again wanted to feel a sense of obligation and duty toward sex that would arise from a muddle of inner confusion: that sucked.

Steve had concerns—having had fundamentally shut down the works for twenty-two years—about what level of basic sexual function and control he was stepping back into. Basically, he was prepared for disaster.[104]

I was worried about being the kind of sex goddess with whom it would be worth giving up decades of pristine celibacy to pursue lofty sexual aspirations. What if *I* turned out to be the disaster he wasn't prepared to contend with, and that underneath whatever veneer I'd finagled, there was nothing but a wet rag?

There were serious reservations lurking around in our midst.

Regarding how hot or not we were for each other, we wrote up lists of positives and negatives, to acknowledge for ourselves and voice for the other what things we found attractive or unattractive. We discussed everything, including how to maintain and enhance the plus factors as well as address the areas where we could, within reason, work to assuage or eliminate the unsavory particulars. This way we could work to heighten the attraction and grease the wheels of the sexual machinery.

On the negative side—for a rather humorous example—he didn't like the way my eyes bugged out at times so I was actually able, with practice, to recognize when I was doing it and work on curbing

---

[104] After two-plus decades of absolute commitment to celibacy, Steve had become relatively facile in dealing with the ins and outs of controlling sexuality in that realm. However, the prospect of engaging physically in sex again was an entirely unknown arena, and he had no reason to assume that once the gates were open, his level of celibate control would have any relevance within the context of this new ballgame, not to mention that he was stepping back into the game with a fifty-year-old body, not the twenty-eight-year-old one with which he was last familiar.

the habit of making said facial expression. I asked him to build up the muscles in his ass a bit, so he began doing lunges at the gym. I agreed to work on creating more muscular definition in general and to allow my hair to grow as long as possible. He agreed to letting me keep his winter beard trimmed to my tolerances and to throwing out the worst of his ridiculously tattered articles of clothing.

We committed to keeping our bodies fit and attractive, as far as reasonably and healthfully possible, because a fit and healthy physique is a very important aspect of a robust sex life, particularly over the monogamous long haul. You will remember that in a previous chapter I said that the bottom line is chemistry, but with a long-term sex partner, I believe that things should be starting out *well above* the bottom-line threshold as there really needs to be a fairly rich variety of additional stimuli to be able to utilize during the spells when boredom shuffles in.

Let's Get It Started

After graduation, I wrapped up my life in Santa Cruz, loaded my station wagon to the gills, and hit the road back to Oregon. Once settled, we got right down to business.

We had tons of sex while, at the same time, taking it very slowly and systematically, following a disciplined plan that outlined progressive phases of a gradually expanding range of activities. This was part of the careful plan to ease us both bodily and psychodynamically back into the sexual domain as well as to allow us the space to observe and address whatever surfaced within and between us.

We began with only kissing, modest flesh nibbling, and light caressing, which we did for numerous months. This allowed us time to just tune into the chemistry and feel how our bodies responded to each other sexually (and, for Steve, to explore how his system responded to firing those pistons again). Next, we added breast fondling and sucking and then, even later, manual stimulation of genitals. After that, we expanded the repertoire to include oral sex. Each phase lasted for a substantial period of time, and we only progressed on to the next when we both felt entirely complete with the last and ready to do so. By the time we both felt prepared to advance to having intercourse in the anything-goes stage, we had already renegotiated our second four-year contract. Our protracted outline was of the utmost significance for both of us to effectively tackle our own challenges.

For Steve, due to the length of his celibacy, the snail's pace was necessary in order to start the engines up slowly. Anything else would certainly have been disastrous, on many levels, just as he had feared. Imagine starting a stone-cold engine for the first time in twenty years in the dead of winter. You wouldn't want to gun it straight away and peg out the tachometer; you'd probably try to prime it as gently as possible, warming it up and checking it out at an idle for a bit, then easing it into first gear, then second, and so on. Furthermore, inherent in our goal of the kind and quality of sex we were going for is an extremely high degree of control in terms of male ejaculation, in addition to the fact that beyond about age forty, the energy loss from ejaculating on a frequent basis becomes much more detrimental. So taking it easy was crucial in terms of his entry into the realm of developing that control during sex.

My role in this aspect was, to the best of my ability, facilitate a smooth transition for him, which I did by tuning into his body, listening carefully to his comments, honoring his requests, and paying attention to every detail of our interaction. This was mostly extremely easy for me because of my love and respect for him, my reverence—and gratitude—for what he was undertaking, and also my high degree of sexual interest. I was deeply honored to be the person in this position of responsibility. Due to what the whole thing represented to us both as well as the extreme vulnerability of the process, my senses were generally pretty acute in this regard without requiring much effort. Nevertheless, I constantly made sure that I was holding all this at the forefront of my awareness—in other words, not snoozing.

For me, the immanent challenges would be all about psychoemotional housecleaning and actually rewiring some of the circuitry, so to speak, which I will discuss at some length. His capacity to be attentive to me in the same way, and more, provided the facilitation that eventually allowed me to successfully clear out most of the blocks in my system (those crystalized inhibitions I spoke about in the second chapter). The nervous system, over time, actually adjusts its activity according to how it is used—or not used—and parts that have become deadened can be reawakened through deliberate practice. In the sections that follow, I will provide full explanations of some of my personal examples of this: my eyes, my hands, my breasts.

The ultra-expanded timeframe we spent having lots of sex within a format of restricted enterprise, held in the arms of a profoundly vulnerable and loving intimacy, was so full of gems of revelation that it has probably been the most deeply informative, multifaceted adventure I've ever taken. It turned out to be the means that made real the idea of drilling a mine shaft. And, as I said before, both the trash and the treasure would be unearthed in this process.

As Tears Go By

In the beginning—probably about the first four years or so—there were many times we simply had to stop in the middle of whatever we were doing and sort through my emotional and psychological stuff.

Over the prior decade, I had done extensive work within myself to address my worst obstacle, which is a deep-seated self-effacement, or lack of self-worth and esteem. I had been ruthlessly and unscrupulously abused by my older sister throughout our young life together, and the heartbreak and devastation from that had infected my being at every level, as I discovered on my journey back to health and wholeness. Although tremendous strides had been made thus far (in fact, radical transformation), the environment Steve and I fostered—through the intimacy between us and the focused vulnerability of the sex we had—became a potent catalyst to further the process. And because we were not just looking to have a sexual outlet but a full participation at every conceivable level, we were not about to go sweeping anything under the rug along the way. So many aspects of myself had become discolored under the murky shadow of self-effacement and so, naturally my sexuality was likewise tainted, inseparable as it is from most every aspect of ourselves (especially with the additional fusion of emotion and sex taken on by females). Usually, at some point during sex, for some obscure reason, I would find myself somehow disengaged from the activity—not participating wholeheartedly or whole-bodily. And it was most assuredly not due to lack of sexual interest in my partner.

I would struggle internally, trying to work it through myself and to get free of whatever had a hold of me, sometimes successfully, but usually—especially in the beginning—not before he picked up on it and asked me what was going on. At this point we would stop and focus the lens on trying to sort it out. Sometimes there was an answer readily at hand—an emotion or a distinct thought process. Oftentimes, though, only a disconnected, disconcerting emptiness predominated. That emptiness conjured up feelings of anger and sadness, a sadness mostly about feeling entirely remote and alien, as if my very heart and soul existed in a realm eternally inaccessible to human ingress. The anger arose in futile defense. It left me feeling darkly detestable, sorry for Steve for not recognizing that he was wasting his time with a ghost of a person who *had no* heart or soul and who therefore didn't deserve anything from him, much less such patient, loving attention. That sensation of hopelessly unmitigated worthlessness is the most hollow sense of despair I have known, and to face this dreaded void was to stare straight into the center of my own broken heart. It was the bedrock of my self-loathing, just a broken pain in my chest latching onto the multifarious negative attitudes about sex and my body that I had gathered and packed in along the way.

Occasionally, I needed to spend some time quietly alone to move it through. But frequently, by way of talking it out together, I would locate a very specific idea or sensation at the root of it, which I could then voice, express, and heal.

Once, after stopping and being unable to speak coherently at first, we lay together in silence until I located something—a deep, heavy, and amorphous grief. Sinking silently deeper into that, I felt my mother, and I voiced that. A moment later, with a flood of tears, came the translation into words, straight out of this inward sensation of my mother—not something that she had ever articulated in words herself, but that I must have simply internalized from her presence—*that there was absolutely no joy or beauty in being a woman.*

I cried as my body shook with uncontrollable emotion, and then it passed. Afterward, and since, I felt such a relief from the burden of carrying the weight of that subliminal notion inside myself, probably for my entire life. Taking all this in, I feel inconceivable gratitude for the blessing of such a superlatively supportive partner who has helped me to heal sexually (by helping me to access the joy and beauty of being a woman through his own profound appreciation of femininity) and sorrow that my mother did not receive such intimate, loving, and healing sexual support from my father.

Each time we circled this route, with one more obstacle removed, we were another step closer to the freedom of the dynamic sexual expression we sought to manifest. The obstructions were always a disturbance to some degree, and sometimes even very upsetting to him, both emotionally and physically. Yet the patience and love he demonstrated over and over, and our consistent work of pressing through the jungle, eventually brought us through the woods out into the open. Now, more than a decade into this endeavor, it is rare that we have to stop and deal with this sort of thing. The work has paid off, beyond imagination.

The thing is, how many times have any of us pushed aside some annoying emotional issue during sex or, worse, continued going through the motions of the act without being fully, bodily present because that annoying feeling has infiltrated and hijacked the unit, only to leave a sense of emptiness rather than fulfillment? Usually, what is there has an important snippet of the story to tell, and what it needs is a moment to catch its breath, get its bearings, and figure out exactly what it has to say. It always has something. "I don't know" is almost never the last word. It just means there's more digging to do.

This can seem to be a daunting task. It is. It takes time. It takes patience. It takes a lot of skill in navigating through really tricky psychological and emotional territory, and it demands tenacious commitment to the expedition. Given the extent of the emotional damage incurred in my youth, I could have never approached, let alone sustained, functioning at this level without having spent so many years prior rigorously engaged in the process of healing that damage and acquiring those skills. But no matter how abysmal it may feel at times, the most important truth I learned through this process is that *it is not bottomless*, and one day, after much digging, we lift our eyes to see that the excavation is basically done, and we are free. (From here on out it's just general maintenance!)

Eyesight to the Blind

One of the things we did a huge amount of during our first phase is talk. There is so much fascinating information to communicate to one another about our sexuality that ends up allowing us to enjoy sex all the more—and all the more intimately—that I can't see any excuse for not passionately doing so.

For example, Steve described in colorful detail to me what it *felt* like to him to have an erection. The impact of that description alone has so greatly enhanced my own growing recognition of what an erection *is*—in terms of what it is to the person who has it—that, ever since, I have experienced a whole new dimension of appreciation for the penis and enjoyment of interacting with it. It allowed me finally to comprehend, with visceral empathy, the feeling of masculine power and even the inspiration for phallic worship manifested in human history.

To be honest, I always regarded the phenomenon of phallic worship—and offhandedly dismissed it—as a quaint historical oddity from an uncivilized era where I could almost visualize brutish males dragging their female receptacles about like living blow-up dolls. I think that as a woman, the idea of phallic worship continues to be threatening because of the extant issues of male supremacy and misogyny still kicking around in our midst, and there is an underlying sensation of contemptuous anger due to a reactive misandry (and, therefore, that resistance to celebrating masculinity). The idea of phallic worship, as a predominant cultural feature, stirs the real fear of living in an environment of intolerable oppression. (I say this now, as the indefatigable cult of the divine fetus continues to feverishly pursue the evisceration of women's reproductive rights across the country, a real threat that prompted me to get sterilized as soon as my childless needs, values and goals became clear.) But, damn! My new appreciation for the experience of a man I love made me want to worship the phallus myself, not just his, but phallus as emblem… and that has only empowered me as a woman who is able to love men even more and to benefit even more from a heightened ability to sense and, thus, receive that power sexually.

The alchemical magic of opening the eyes to this dimension is that it opens up the more subtle capacity in sex to receive the *essence* of masculinity—or femininity, since the same is absolutely true for the man interested in tuning into his female partner in the same way, or anyone for that matter, interested in tuning into sexual energy and essence with any given partner. (In fact, part of my education was absorbed in silent observation, simply experiencing the way my partner was so deeply, receptively, tuned into me.) Now this is something to blow your mind. This brings every cell and fiber of the body awake to really *feel* the chemistry at the hormonal level with all the constituent subtle energies vibrating and resonating. This brings sex to the level of ecstasy that is hinted at in sacred texts.

But it absolutely cannot become manifest while we are still caught up in hating, fearing, fighting, or holding out on one another, *at any level,* in that us-and-them paradigm (since ego is far too preoccupied for that "sacred" element to exist). I am not preaching here about loving everyone, or "becoming one", or any of that mumbo-jumbo that is really so limited in any real, practical sense (remember, after all—we are the world, we are the compost). Therefore, I am talking about clearing out all the trash and cleaning the house so that, with the burdensome impediments that clutter and cloud the works removed, the place sparkles with the pristine reflections of what is actually happening physiologically and energetically, rather than psychologically, mentally, or emotionally.

My new appreciation for Steve's anatomy and his sexual experience came into play at every level of the sex we had. This is because it peeled off an invisible layer of film that, in this case, was a fear-based prejudice against the phallus, of which I was previously entirely unaware.

In fact, in the process of opening myself up to a deeper affair with the penis, I unearthed a very old memory of tittering with some young female acquaintances (a rare moment in my teenage life!) about the "ugliness" of the penis. "Women are beautiful!" we giggled, "but look at what we have to deal with!" I was surprised to reflect on this moment in time and realize that there was still a perceptible trace of that prejudice, showing up now as a subtle aversion. In a sexually enlightened society, I believe the juvenile squeamishness toward sexual organs, if present at all, would dissolve naturally and completely with maturation, while in our sexually stunted culture they'll just stick in the dark crevices, undetected. This faint reluctance felt like the flimsiest film of avoidance, and yet, as I blew it aside with a gentle puff of recognition, I could feel myself open to a whole new dimension of sexual receptivity.

Once again, I was dumbfounded by the earth-shattering effect of removing a dinky little obstacle I didn't even know was there. I was learning the deepest of secrets about sex, life, and practical psychology. This stuff cannot be fully accessed by lying back comfortably on a couch in talk therapy, because it requires the bare-assed vulnerability involved in relating intimately within the context of our greatest exposure—the bedroom. Because of what it opened within me, I was able to really up my game, dialing in my awareness to discern every nuance taking place moment to moment under the skin of his shaft, whether through my palm, my mouth, or ultimately, my vagina. (Like a condom, emotional hang-ups are a barrier that will indeed decrease sensitivity—yet, in contrast to the condom, whose usefulness is irrefutable, hang-ups are only trouble!) Through fully tuning into this feature alone, I have experienced full-blown genital orgasm by manually stroking the throbbing cock and striving to absorb every component of what it generates and represents.

This sensitivity has turned out to be the most critical piece for us in the ongoing practice of his ejaculatory control. The endeavor is so mercurial at times, with fluctuations that can be instantaneous,

that a lack of awareness on my part of his moment-to-moment condition—and my own fluid ability to adjust accordingly—can make
all the difference in his level of success. He has often been apologetic
for the trickiness I contend with, but that always makes me chuckle
tenderly, because I truly love every part of it. The heightened attention I pay directly enhances my own arousal. It's magnificent that
way.

There have been a small handful of times over the past thirteen
years when I've felt constrained and physically agitated by having to
make accommodations, which is bound to happen at times due to
the way sexual processes unfold in the body. However, the disruption
that occurs when he gets far too close to the edge is much greater,
when he must go to great lengths to restrain the ejaculation. Then
that is not only a gross disruption to what we're doing, but also to the
flow of his own energy—due to the forceful clamping down he has to
do muscularly—and therefore my own.

Continuing with our elaborate communication, he described
to me, with great specificity, the sensation of ejaculation, from the
building of pressure and the mounting demands of the physiological urge, to the threshold of the moment-of-no-return and beyond,
with the internal ejaculatory release and the movement of the semen
through the shaft and out the end.

I described for him, in as much detail as I could access, all the
different kinds and qualities of orgasm that I experienced, including
my own ejaculation of fluid. I described what it felt like having tits
(once I actually became associated with them) and a horny vagina,
and all my bodily sensations of yearning and burning, of satisfaction,
dissatisfaction, and insatiability.

After having sex, we discussed it at length—responses to each
other's body parts and the various positions and manipulations we
came up with, orgasms, emotions, thoughts, desires, inhibitions, and
generally where our heads were at—comparing and contrasting our
personal experiences and impressions of each other's experience with
what we actually described. Many times, we found out we were on
target in our sense of each other and our experiences were in sync, but
other times we realized that each of us had an entirely different expe-

rience! (Sometimes he'd think we were both having a great time, only to find out afterward that it was a little lackluster for me, or I would think he was not really interested when he was intensely absorbed, and vice versa and so forth and so on.) But this kind of disjunction happened much more in the beginning, because the communication helped us to understand each other that much more over time as well as to address, if possible, whatever issues caused the discrepancies.

For me, the exhaustive communication not only allowed me to "see" him and understand his experience, but it gave me a far greater vision and understanding of myself and my own sexuality. The process of struggling to communicate my own experience—bodily, emotionally, mentally, all of it—was like bushwhacking through the brush, helping me to forge much stronger inroads of connection with my body and disentangle some of the chaos of the wiring.

Stroke Me

During the first, most limited, phase of our plan, I began to notice something astonishing taking place in my hands. I felt erotic pleasure coming from them as I ran them over the contours of his body. Appallingly, I had not realized that the hands could be sexual organs. It was as though they had never before been "awake" during sex, like someone on the assembly line was just checked out for lunch and everything beyond that point just shot to hell. I still marvel that I'd never gotten this part before, like the awareness exercise where you count how many times the basketball bounces, only to realize later that you never saw that gorilla jumping all around on the court!

I still have not figured out how a person, as sexually explorational as I had been (not to mention a massage therapist, intent on enhancing palpation skills), could be so shut down in this critical area and remain oblivious to it, as I had done. Power of habit, I suppose, and perhaps even *because* I was a massage therapist, so ultra-cautious about maintaining proper professional boundaries. Who knows. I also think that we just get into patterns that channel our attention into ruts where we will stay until we mix things up enough to wake up.

At any rate, the sexual discovery of my hands is still enchanting to me with the amount of sensory input it channels into the system during sex, not to mention my gratitude for my partner's muscular contours for providing quality fodder. And the fodder bit is serious business. The more my senses awoke, the more I realized how significant—to the humming of the immaculate machine—was each data byte they collected.

The most important point is that wherever we have awareness disconnected from body parts, there will be a missing element, a gaping hole, in the quality of the sexual experience. And what that indicates is a compartmentalized lack of wholeness somewhere within the being.

It has been said that the brain is the biggest sexual organ. Typically, that tends to be a comment on the power of imagination, but I think of it in terms of awareness. The more conscious attention we bring to the act of sex, the more dope those clever neurons in the central nervous system have to work with in order to contribute *their* thing, and since the whole organism is sexual, through and through, we finally get to see what we're made of…and what we're capable of experiencing.

Eyes on the Prize

Resuscitating my dormant hands felt very similar to reviving my connection to visual arousal during sex. With my hands, I felt the awakening begin in the corpuscles of my flesh, progressively tapping a wire back to my brain, igniting that region, and sending electric charges throughout my sexual body. The visual, being much more immediate, fired up my brain like a reflex, and my devout attention to it helped me tap into the nectar pulsing through my gonads. I could begin to feel the erotic sensations happening in my vagina just from literally opening my eyes. This quiet little riot came about by simply slowing things down, availing myself to new sensations and paying attention to all the details and subtleties.

Prior to this chapter of my life, my first experiences of hands-down visual arousal (besides "sex" scenes in mainstream movies) were, interestingly, in strip clubs. When I was living in the Bay Area, I took to visiting the strip joints in North Beach and was so moved by the erotic dancers that I would literally begin to lubricate. This reminded me of my experience with the doll at three, in that these women—rather than actually being outright objects of sexual desire to me—represented, in their femininity, something with which I could identify, and the arousal flowed from there.

Now, in a very different context, and in the pursuit of deepening the exploration with my partner, I would take deliberate pause to sit back, at least two or three feet, and simply look at him there—naked and erect, flush-faced, and hair all askew—and realize how incredibly *hot* that was visually, and just be with it.

At first, though, it really wasn't a fluid, simple thing like that. Even though I had for many years practiced having sex with the lights on and my eyes open (literally), there was still a layer of fear and vulnerability to penetrate. And part of this was the fact that I knew this man saw right through me in every way, with his piercing awareness and depth of familiarity with me. I felt as though there was a cloud, a lack of focus, some foggy resistance keeping me from the full experience of consciously focusing my vision upon him. It was wrapped in a haze of self-consciousness, a very well-hidden fear of *looking*, and beyond that, of *responding* to what is seen.

It was as though the visual experience was being hastily, almost surreptitiously "overlooked," as something squeezed in between here and there but not taken as a meaningful thing in itself. There was even an ostrichlike sense of hiding, as though by not seeing him, I'd be less conspicuous myself—although it's true that when you sit back a few feet, your partner can naturally get a better look at you too. But I could see I really wanted to hide rather than just sit back and take it all in. I had to pull myself away like a magnet that has no inclination whatsoever of moving this way, and hold myself against collapsing back into its force.

It has taken purposeful practice, just like this, with many variations, to nourish and cultivate visual participation in sex. Like the irony of being a massage therapist oblivious to her hands, this visual disconnect, coming from someone highly right-brained and fairly steeped in the visual realm of art, is an odd sort of humdinger. Again, the compartmentalization of sexuality knows no bounds! And my experience brings to mind the plethysmograph experiment because I, like all those subjects, had become so disconnected from the workings of my own body. Yet my experience also makes it clear that this disconnect can be remedied. The brain is highly malleable. The method is a practice of watchful awareness. Now, I make sure I remember to utilize my eyes throughout the sexual encounter to pull in those data bytes and process them all the way through—no holds barred—again, acknowledging with gratitude that my partner keeps himself in appealing condition. The more fronts that are open for business, so to speak, the more thriving and resilient the sexual economy (something I'll pick up again later).

Experimenting with the use of pornography to enhance the sex we have together has put an even wider selection of these juicy bytes—as well as a few other interesting tidbits—on the table to chew on. For both of us, there has been something about pornography tending to call up a bashfulness that hearkens back to a "what would my mother say" sort of vigilance in the psyche. And then, for me, there's also the sideshow racket about how nasty *nasty* girls are, and the tendency to then turn that inwardly into a feeling of shame, which is the most surefire way to shut down the whole works—that's why shame was invented for us![105] From this matrix of prude notions arises within me an argument against the value of even venturing into the realm of pornography. "Why go there?" it says. "Why *that*

---

[105] It may be more correct to acknowledge shame as a "socially evoked (biological) affect…a complicated affect whose…stimuli often have to do with maintaining hierarchical relationships in highly social animals, and is the submissive response to rejection by the hierarchical group…(most) obvious among the primates, and particularly in human beings." Even though it was "invented" at an unconscious, biological level, human consciousness has blown it up, infused it with *guilt* (mental imaginings of past and future ethical "wrongs," or *sins*, and their consequences) and maximized upon it to manipulate the masses, especially with regard to sex. I have taken these quotations and paraphrased ideas from the afterword of the first Mariner Books edition of *The Origin of Consciousness in the Breakdown of the Bicameral Mind* (Boston: Mariner Books, 1976, 1990) by Julian Jaynes.

when there are plenty of other things to do….And what about women's lib, for crying out loud?"

Remember what I said about things that make you squirm? That's the answer that I give back to myself, and then I just keep turning the whole thing onto its ear by affronting its poor fragile little sensibilities. Enter: the rebel. She's quite an ally in this whole operation. But then, even she has to go, because the shadow of any particular identity will distort the real picture. The good girl and her cloak of shame will dim it down to nothing; the rebellious charge, with her penchant for the dramatic, will overinflate everything. We're just looking for the facts here.

In addition to all this good stuff, pornography has been great for, once again, the dialogue that gets us, as partners, more in touch with each other sexually by sharing the details of our own responses. Best of all, though, it's a perfect venue, particularly in print form, for spending the time to really pay attention to exactly what responses— sensual and censorial alike—are taking place. Regarding Bergner's book again, it is exactly this kind of attentive exploration that can prove to each of us women who may be in doubt, one by one, that we have all the working pieces in place, not only for visual sexuality to take place within our bodies, but also for us to actually have a vivid awareness of precisely what, why, how, and to what extent it turns us on…*at a primitive level…beyond the obfuscations of the mind.* Now we're back in business—and *this* is women's lib!

I know some of my own impediments to the visual experience were exacerbated by the self-effacement issue. But I also know that, absolutely, at its very basis, is that cultural indoctrination denying women—by false claim of biological fact—this aspect of sexuality. The most powerful influences that form our ideas about the way things are—such as this very kind of cultural mind-set (that women do not get turned on visually) within which our lives unfold—are the ones that work so imperceptibly and so convincingly as to raise no notice nor inspire any speculation whatsoever. Therefore, we usually remain obliviously faithful to the silently established elements of said mind-set. But…if the presumed visual deficiency of female sexuality were a biological fact, based on a genetic blueprint, preventing women from responding sexually to a vast array of visual stimuli (forgetting the frank results of the plethysmograph experiment), it would take far, far more extensive manipulations to alter than merely slowing down, observing, and pushing past a few psychoemotional obstacles, don't you think?

More Bounce to the Ounce

The most outstanding instance of the actual "rewiring" of my electronics occurred during the second phase of our outline when we spent lots and lots of time focusing on my tits.

Prior to this chapter of my life, the modest little fatty blobs on my chest—once I got through the horrors of puberty—were little more to me than something I was thankful were not burdensome to contain. In terms of sexual pleasure, they were barely so much as an afterthought, that some partners enjoyed more than others, and those that did obviously did so more than I.

At least with my breasts, I can easily understand the disconnect, which I'm sure began as soon as puberty with my willful denial of their budding existence. But it's still quite striking to me that when I strain to remember my sensations of them at all during past sexual encounters, I can only grasp moments of noticing whether the person handling them did so *comfortably*. The main outstanding feature I recall is that a lack of outright discomfort amounted to a tolerable experience, and I remember on such occasions watching with a detached curiosity and amusement, sometimes almost feeling pity for the one who seemed to think they were something worth getting enthralled about.

Well, those days are long and happily gone. What happened during Phase 2 with Steve has dramatically altered my affair with these organs of my anatomy—and so thankfully, not only for myself, but for us as a couple, since he is an inveterate enthusiast of the objects at, er, large.

Genuinely understanding his enthusiasm helped a lot in the beginning by giving me that added incentive to look into the hidden possibilities, so this goes back to emphasize the important ingredient of communication.

He had spoken to me at great length about his lifelong fascination with breasts, including his history interacting with them and the incomparable sensation of feeling their soft weight in his palms. He spoke to me about his response to my own, including the various positions in which he found them particularly interesting. He effusively expressed his pleasure with them whenever it came up during sex and also communicated his responses throughout the day. Both understanding and feeling *his* pleasure integrally worked to enhance my experience of opening to them myself. I was at least now beginning to pay some attention to them.

By way of spending a lengthy chunk of time during which fiddling about with my breasts was just about all the menu afforded our appetites, things gradually began to shift. Being the breast buff that he is, in addition to having an interest in and capacity for sexual dexterity, he was able to serve up my breasts in a delectable variety of ways, manually and orally, so that my nerve endings actually began to come to life and to route their connections both north and south. I realized there was not only pleasant tactile but distinctively sexual sensation going on, not only at the nipple, but around the whole sphere of the breast and into the cleavage onto the sternum of my chest.

The restricted scope of our activities forced me to view breast stimulation as an end in itself (since, when that's really all you're doing, if you just look right past it, you got nothing, girl). So I brought everything to bear upon my awareness of the experience with no distractions. We ultimately spent enough focused time with them to allow something to occur that put everything into vibrant perspective regarding the sexual nature of my tits: I began to have orgasms from them, in them, and through them. Of course, this blew my mind to smithereens, given where I'd started.

During that phase, since we were not having any direct genital stimulation, the sensation moved—sort of via my navel region—from a hot full feeling in my breasts into my vagina, causing orgasmic movement there and, then, with orgasmic release, more hot energy shooting out through my nipples. The feeling was like coming through my tits, and I desired an ejection of fluid through them (something which has yet to happen).

Now it's common knowledge presented in virtually all modern guides to female sexuality that the breasts are dynamically linked to sexual energy and arousal in the vagina, and that they are not to be ignored. I'd encountered this stuff before, but the information itself did nothing for me in any practical way because of the effective barrier I'd erected to disidentify with them. What an incredible lesson in recognizing the power of the mind to completely dictate our experiences, right down to bodily sensation. (You can hopefully see why I harp so much about questioning everything, withholding all assumptions, and pressing deep into explorational frontiers.)

Now that my breasts are sexually enlightened entities, they have gratefully become part of my conscious living, breathing body. These "fatty blobs" on my chest have a venerated presence there now, and we all have a much more vibrant existence as a result. They even swell when they're happy to see you! I have tapped into the bodacious powerhouse that resides mysteriously within their glandular matrix, and I have every intention to continue doing so. I'm more whole, more integrated, more in touch with my personal *and* sexual power, period.

Sex Machine (You Shook Me All Night Long!)

On the ranch, I grew up operating all kinds of heavy machinery. We always had a range of equipment—much of it on the end of the spectrum closer to the junkyard—with which we got by. Generally, the farming part of our family operation was never much of a turn-on to me, as I found the animals to be much more personable (no, I'm not suggesting I was into the practice of bestiality, although I admit I did occasionally acknowledge—observing the accessibility of a ewe's cute little vulva—the inspiration for the widespread groaner about farmers and sheep, and I blushed occasionally at the generous unsheathed endowment of our geldings). But had I discovered the vibratory joys of rustic machinery earlier on, I might have had quite a different response to farming.

The first time I experienced female ejaculation was in my midtwenties raking hay in the upper alfalfa field. This was around the time I was just beginning to come out of my drab shell to explore the wide world of funkalicious technicolor, so I felt freakishly daring as I stood up on that little blue Ford and pressed my pubic bone, just forward of my clitoris, onto the firm edge of the steering wheel, hoping the neighbors wouldn't just happen to drive by on the county road and notice something of a spectacle. The orgasm itself was truly out of this world as it was—we're talking about a one-ton, *fifty horsepower* vibrator—but the sensation of hot liquid shooting out gave me a thrill I'd never even approached.

All right, I'm ready to take on the hot topic and knock this thing out (with my American thighs). Although acknowledgment of female ejaculation goes back more than twenty centuries in the literature, it still remains an issue of sizzling debate. There has been intense controversy in our midst, from scientists to libbers to censors of obscenity, with conflicting information and inflamed opinions.[106]

A 2007 study,[107] performed using ultrasound imaging of the bladder and biochemical testing of the fluid ejected at orgasm, concluded that the fluid contained constituents from the female prostate (specifically, PSA and PAP) that are not found in urine. This called for further recognition of the existence of the female prostate

---

[106] Certain women's libbers have attacked the notion of FE as a fantasy projected onto women for male enjoyment. In 2002, and again in 2014, the BBFC (British Board of Film Classification) banned porn depicting FE on the contention that it was actually urination, which was officially designated "obscene." British porn filmmaker Anna Span challenged the board with scientific evidence for it, and won.

[107] F. Wimpissinger, K. Stifter, and W. Stackl, "The Female Prostate Revisited: Perineal Ultrasound and Biochemical Studies of Female Ejaculate," *Journal of Sexual Medicine* (Sept. 2007), 1388–93, http://www.ncbi.nlm.nih.gov/pubmed/17634056.

"officially" discovered and named[108] by Slovakian scientist Milan Zaviacic, author of *The Human Female Prostate*.[109] Zaviacic proposed that the tissue is not the vestigial Skene's glands and ducts, as thought, but a prostatic gland that is located *in* the walls of the urethra (the male prostate is *around* it), functions like the male prostate, and is an erotogenic zone that "participates in the female ejaculation phenomenon."[110]

British porn filmmaker Anna Span (with her crew), having witnessed the ejaculatory event, asserts that the "speed, volume, viscosity, smell and sight" of the fluid are all very different than urine[111] (and with this, I absolutely concur). When she convinced the British Board of Film Classification (who were about to censor her film capturing the moment) that her explosive heroine was not indeed urinating, they allowed her to release the film.

With so much ado about the composition, and the meaning, of what exits (or does not exit) the female urethra during an explosive orgasm, you have to wonder what it's all about. Perhaps some of it is a sexist reaction against female pleasure. Perhaps, being unfamiliar, it's just too close to kinky. Some paranoid feminists have simply

---

[108] Seventeenth-century Dutch physician and anatomist Regnier de Graaf originally associated female ejaculation with the erogenous zone now known as the G-spot (named after, not him, but German gynecologist, Ernst Grafenberg) and likened it to the male prostate.

[109] Milan Zaviacic, *The Human Female Prostate: From Vestigial Skene's Paraurethral Glands and Ducts to Woman's Functional Prostate* (Bratislava, Slovakia: Slovak Academic Press, 1999). The term "female prostate" was officially accepted by the Federative International Committee on Anatomical Terminology in 2001.

[110] http://www.radio.cz/en/section/ice_health/milan-zaviacic-the-slovak-scientist-who-discovered-the-female-prostate. Zaviacic says the female prostate mainly gives sexual pleasure but has further medical significance in that it is subject to the same diseases as the male prostate, so recognition of it is critical for accurate diagnosis and appropriate treatment of urogenital diseases in women. (Other sources maintain that the female prostate is a bristly tube enveloping the urethra.)

[111] "Violet Blue: Woman Porn Maker Anna Span Challenged the BBFC Over a Controversial Sex Act, and Won," October 8, 2009, http://www.sfgate.com/living/article/In-The-U-K-Female-Ejaculation-Is-Not-Obscene-2474912.php. (Other sources confirm the taste, too, is different: sweet, rather than salty.)

blitzed the whole topic, assuming it's just another patriarchal attempt to "masculinize" female sexuality! In any case, all this hullabaloo appears to represent yet another symptom of our pandemic sexual neuroticism. And the fact that science has been so sluggish to come around to full-blown enlightenment on the topic surely reflects on all the prudish—often brutish—denial of feminine sexuality over the centuries.

Therefore, in the meantime, while the mainstream is all tied up in a tangle, we mustn't let it impede the flow of this magnificent stream of our own. It's imperative that we each simply separate the subjective aspect of female ejaculation from the objective realm, laden with all its worries. Subjectively, it is (literally and figuratively) a *blast*. So, in the name of liberation, it's high time to unplug the waterworks and "come" undone. Personally, I think it's such a liberating and extraordinary sexual experience that I'd be all gushy over promoting a tradition like the Batoro people of Uganda, whose elder women teach pubescent girls the art of *kachapati*, or "spraying the walls." Let the men paint 'em white and then let us spray 'em down! Sounds like good times for all.

My first time, on that little beast of a machine, I wasn't sure what to make of it, and it didn't happen again until several years later. Even then, it was an isolated, although extended, instance: a summer road trip with my boyfriend, when I found myself squirting liquid repeatedly for forty-five minutes, as he fingered me while driving. (I should have been completely desiccated, right? Yet even after something like this, a woman will find that she still has to pee—more evidence, clearly, that she is not urinating.) Beyond that incident, it wasn't until a few years later that I became comfortable enough with the marvel of ejaculating to allow my body uninhibited release. Practicing it while masturbating was integral. Then later, having a partner who really loved it encouraged my exploration of the phenomenon even more. But reaching my own full capacity to let loose with the liquid assets involved revisiting and cultivating the capacity for continual climax.

That road trip was my first experience of an out-and-out continual orgasm, and those did not occur again with any regularity until my current relationship with Steve, when we really began to get the *motor clean*…so I could *stay on the scene* (to mix my lyrical metaphors)![112]

At this point, it is common knowledge that women are geared for multiple orgasms. What is not so widely acknowledged in the mainstream is our capacity for continual orgasm, climaxing that goes on nonstop without any refractory period whatsoever. Now, because I just read a book entitled *Extended Massive Orgasm* (or EMO),[113] I have to make it clear that what I am referring to as continual orgasm is distinctly *not* what these authors are describing. I am not redefining orgasm to mean that you are just focusing on the pleasure of your genitals. I am not talking about *approaching* an orgasm and backing away, approaching and backing away, over and over again. These are fine ways of having sex, and approaching orgasm, but these are not *continual* orgasm. Continual orgasm is an orgasm as we know it—the genital musculature contracting intensely and involuntarily in response to the nervous system firing off—that continues rhythmically and indefinitely, without a refractory period and with mildly fluctuating peaks and valleys.

There is a high degree of consciousness, or bodily awareness, involved in (and required for) manifesting this type of orgasm reliably. This means all that hard work getting things back in order has the potential for big payoff in the "O" department since, for a continual orgasm to take place, a woman must be able to put everything aside and let it roll, baby, roll, which is why it helps so much to clear out all the obstacles.

I remember, at age twenty, in my first sexual relationship, that this experience was just peeking through then. After intercourse and his ejaculation, he did what guys are apt to do: he fell asleep. It was at this point, when my body was still sexually aroused, that I would lie

---

[112] Referencing AC/DC, "You Shook Me All Night Long," Atlantic, 1980, and James Brown, "Sex Machine," King, 1970.

[113] Steve and Vera Bodansky, *Extended Massive Orgasm,* 2nd ed. (Alameda, CA: Hunter House Publishers, 2013).

draped over him, experiencing wave after silent wave of intense plea-sure just in response to his vital signs. I have to admit that this time while he slept was probably the most richly rewarding sexual aspect for me, simply because it was the time when nothing else was going on—no distraction, no sense of "performance," no emotional inter-personal dynamic upstaging the pure sexual movement, no rush to the finish line—all the things that typically get in the way of how sex really should unfold, only while both parties are conscious! I just lay there and let things unfold naturally in my body. But the situation—namely, my partner's absence from the scene—didn't encourage my full orgasmic development at that time, when my sexuality and how it would come to manifest were taking shape, and so it receded fairly quickly from the picture. By the time I found myself sharing a bed with the next boyfriend a few years later, it was all but forgotten as an odd aberration of the distant past.

To bring continual climax to the fore in a sexual partnership, both people really have to be fully participatory. My eventual success in manifesting continual orgasm (as well as ejaculation) as a regular part of the orgasmic fare in my current relationship involved both of us in full collaboration but also something more.

About nineteen years ago, I began practicing the Taoist exer-cises outlined in *Cultivating Female Sexual Energy*, by Mantak and Maneewan Chia,[114] and this foundation of solitary work learning to "pump" and circulate the sexual energy within my body became central for the establishment of that quality of orgasmic experience. Through those exercises, I got meticulously familiar with the intri-cate musculature of the pelvic floor and vaginal walls. I became con-scious of the deeper physiological and energetic sensations of my sexual anatomy, including the vagina, cervix, uterus, and ovaries, and developed awareness of the central energetic column known in Eastern terminology as the *sushumna*, the subtle channel through which the not-so-subtle electric energy moves up parallel with the

---

[114] Mantak Chia and Maneewan Chia, *Healing Love Through the Tao: Cultivating Female Sexual Energy* (Huntington, NY: Healing Tao Books, 1986).

spine from the perineum to the crown of the head. (Knowing the way around your own pelvic floor helps isolate the muscles involved in ejaculation, and attuned awareness of sexual energy movement comes in handy for jumping the train of continual climax.)

I had no idea at the time I started that I was paving the way for what I'm talking about here. In fact, as far as I could tell, it never made any difference whatsoever in all the sex I had for the first ten of those years. But I kept doing it, at least enough to keep the practice relatively facile, and then, when I moved up to begin with Steve, I got that book back out and recharged the discipline.

What I've gleaned from both study and personal experience is that an important piece of orgasm for many women—and doubly true for continual climax—is an environment of spaciousness that involves the lack of a goal. When there is no pressing issue of *going somewhere* or even the idea of *doing something*, the body-mind awareness can more easily expand to include a far greater expanse of stimuli, the conscious brain can accommodate and process more of it, and then the entire system—the labyrinth of nervous and energetic conductivity—can be left to its own devices. So what this means is a more leisurely, expansive attitude toward having sex from both partners' perspectives, as sort of an attentive, in-the-moment revel in pure sensation.

To maintain this attitude in a long-term relationship requires work: work to fend off all the other aspects of shared living that tend to encroach upon this precious territory, and work to address the issues that can turn the sex into a feeling of obligation, drudgery, or mechanical habit. And this, of course, requires the ability to remain present in the moment, which, in turn, requires a large modicum of internal quiet. So we end up back at the realization of the importance of cleaning and degreasing the equipment…just can't get away from it!

Men have to be skilled in ejaculatory control and attentive to following the woman's body deep into the orgasmic wilderness. Women have to come undone at every level and simultaneously attend to the man's orgasmic whereabouts to help him succeed in his own control.

What I learned about coming undone in this way, both for fostering ejaculation and continual climax, was that I had to allow myself to go places that were way out of my comfort zone. I had to create a whole new relationship with my pelvic floor—one that involved relaxing musculature that my mind and body had become convinced is only appropriate when seated securely on the toilet! I had to let go of my fear that maybe ejaculation really was urination (because it does feel disconcertingly similar, since the mechanism involved is part of the urethra). I'll admit to having suspiciously sniffed around many times over, before being convinced that it wasn't just the golden shower. With Steve's amazing support, I was also able to look straight at my level of paranoia around the issue in order to recognize it as just another piece of baggage containing more of the same old uptightness around sexuality.

Importantly, when Mary Jane Sherfey discusses the limitless orgasmic capacity of women, she emphasizes that it all has to do with the engorgement of the tissues with blood, or *vasocongestion*, that is associated with the action of bearing down (which is actually one of the things the body naturally wants to do during climax). My own experience corroborates this—which means, however, that I've also had to confront the fear that I might defecate, as well, when bearing down in this way, bringing more pleasure and more orgasms. I'm able to face the fear of undesirable bodily functions and downsize my anxiety by remembering to loosen up, lighten up, and grow up (something I need support with at times). Hey, as far as we're concerned, a turd in the punchbowl doesn't have to ruin the party! In that possible-yet-improbable event, I can always take to the shower and try again, if necessary.

So, in this odyssey to orgasmatopia, we have to throw caution to the wind, lash ourselves to the mast, and listen to the song of the sirens (watch out—it might sound like AC/DC, or James Brown!), letting ourselves become shipwrecked, if necessary, so that we can demolish the crowded container into which we've crammed our sexual selves.

When the inhibitions are removed, and a woman's body is given the appropriate attention (which will vary greatly from woman to woman, meaning each woman must know her body well enough for this), it becomes possible for her to reach a unique state of arousal—a whole new gear entirely—in which her body is humming along at such an efficient, frictionless level that the type of further input then matters very little. She is then just about running on the fumes of her partner's vital signs! Steve knows when I'm in this zone, that he is literally free to do anything…he could rub my elbows and keep me going.

The experience of continual climax always brings me back into contact with insatiability, demonstrating again the vast horizon of sexual capacity and desire. Now here's the full quote from Mary Jane Sherfey: "To all intents and purposes, *the human female is sexually insatiable in the presence of the highest degrees of sexual satiation*…the more orgasms a woman has, the stronger they become; the more orgasms she has, the more she *can* have."[115] This is a very significant statement, and one that my own experience has certainly validated. I believe that acknowledging this as a healthy possibility is an important step for any woman beginning to approach an exploration of unrestrained sexuality and the unleashing of her orgasmic capacity.

And, for the super freaky *Super Freak*—as promised in that chapter—richer still is that territory! (Wouldn't let your spirits down, would I?) There is something about the degree of abandon within the mind, allowing the body to function with total unrestraint at the level of the sought-after perpetual motion machine that calls up a razor's-edge experience combining a lucid freedom (from the tangle of the usual self-identified relationship with the sexual body) and a direct line to the source of that body's carnal desire. (At this point, we are elevating the quality of awareness to that which actually makes sex a holy act, the genuine article. And in this realm—truly, my sister—*blessed art thou among women!)*

---

[115] Sherfey calls this "satiation-in-insatiation," attributing it to the pelvic anatomy and sexual physiology involving an increasingly high degree of perineal edema and vasocongestion that facilitate perpetual arousal and orgasmic activity. She suggests that women, like their socially unencumbered primate relatives, would manifest a more voracious sexual insatiability if their civilization allowed it (Sherfey, 112).

This fascinating experience juxtaposes total psychodynamic contentment and unlimited bodily desire (or "satiation-in-insatiation"). And this (a lucid, nonattached awareness observing the pure flow of natural desire) is the perfect environment, if one is so inclined, for the firsthand study of the nature of desire itself and therefore a deeply informed and enlightened understanding of the experience of our lives.

For both Steve and myself, this defines the general intent of our sexual objective. What it embodies is the expression of mental, psychological, emotional, and sexual freedom that results in the practice of relational and physical intimacy at our utmost capacity.

PRESSURE DROP

There's still much more to be said about all the things that happen when the initial intensity of excitement wears off, because that part does, after all, comprise the overwhelming bulk of the long-term sexual relationship! I considered inserting this into the earlier section discussing boredom, but I think, with everything else under our belts between then and now, we're better equipped to delve deeper into the topic at this juncture.

Just Like a Woman

When I reflect back on the six-year open relationship and the distressing obscurity I began to experience around my sexual desire for my partner, it brings up a question. Why would this stuff rise up within a relationship of trust and intimacy, and not with unfamiliar men, with whom a woman—one would think, given her delicate feminine needs (ahem!)—would feel much more vulnerable and insecure? Because, I assure you, I never struggled with this issue with any of these other fleeting men.

The most obvious answer is boredom. But there is actually a lot more psychoemotional texture to it than a simple, straightforward answer like that. I mean, we're *women*, what did you expect! All joking aside, however, I want to remind everyone that the excessive, seemingly insurmountable complexity of female sexual psychology is due to the extravagant training we have undergone throughout our lives, forcing us to wed our sexuality to our emotionality.

Emotionality is complex. Choose any given male, ask him to speak cogently about the ins and outs of his emotional existence, and, chances are, you'll quickly get my drift. It's just that he's been spared the additional calamity of constantly superimposing this fracas onto his penis…which is, in all likelihood, part of why men often have a much easier time ignoring their emotionality. Besides this, men are still generally taught that emotionality is an emasculating weakness, which therefore encourages detachment from it. Since it is then not *unnaturally* cemented to something as irrepressibly front and center stage of our lives as sexuality, male emotional dysfunction can much more easily recede from the picture of his overtly evident functionality.

At the same time, perhaps it is partly because women are forced to contend with it in precisely such a way that they tend to *be* the more emotionally literate bunch. Furthermore, it is probably testament to just how *highly sexed* women are that they appear to be so *highly charged* emotionally: this is the chute into which female sexuality has been herded by all the good shepherds!

So, returning to the point, I believe my own disconnect from desire (and also that of many other women, most likely) was largely the consequence of all the unresolved psychoemotional garbage—the confused compartmentalization, the cross-wiring, short-circuitry, female cultural training, and so forth—floating around inside that accompanied and exacerbated the natural condition of boredom. I want to pick up again the idea of the sexual "economy" I mentioned earlier, because it's going to be a nifty concept to elucidate the point I'm about to make.

Obviously, both men and women get bored at some point. But, more often than not, it seems that women are much more vulnerable to it collapsing their entire economy and causing an overwhelming problem, because it is propped up way too precariously. Just as I discovered with myself, all fronts are decidedly *not* open for business…because a whole slew of scoundrels (from Saint Paul to Walt Disney) have banded together and monopolized the show, beating all the competition into the corner. Female sexuality has been squeezed out of business in ways that are difficult, but not at all impossible, to access. A woman has to do the work herself (such as exploring and experimenting beyond the sexual identity she has assumed) to sort it all out and reopen the boarded-up fronts—whatever they happen to be for her—in order for her sexuality to thrive and bustle through a recessive downturn such as boredom.

Part of my theory about women and boredom in the bedroom is that I don't believe they interpret it correctly. First and foremost, it may never even occur to a woman that she is simply bored and wanting sexual novelty, because that goes against every grain of her training about who she is and what she ought to want as a female. The unspeakable irony of the whole bill of goods women, in particular, have bought into about security and all is that *familiarity can be the most fertile ground for insecurity.* So we really get taken to the cleaners, both coming and going (as, of course, do the men).

It works like this: less excitation of the nervous system means more space in the brain for other things to rattle around in there—which they do. Basically, boredom abhors a vacuum, so when this abhorrent space arises, it invites all the neurotic little gremlins inside, and they begin to wreak havoc. I'm referring to all the myriad things women have learned about *what it means to be women* from a noxiously misleading and frequently misogynistic (ultimately disempowering) world and the ways in which we silently carry the resulting affliction wrapped tightly around our sexual identity, just as I mentioned in the beginning of this book. How we have come to terms with being women (or simply being sexual entities who happen to have female anatomy) has been profoundly defined and distorted by this world, and requires penetrating investigation.

Getting familiar with a partner means there's no more beguiling mystique to mist over the vista and placate the little beasts that gnaw at well-being and sexual self-esteem and there's less of the aggressive heat from the strange factor to burn through it. Because of the brass-tacks nature of things at this juncture, the sharp points (such as emotional-sexual insecurities) start to pierce objectionably through the romantic gauze and grate on the tender spots. The increased vulnerability can cause a woman—as her self-critical insecurities escalate and underlying problems crop up—to close down sexually to her partner, bit by incremental bit, if she doesn't go straight after each little gremlin as it enters (that means stopping in the middle of whatever you're doing and addressing it), with a compassionate and intelligent understanding of what's going on. This work is nicely facilitated by a patient, honest, and sensitive partner, but it's tough work, no matter how you slice it. It cuts right to the quick.

Also, getting familiar almost always brings the development of dynamics around interpersonal difficulties. The dynamics that form unintentionally are frequently—and most unfortunately—dysfunctional, arising from our reactions to the contrasting (annoying) ways people function. The accumulation of such dynamics becomes an obstacle to intimacy. Obstacles to intimacy, over time, become obstacles to sex, because when the honeymoon excitement naturally simmers down, what's left is how open and generous we can remain with each other interpersonally.

Because a woman has to access a high degree of abandon to fend off the indoctrination and have great sex, the places where she is shutting out and closing down to her partner will be magnified, and she will be fragmented and compartmentalized internally, resulting in an incomplete participation in sex. This experience will tend to become unpleasant, leading to dissatisfaction on her part (both with the sex and with her partner), and less inclination toward having more sex in the future, which, of course, then leads to dissatisfaction for him as well.

And don't get me wrong, the same problems with familiarity may arise for men, who will also tend to sense their vulnerabilities when excitation isn't all-consuming, especially when facing a partner's waning enthusiasm. We have the same underlying psychology, after all, and he, too, is liable to find he has emotional and psychological baggage weighing on the sex that must be dealt with.

So we all have to get busy in relationship to resolve the issues that obstruct intimacy, if we really expect our sex lives to unfold happily ever after. (The "happily ever after" part we were never taught is all the effort it takes to maintain intimacy!)

I Get By

Some of the toughest work is actually around the honesty of your partner (being able to hear their candid feedback and responses). And I know this calls up the stereotypical male conundrum of being caught between a rock and a hard place: damned if you do, damned if you don't. She demands to know how you feel and what you think, but she can't stomach the answer, either (1) because she can't believe you would actually tell her the truth if it was negative (so you probably really *don't* think she looks good in those pants, you're just saying that to appease her), or (2) because it's so devastating to her that you actually *do* think she looks plump in those pants and you honestly told her so.

As a woman who really values honesty and the undistorted reality of things, I have struggled mightily with this rascal. Because I know my baby will unambiguously tell me the honest-to-goodness, god-awful truth, I don't have the option of not believing him, which is great when it comes to positive feedback—I have to *let it in*. But it's only my commitment to cleaning out my own cluttered closet that forces me, when it comes to the negative feedback, to let it in and handle it skillfully, which looks like acknowledging and addressing the data and *letting it go* emotionally. And that's hard. Some disgruntled little demons try to linger about and stir up trouble in Paradise, but with a deep commitment to accepting full responsibility for my own emotional maturity (and my *sanity*)—and with a little help from my friends—it eventually gets done.

We Can Be Heroes

For me, a huge necessity has been extricating my sense of worth from my (critically measured) sex appeal, something that is increasingly foisted upon us all but is generally much more heavily weighted for females.

Jessica Valenti, again in *The Purity Myth*, describes with disturbing accuracy how women are taught "that, one way or another, their bodies and their sexuality are what make them valuable."[116] We have been so deeply indoctrinated to evaluate our worth as human beings in terms of our sexual appeal and utility, which must be (impossibly) spectacularly open and available while at the same time being exclusive and discreet, of course, as moral creatures. So naturally we've lost sense of a greater more realistic frame of reference.

When the entire measure of one's human worth is wrapped up in sex appeal, the usual run-of-the-mill insecurity can get infused with a more hysterical quality of fear. This hysterical charge overlaying a deep fear of inadequacy, I am convinced, comes directly out of the sexual disempowerment of women rife within our culture. All of the erotic feminine power, the sweeping tidal wave that it is, has been choked and squeezed tightly into a tiny, little tube of flimsy whimsy, resulting, essentially, in a caged wild animal.

The devious idea that sex appeal equals worth turns every minute detail into something of dire consequence, inordinately—and indiscriminately—overinflated. But this is where a little reality check pays big, showing me immediately how preposterous it is and how deranged I am for swallowing such a concoction. The reality check has to do with the simple understanding that I cannot, unlike my Saul of Tarsus, be all things to all men. *Nor, thank heavens, am I obligated to.* At this point, I snatch the damn booty and beat cheeks, shrieking all the way to the bank! (I'm saving so much money on beauty products. In fact, speaking of economy, I want to put the fear of god into the market that dreads our enlightenment while making bank on all our sexual insecurity…call it *The Ulta Challenge*.)

Another important piece of the reality check is that sex appeal is actually a very well-rounded, voluptuous entity itself. It isn't shot to hell by a trace of cellulite on the thighs, an extra pound in the middle, an additional wrinkle on the forehead, or a bit of premenstrual bloating, all the little things we will fixate on, obsess about, and otherwise allow to ruin the day. The fact is, the only one of these things that will ruin the *sex* is the debilitating fixation. Sex appeal has to do with a person in entirety, including every aspect of inner

---

[116] Valenti, 10.

well-being and physical health. When we gravitate to fixation on the petty minutiae, it is at the expense of greater well-being, sensible reality, and personal power. In the long run, it's these things that tend to *result in* sex appeal anyway (as usual, we've got it ass backward, chasing our fancy, fluffy tails into impotent oblivion). So, with a deep breath and a big glass of water, bottoms up to health and well-being. And now we can power up the focus on the "housecleaning" within. (Once we detonate the major obstacles, so much of working on ourselves, retraining and reinventing ourselves, has to do with the diligent, wholly mundane practice of simply redirecting our attention, over and over and over again.)

If we're really serious, we can even take the reality check a dimension bigger, to remembering that we *are* alone, and ultimately the whole pot of stew boils down to "I and I" so that who and how I am, in relation to myself and myself alone, is beyond any doubt the most significant problem to solve (because "nobody else is a constant"[117]). In the scheme of things, whatever that may actually be, those who have addressed this issue will not have done so in vain. When the house is clean, it is a joy being in it. If guests arrive, they can appreciate it too. But then, if nobody shows up, who cares?

All She Wants to Do Is Dance

Sexual boredom for women has to be exposed for what it is. It can no longer hide behind sexual and emotional insecurities, boarded fronts of psychosomatic blockage, confusion between what is emotional and what is sexual, and delusions about deficient libidinous appetite.

The notions behind all the insecurities, tangled up like laundry that's been stuck in spin cycle for centuries, must each be individually extracted, hung on the line, and ironed out. That means putting

---

[117] Full quote by Mohadesa Najumi: "Aloneness is a gift. A beautiful gift to the human soul. True and consistent satisfaction comes from the bond you form with yourself. Nobody else is a constant."

Sherlock's lens to task looking at dark and mysterious ideas about our identities as women that prevent full, uninhibited participation in sex, and asking probing questions that get right under the delicate skin.

The mental and emotional blocks that prevent the full dynamic extent of bodily responsiveness have to be recognized, identified, and ratted out; each and every nail that's been sunk into the boards covering the portals of sensual passage must be pried out with sturdy claws. This involves getting naked—bare-assed naked and fully exposed. It's done by taking the time to slow down and give undivided attention to the sex act in general, and to forgotten regions of the body specifically, watching closely what transpires inside and out, and shining the light of knowledge and compassionate reason upon the process to understand patterns and to trace the roots of each issue as far as possible to the source.

The crippling confusion between emotionality and sex has to be totally deconstructed to get that preposterous monkey wrench out of the works. That means taking a sharply critical scalpel to the massive body of ideas we have about love and romance, marriage and monogamy, security, intimacy, and commitment, and excising sex from this fibrotic mass to get a clear idea of what it is and how it actually works when left to its own devices. Finally, with this excess of rubbish sorted out, all delusions about the wan female libido will actually be dispelled as a matter of course. The sun is always shining behind the clouds, you know.

Why so much ado about boredom? Because once we can see clearly what's going on, and along the way develop a more integrated, healthy, wholehearted participation in sex, the natural boredom that starts showing up will not be the kiss of death to your sex life… because when it is overwhelmingly burdened with all the undue baggage we carry, this benign entity turns into the grim reaper. Save our souls!

I Need a Man

Hey! Is this my tune?[118]

I want to talk about my favorite thing again—masculinity. I do, because it is, I've found, a terrific antidote to pure (meaning undistorted by all the other crap) boredom with your partner.

Once we've opened up enough of those shut-up fronts, cleaned up the frayed, corroded, and tangled wiring, and reenergized the circuitry, then we can open fully to the dazzling essence of our own femininity, which is, for strongly heterosexual women, buzzing with masculinity receptors. (And listen, if masculinity's not your thing, please just go ahead and substitute *your* thing in this section, because it all works the same way.) If there is enough of it in him, your partner becomes a *representative* of manhood, and that statement transcends the boundaries of individuality. What this means is that when you have cultivated your own sensual capacity, tuned your equipment finely enough to perceive the minutiae of essence, you are now able to appreciate the affair at a more transcendental level, beyond all the limiting identifications. You can recognize that you are Woman having sex with Man, so exactly *who* that man is—as long as he adequately represents it—becomes fairly inconsequential. Same is true of man to woman, woman to woman, and man to man.

This, I've found, can actually dredge up some more of the deepest sediments of sexual guilt. At times, I've experienced that alongside this untethered and shameless affair with pure masculinity (while having sex with my *monogamous* partner, no less!) arises a disconcerting sensation of chagrin, a self-reproaching condemnation informing me of the arrant disgrace of my slutty spirit. A message like this goes extremely deep. I address it by consciously acknowledging its presence and its impact within, whether that means stopping in the middle of the activity or not, in order to do whatever it takes to figure out what's going on and deal with it, eyeball-to-eyeball. Talking, writing, *expressing,* meditating, contemplating, and the practice of tuning into heart, mind and body are my best tools. And gradually, bit by bit, I remove all this rotten rubbish from the morality archives, relo-

---

[118] Eurythmics, "I Need a Man," RCA Records, 1987.

cating it directly into the circular file, and consequently, streamlining the *reality* portfolio! (Thus proceeds the comprehensive overhaul of the irrelevant, outdated, and totally misinformed inner archives of our most personal sexuality. Diligently done, the process reveals all sorts of astonishing little things slinking about under the radar that will otherwise quietly prevent the quality of abandon required for the fullest sexual expression.)

To keep enriching our ongoing familiar affair without censoring or repressing the wider reality of response and desire, what Steve and I do as a practice is notice all the outside stimuli, and then utilize it with each other. We pay attention to all the sexual responses we have going on day to day out in the world, watching how they stimulate us, allowing them to do so, and then willfully channeling the drive back toward each other.

For example, I see a well-built character striding shirtless down the sidewalk and my head turns. My eyes feast on the appeal, and I feel my engines begin to heat up in a flush. (It's amusing to watch the mechanisms at work, just doing their thing.) Then, just before I indulge the mental urge to follow Mr. Shirtless down fantasy alley and into the bushes, I deliberately call to mind something particularly masculine about Steve—his shoulders and chest or a full erection— and, instead of merely becoming distracted into fantasy, I sketch an *intent*, or a mental visual of unleashing my desire with *him*, the bird in hand. I usually tell him about the response I had earlier, and, when we are actually having sex, sometimes that visual springs to mind with a tingle, and it just feeds into the stimulation of the moment with Steve, kind of like the pornography of life. I have responded to a representative *image* of masculinity, and I am interacting with another *physical* representative of it, and the translation is quite direct and totally satisfactory—even if the particular image I saw on the street was bigger, buffer, blacker, younger, whatever—because what I'm interacting with is *sufficiently masculine*, and my body gets that need met.

It's extremely important, though, to note the huge distinc- tion between what I'm describing and what would otherwise be merely fantasizing about something—or someone—else during sex.

Fantasizing during sex involves *actively perpetuating and embellishing* the imagination to the exclusion of full attention to the present partner/activity. *Using the pornography of life*, on the other hand, involves *observing* the thoughts and the sensations that come along with the outside stimuli and, without delving into daydreams, bringing full attention—along with the added arousal—directly back into the present moment with the live entity at hand. This is an active, willful practice, and what I'm describing takes concerted effort to orchestrate. Again, there is no lazy-man's guide to this. But it's not rocket science either; it just requires practice, attention, and the desire to make it work.

What if you find your partner *doesn't* have enough of it in him to be an adequate representative (and this will obviously vary radically from woman to woman)? Well, darling, the truth must be told, and this is always where the rubber meets the road. This is the riskiness of the business, and this is why not many people will venture the capital. But, to take it all the way, everything is put at risk—that's the way this works. In the *real* world, it doesn't have to be the end of a compatible, working relationship, although it probably means the end of a *monogamous* one. This is where the uncoupling of our emotional and sexual needs serves us very well and can allow us the relational flexibility to accommodate our loved one's needs, even if that doesn't directly, or exclusively, involve us. (Of course, men too must be making similar evaluations about the meeting of their own sexual needs.)

Ultimately, however, when things are adequately aligned, this translation of desire for other men into a desire for masculinity itself results in an infusion of freshness into the act with a familiar partner. It's that refreshing sense of newness that Webster called virginity. Here we are, back down to the birthday suit of childlike sexual innocence, only we are now fully developed, mature creatures capable of harnessing all this raw power in an act of sexual intercourse and communion that has classically been reserved for divinity.

It's very real, but it's also a very fine line to tread successfully, which is why we can only even talk about manifesting things at this level when enough clutter has been removed, in earnest, from the premises. I don't even know if it's a permanent solution—I cannot attest to that—but I do know that it can be a powerful component of monogamous sexual contentment and fulfillment on many, many levels.

Strange Brew

Surprisingly, perhaps, the best time to get to know yourself and each other is when you become bored. This is when all the other things hidden inside have the chance to be exposed, discovered, explored, and either extinguished or exploited. Excitation is that *"witch in electric blue"*[119] making a big scene so that you can ignore everything else. In other words, when you're all excited, it's easier to remain out of touch with what is going on inside you at deeper levels.

This phenomenon is behind things like the wicked midlife crisis, the catastrophic moment of truth that happens at that point in life when youth's edge of excitation has worn off, many of life's eagerly anticipated goals have been achieved (the titillating romantic pursuit has become the sensible spouse, the chirpy vision of bouncing children is now the demanding reality, the dream job has become the daily grind), and one begins to fear that something is drastically amiss. It's all just because the wilderness has been domesticated, there is a cessation of excitement, and so up percolate the bothersome nags hiding just under the surface. The bottom line is, whether it's a midlife crisis or the settling into comfy, companionate familiarity, we are all "amiss" in one way or another to varying degrees. It is because we all, men and women alike, have these complicated emotional and psychological inner lives that actually require a reasonable level of attention, reflection, and understanding in order for us to be fully functional and satisfied in our outer lives. Most of us have either been ill-equipped or ill-inclined to dedicate the time and energy necessary to achieve this kind of well-being.

So, if you have the interest, here's the opportunity. Look squarely at the boredom and see it for what it is (the inescapable

---

[119] Cream, "Strange Brew," Reaction (UK), Atco (US), 1967.

biological reality of craving for new stimuli) and then discover what other things are attached to it. Whatever you do, don't react to the disgruntled feeling without seizing the opportunity to sort things out head-on. Feel into it, talk about it, write about it (hell, scream, cry, and throw a fit if it helps—lord knows I have!), just buckle down and take bold steps to address whatever is necessary. But, *lawdy mama, don't* check out into mechanical monotony. Burbling up beneath that craving for strange may be your very own strange brew crying out for merciful attention. The resolution of each and any issue will create spaces inside for the wilderness to begin returning to a more natural, harmoniously feral state.

SHAKE YOUR MONEYMAKER

When I was nineteen and twenty, I attended Lewis & Clark College in Portland, Oregon. At that time, circa 1990, it was already known as a *liberal* liberal arts school, with a predominant Bohemian culture and a very strong Women's Studies program.

When a friend of mine announced one day she wanted to try stripping, our circle of female comrades from this milieu did not take this news in stride. They were utterly scandalized, because it represented to them everything degrading to their idea of feminist power and freedom. They were certain that her deranged inspiration could only be oozing out from a festering disorder likely born of childhood sexual abuse.

I was surprised at the time, myself, as an unsophisticated farm girl with no exposure to that world, but when I talked at length with her about it, I didn't pick up on any of the disgruntling vibes or distressing undertones one would expect of someone so troubled. I saw a woman who was—in addition to having a gentle, playful, and generous spirit—beautiful, daring, and quite comfortable in herself. I was in full support of her endeavor. I admired her and felt genuinely excited for her.

I was thirty-three when I took an erotic dance class in San Francisco taught by an ex-stripper from Canada,[120] whom I'd met through an extended community in the Bay Area, and it was during this class when it occurred to me that I needed to be doing it on stage, in public. I toured all the clubs I could locate in North Beach

---

[120] That would be the lovely Ms. Catherine Rose, formerly of Slinky Productions.

and took it all in, bought some lap dances for myself, and relished the ladies strutting their stuff. I got some lingerie and booty shorts and practiced to my favorite funky music in front of the mirror in my room back in Santa Cruz. I visualized auditioning in the city but continued putting it off for every conceivable excuse but the real one—which was that it scared me shitless.

My first experiences of lap dancing for someone were a sweet sensation. I had started seeing a man sexually—a friend-of-a-friend setup that was a gorgeous success. We hit it off immediately, unable to take our lips off each other. Furthermore, we both had the same limited time to give. With me coming to the beginning of my six-month celibacy and him approaching tying the knot, we were each acknowledging the end of a significant chapter of our lives. So we gave it all, for a limited time (an arrangement he had made with his fiancée).

His excitement and enthusiasm for my dancing, as well as being able to incorporate this new flair directly into the sex with him, helped me to easily and naturally slip bodily into this emerging part of myself. Moving my body with the music—adding a little strip tease, gyrating to the rhythm of my desire, grinding into his crotch, adding a blow job here and there—turned me on as much as him, and we let that stoke the fire between us until we had no other recourse but to throw each other around for the rest of the night. It was incredible fun and an exquisite, intimate way to initiate myself into what would eventually become a professional enterprise (minus the blowjob part).

Time Waits for No One

After the celibacy and by the time I'd moved back to Oregon to be with Steve, I was beginning to feel again the stirring within of my desire to strip. The usual reservations had their way with me for about a year, but then, one day, while out digging around in the dirt, I had the frank revelation that I was thirty-six years old (which is already getting pretty long in the tooth for a stripper) and my window of opportunity for acting on this was, in fact, getting smaller with the relentless march of time. Most importantly, I knew I would truly regret it if I let it pass me by.

So Steve took me downtown to the one and only local titty bar to check it out. I remember the first time I walked through the front door and sequin-curtained lobby in the middle of the day, taking in the dark and dingy details of the grease- and smoke-infused environment. My sinuses squirmed in sync with a cold, unctuous pulse in the pit of my stomach as I sized up my surroundings like a slow-moving, heavy-headed reptile. We ordered the obligatory drinks and settled into a couple of extremely well-used chairs to generate some night vision and get acclimated—for me, to the idea of finally actually doing this thing in real life, which under the black light, amped up the pallid green about the gills to a verdant phosphorescence.

The second time, I went in alone and hit the door girl in the lobby about getting a job dancing there at The Office: Gentleman's Club. She directed me inside to speak to the manager, an enormous man who, although overbearing in size, was as intimidating as an overstuffed teddy bear. Weekdays after opening, between twelve and two, he said, were audition hours and he would be there, so just come on in.

This seemed awfully informal for show business, I mused, but it was what he told me the next day before my audition that delivered the unvarnished bottom line of the indecorous enterprise. "Don't worry, honey, if you can't dance," he said reassuringly. "If you can take off all your clothes up there on stage, chances are you got the job." Obviously, talent was not a criterion…nor much else, for that matter. Then, for added encouragement, he offered, "So try to take everything off."

I was escorted through the establishment past the main stage in the center and a mirrored half stage against the back wall to a tiny dressing room in complete disarray around the corner behind the DJ booth. I worked out a space on the wraparound counter under the naked lightbulbs just big enough to set my things on and, in a cold sweat, fumbled my way out of my street clothing and into my attempt at stripper garb. Then I nervously ventured back out, handed the DJ an audition CD on my way, and wearing my Dress-for-Less lingerie and a pair of fuck-me heeled shoes way beyond my skill level, managed to find myself ascending the stairs to the center stage as the DJ barked a barely intelligible introduction through the microphone over the music.

There was only a small handful of customers in the club at that hour, but nevertheless, when I got on stage, the severity of my nervous condition made me feel as though my body were experiencing an odd form of rigor mortis—*en vivo*. There seemed to be serious obstruction at the motor synapses, and I felt very little familiar corporeal feedback, which added to my sense of total awkward disconnect. My panicked psyche darted about like a wild rabbit, wondering how I might manifest a disappearance, while my body fumbled to obey what may as well have been somebody else's commands…whatever genius it was who came up with this big idea.

The complete removal of my clothing was, given my state of bodily inelegance, more a feat of physical dexterity than courageous grit. Because my own and others' nudity is something with which I'd become quite comfortable by this time in my life, the exposure of my buck-naked body was *not* the issue underlining my terror. For me, what was profoundly pressing my panic button was the idea of viewing myself—and the unthinkable audacity of *presenting* myself—as an erotic entity with the racy chutzpa to be performing and flagrantly "selling" my sexuality to the public. "Who's gonna buy that?" shrieked a voice in my head, because I sure didn't.

I floundered around on stage for the most bizarre seven minutes of my life, saved by that blessed brass pole from several near crash-and-burn skirmishes with the linoleum. When my two songs came to an end, I realized that I'd managed to successfully fulfill the critical mandate as well as adhere—within some semblance of reason—to the stage rules laid out by Big Poppa beforehand, although just before I dodged back into the dressing room, one of the girls pointed out to me that I'd forgotten to collect my tips—six big ones, I'd made, on my debut!

Back in the official quarters of The Office, the big fella beamed at my breathless anticipation and assured me that I'd gotten the job as he handed me a half-inch stack of paperwork to peruse and autograph. In addition to the exhaustive state, county, municipal, and OLCC (Oregon Liquor Control Commission) regulations, it presented the legally-required options of signing on as an employee ("House Nude Dancer") or as an independent contractor (hereinafter "Nude Dancer"), stipulating, however, the most restrictively unpalatable details of the former in no ambiguous terms. Of course, I chose the latter. (I have never encountered any stripper yet who has signed on as an employee—at any establishment.)

Three hours later I, Nude Dancer, stepped out from the dusky underworld into the daylight on the street. For whatever it was worth (and I had no idea yet), I'd done it.

What It's Like

Plainly put, my entry into the industry was culture shock. At heart, I was still (and may always be) a soft-spoken, wide-eyed, country-bumpkin sort of gal in spite of my relatively audacious undertakings and depth of inquiry. A friend of mine at Lewis & Clark used to liken me to Winnie the Pooh, who toddles around in benignly innocent yet comical naivety, somehow always managing to get by in spite of himself. I'll admit, I often marvel at my own good fortune, wondering how many near-disasters I've narrowly evaded trundling along my merry way.

The environment was caustic to my subtle sensibilities, which I realized had become considerably rarefied in the last dozen or so years by a contemplative, clean-living lifestyle. In 2007, the year of my momentous audition, public establishments in Medford, Oregon, were not yet designated smoke-free, so the poorly ventilated facility was a veritable secondhand smoke factory. It reminded me of living, at twenty, in Cuenca, Ecuador, where the total lack of vehicular emissions control made the air quality so poor that I saw little distinction, or consequence, to my growing taste for sucking tobacco smoke from the filterless cigarettes I purchased individually from street-corner vendors. What's the difference? I had pondered, rationalizing my toxic indulgence. Although I didn't take up smoking again, I doubt my lungs could make much distinction.

My sensation of the alcohol consumption within the club environment was similar, in that I literally felt hungover the next day as though I had gained a secondary sort of intoxication—the backside downer without the forehand fun—from the liquor-laced carbon dioxide exhalations of workers and patrons alike. Also, in those early days at The Office, there were a lot of drugs circulating among both customers and entertainers—from pot to crystal meth and cocaine (at that time, Medford was a hot center of methamphetamine production and distribution)—and police raids were not unheard of. Furthermore, the dressing room was teeming with germs as that early collection of girls coughed, sneezed, sniffled, and puked with a seemingly constant string of cold and flu viruses and various gastrointestinal distresses from food poisoning to alcohol excesses. A seven-hour shift twice weekly spent inside this petri dish rendered me ill for the better part of my first year of exposure.

Oh, but I was having so much fun!

Believe it or not, I actually was. As my nerves evened out on stage, I felt myself stepping into the full embodiment of what I had tinkered with a lifetime ago with my high school girlfriend, and what emerged was the inarguable fact that nude entertainment and erotic dance were perhaps the most joyful and authentic expressions of who I am. I reveled in it. With this experience, I could plainly see why it would have been such a shame to have let time pass me by on this one.

Part of my initial culture shock was the crass, in-your-face attitude among the strippers and the shit-talking trash flying around the dressing room. But the willfully indelicate attitude, the incisive sense of humor, and the earthy camaraderie pervading it all, win me over to this day. I've taken great pleasure in the fusillade of spirited dressing-room commentary bursting in and out of the swinging door that narrates a day in the life and knits the community of women together like a flamboyant, colorful scarf defiant to the blustery winds of the world. These women are really something to reckon with, and I love them wholeheartedly for that.

Of course, right off the bat, there were some ladies who played the nasty power trip of attacking the tenderfoot, but since I didn't play into this, it never went too far. On one of my first days on shift, I did the unthinkable, taking a customer from the stage during a girl's set and, back down on the floor, she tied into me like a junkyard dog. Although, in this case, it had been the customer who had grabbed me for a dance as I passed, I understood exactly what it meant in terms of stripper etiquette (you just don't do it, period). So rather than try to argue the point, I thought it better to swallow my humble pie and chase it with an apology. When I approached her in the dressing room, she bristled, prepared to fight. But my peace offering landed somewhere completely outside the cage, and I watched her entire persona rearrange to process the unexpected state of affairs. I really meant it, though, and after that I strived to be very conscientious about all aspects of unfolding transactions with customers. If you're not paying attention, chances are you're stepping on toes and making unnecessary drama. When trouble is just waiting for you to do something careless, a little forethought goes a long way.

On the flip side, I had to strengthen my stance and protect my own toes at times from coworkers and customers alike in a balancing act between getting along and having a vertebral column. While most of the fighting that goes on is unwarranted, some battles must certainly be chosen—or, Tut-Tut, Pooh gets trampled in the mud—and it takes keeping a sharp mind to make that distinction on the fly.

She Works Hard for the Money

The reality of working as a stripper offered up some other surprises. One was, indeed, the length of the shifts. I had conjured up a fantasy of spending two to three hours or so at the club, flitting on and off the stage, collecting my tips, and then breezing out to call it a night, so I was a bit rudely awakened to learn otherwise.

The morning after my first full shift, settling onto the toilet for a pee, I looked down and gasped in horror to see the deep mottled shades of blue and purple covering the two swollen stumps that should have been my knees. I got up and proceeded to examine the rest of my body, discovering numerous other colorful markings over elbows, forearms, thighs, and hips. Deeply disturbed, I seriously questioned whether this was really okay. My body was racked with aches and pains, and I looked like a victim of assault and battery.

The next eye-opener was that stage performance is only about 10 percent of the work, if that. The other 90-plus percent of the job involves direct engagement with customers—meeting, mingling, socializing (otherwise known as "hustling")—because the lap dance is where the real money is made in the business. (Although occasionally it does *rain*, stage performance is mostly the arid "advertisement.")

This kind of thing, basically acting as a social butterfly, slipping in and out of easy small talk with an unimaginably diverse selection of humankind, was a skill I was distinctly lacking. I really had no idea how to make this work—walking up to someone and fabricating an easy conversation out of thin air—and just the idea (let alone the reality) of doing this for hours and hours at a stretch both intimidated and exhausted me. I felt I could be quite content (were it not for the stifling quarters) to pass my entire shift as the minors[121] were required to do: lounging about in the dressing room until their turn in the stage rotation, and permitted—by specific customer request—to perform lap dances on the back stage under surveillance of the DJ booth!

But, here I was, and it was rapidly becoming clear that my quiet reservation was not going to make my gambit as a stripper a very lucrative endeavor. While this was certainly true from a monetary standpoint, I could sense that it would also be far less enriching as a living adventure.

So, it began to look like walking the talk—already pushing my envelope with a presumptuous parade of my sexuality—might actually be easier than learning to "talk the walk," so to speak. This was turning things inside out and every which way in my interiors, demanding a restructuring of myself at levels I had not anticipated.

---

[121] In this industry, "minors" are below legal drinking age. The legal age to work is eighteen years of age, so they are not yet able to freely range the facility, which serves alcohol.

It forced me to oblige myself in ways I had always rejected. As a teenager, I'd established a disdain for small talk in general, which I'd inadvertently cultivated throughout my entire adult life, never seeing enough value in it to consider my aversion something worth overcoming.

But as I watched the other women slide up effortlessly next to the customers, chatting breezily and waltzing them, with seamless panache, back into the lap dance area, I began to admire this level of ease and social aplomb. I began to see that my social reticence had an aspect of hiding in it that I had overlooked in my self-justifying dismissal of "superficial drivel." And so, as a result of my reluctant revelations, I began to put serious effort into building that skill and confidence in myself.

As I did so, I realized I appreciated the fact that our little club in Medford, located right off the I-5 corridor, was the only one in the entire Rogue Valley area. This meant that anybody and everybody within a wide radius who had any inclination toward this kind of context ended up at The Office—which resulted in a pretty wide spectrum of humanity as a customer base. This cultural diversity brought out the inquisitive social creature inside myself, and I uncovered a knack for pulling out the information that interested me in people. Since I can take an interest in almost anything, from a purely humanistic standpoint, I used that as the basis for my "hustle."

Mostly, I listened, and since most people really enjoy talking about themselves, it is easy enough to keep them going with the right kinds of questions and attention. On the other hand, I also encountered customers who, with their own evident interest in what I had to say, turned this table on me and got me to prattling on and on about myself.

Astonishingly, within the shadowy environs of the little old Office I stumbled upon the crossroads of the earth, meeting people from every corner of the US and the world from Barrow to Key West, New Zealand to The Ivory Coast. I heard stories from bull riding, stock trading, drug smuggling, and smoke jumping to building ice roads over the Arctic tundra and wrestling alligators in Floridian swamps. I met "fetish freaks," who were typically the most grounded, straightforward, and respectful bunch of people around sexuality that I've ever encountered—honestly, making the rest of us look all the more like freaks. Many individuals moved me significantly, grabbing hold of my line in completely unexpected ways, then disappearing forever into the blur of the rushing stream. One man, whom I'd at first pegged as painfully awkward, turned out to be the most fabulously intelligent, engaging, and interesting person of all, giving me several pertinent leads in the writing of this book.

At the end of the day, I found enough personal and social inspiration—as well as cash incentive—to keep me hustling my butt. This line of work is all very unpredictable, though, financially. From Dire Straits to Bob Dylan (literally, money for nothin' to crawling across cut glass to make a deal![122]), some days the money flows like a river of generous bounty while other times it's a thankless basket of bloodless turnips. Sometimes I've felt like a movie star and other days like I'm flailing somewhere in the range of invisible to repugnant. Baby, sometimes you're *hot*…and sometimes you're *not*. Best to just hop on that ride—get in, sit down, hold on—and leave your whining ego at the gate, because everything in this honky-tonk depends solely upon who walks in the door.

About a year into it, I noticed I was feeling tense and agitated on the floor. I had become fixated on the money. I was overcalculating my hustle—visually scrutinizing the customers, sizing them up with dollar signs on my eyeballs, and feeling burned over my miscalculations, as when I saw other dancers make good on my "rejects." I spent more time glowering at people from the shadows than actually working and entertaining.

I laugh at myself as I describe this, but it's embarrassing, considering I wasn't even in it to pay the rent or feed my kids. I think part of what happened was that because it did take such a toll on my body, I felt the job had better pay me up well for the battery. But also, it just showed me another aspect of desire (uh, greed), and since I was in it for fun (not my bread and butter but my *jam*!) as well as for personal growth, I jumped on that puppy and put my attitude back on

---

[122] Bob Dylan, "Sweetheart Like You," Columbia Records, 1983.

track. I brought my focus back to enjoying myself and my customers, as much as possible. I didn't throw away the intention to make money—I still view it as a job—but I loosened my grip. It made an immediate difference in the quality of my experience—and not a damn bit, from what I could tell, in the amount of money I made.

Shelter from the Storm

Most rewarding to me socially in the line of work has always been the sexually charged atmosphere. The environment gives license to the recognition of sexuality in a way that a regular public establishment does not, and I relish the fact that blunt talk of sex intertwines easily and naturally throughout conversation—*the way, of course, it should if we're functioning as whole human beings together*. I began to appreciate what an important outlet is provided by this type of venue, and the things my customers would express to me made it more and more clear what a significant position I was in with regard to supporting that outlet, protecting it, and nurturing it.

I cannot overstate the importance of a public social place where people can freely and unabashedly communicate their sexual responses. It's really so stifling out in the rest of the world where we are expected to be so buttoned up about it, feigning aloof oblivion to the presence of these responses. Really, all the chafing, disrespectful, sometimes even frightening cat-calling out on the street, with its undertones of angry aggression is just so much compressed steam blowing out of those buttonholes. Our social, sexual, political correctness has invaded our inner worlds to prevent more immediate, personal—yes, intimate—expressions toward one another.

A surprising lineup of customers at the strip club have expressed shame and guilt for even entering such a place, certain that I (ironically) am convinced they are perverts by sole virtue of their being there. I've had men apologize to me for being unable to resist looking at my "private parts"—again, ironically, since I have obviously chosen to take them public and that's, well, pretty much the point. They have apologized for enjoying the nudity and appreciating *my body* (as opposed to my magnificent mind, my luminous aura, or my electrifying personality), because they have been trained about the abomination of sexual *objectification*. There is incredible confusion—and consequent suffering—around the way we have all learned to categorize and discern what is and what is not sexually correct and appropriate, and this is one of the most obvious places it shows up.

Anyone involved in the sex industry should hold within themselves the understanding that nearly everyone on two legs is probably in some way sexually unfulfilled, since the general environment in which we live offers little beyond restriction and repression. In the industry, you see the wide array of examples comprising the spectacle of this woeful reality. Therefore, having a grasp of the ins and outs of the whole situation fosters the humanity necessary for the kind of exalted perspective that is so badly needed, curbing the reactive recoil of savage vilification that fuels the drama. Who's to judge a married knave seeking surreptitious stimulation? Who's to blame the angry scoundrel looking for trouble; or the gropey lecher sticking his tongue in your ear; the man who begs you to marry him, take him home, prostitute your wares; the screaming, obnoxious ingénues; the venomous vixens? Because there's so much pressure behind the jetty, the small fissure of outlet offered at a strip club can unleash a torrent of flotsam and jetsam that should not surprise anyone. You may not like it and it certainly doesn't mean you passively allow yourself to be jerked around. It just means it doesn't offend you so deeply because you know it's really not personal (as your ego stays obediently at the gate, watching).

Over the years, many a man has vented his frustrations, revealed his grief, and articulated unfathomable gratitude for the services and the sensual presence of a woman with whom he can have some form of interaction and, albeit limited, expression. With the background I have sexually and the insight from my own journey of sexual healing, I am positioned to offer a great deal, and I view it as my utmost responsibility to hold and to handle whatever arises with as much awareness, respect, and compassion as I can possibly summon, which is another reason why my money fixation early on began to feel so out of whack. Any fixation narrows awareness down to nearly nothing (other than a hypervigilance around that fixation), and that's a fact.

After I told her about my new calling, a friend and professional colleague handed me a book. *Candy Girl: A Year in the Life of an Unlikely Stripper* is an accurate account of the industry from a totally different perspective, and reading it contributed to my growing impetus to share my own, radically dissimilar, experience of stripping. Inevitably, I've developed a great appreciation for the courage involved in publishing any kind of revealing memoir, and anyone willfully exposing herself to the pandemonium of working in the sex industry is automatically part of my sisterhood. But I felt uncomfortable with the fact that the author, someone from the "outside" like myself, had immersed herself in this world—hidden to so many, behind the layers upon layers of mystery, cliché, fear and loathing—and emerged from it to tell the rest of the world about it with a pointed lack of compassion. The derisive commentary about her customers, the flavor of her own disgust toward them—their vulnerability, their eagerness, their sexuality—saddened me, as I saw it deepening the stigmatic crevasse. I love a sharp wit and a good laugh, but by just getting a big kick out of it, so much is missed. And it concerns me that bald revelations in this domain, unmitigated by sensitivity, land hard in tender places and deepen the extent of our social-sexual injuries.

I once described stripping—to a young friend of mine curious to give it a try—as *a carnival of horror and delight*, and I really love that description. Within such a highly charged atmosphere, there is so much stuff flying around it can be a hell of a lot to process.

The delight is in the exciting mixture of music and people and money, the electric charge of sex in the air, and the exhilarating unpredictability of this volatile concoction. It lies, for me, within the joy of erotic self-expression and the kinky, I suppose, thrill of exhibition. It explodes intoxicatingly in my neurons when I lavishly embody the function of sex symbol and object of desire. It emerges when I make meaningful and unexpected connections with men and women alike, and in interactions with both customers and fellow strippers. It stretches my envelope. It pushes my buttons. It cracks me up in the dressing room and inspires me on stage.

The horror surfaces within sudden moments of assault upon your person from any given source, and in any manner of disturbing or otherwise unfortunate incident you might find yourself privy to or involved within. Ever present in the mélange, as an undercurrent palpable to the perceptive, lurks that horrifying condition known as the human predicament, spiked with the poison of toxic sexuality, which burbles up in full glory as a result of any alcohol-induced state of decreased inhibitions. And this horror—it can stretch the tolerances of anyone who is empathetically tuned. While the work I'd done on myself and with others had built on a capacity for empathetic sensitivity, my exposure to the storm in this world expanded my girth to some painful dimensions.

In the beginning, I found it emotionally overwhelming. Many times I'd come home so upset I could not sleep for hours, and the next day I'd have to cry and then talk it all out with Steve and others. Sometimes I still do. Witnessing and having direct contact in a concentrated environment with the level of suffering and alienation due to sexual repression and misunderstanding—the drama, the confusion, the chaos—has been a direct impetus to the writing of this book.

It Ain't Me, Babe

There is, indeed, the full spectrum of characters, and I would be remiss to omit mentioning the crummier bunch. However, in good conscience, I need to emphasize that in my experience, there is *not* a greater proportion of shady characters to be found at a strip club than at any other kind of public venue, contrary to common belief. I can't tell you how many guys come into the place thinking they are a totally different type of creature than all our other customers. Who told them that? The movies, the preacher, television, peer banter? Well, I make it a point to tell them otherwise.

I have defused some drama bombs simply by withholding judgment and reactivity. Mostly, I find what I seek out and generally avoid the rest. But honestly, there are simply some crummy people in the world at large, so of course I've encountered them at the club. Furthermore, putting oneself out publicly as a sexual object, given the troubled and confused reality out there, is a very vulnerable move. It can be brutal at times, depending merely upon who chances to walk through the door and what they bring in with them. Some people are looking for trouble, to inflict pain, or to otherwise fuck with your mind. So, while the element of sympathetic understanding still informs the overall perspective, it doesn't mean that you suck it up and stick around. In many cases, that's just plain poor judgment!

Many people in the industry claim to have developed an eye for reading individuals at a glance—judging whether or not they have or will spend money, what kind of character they are, star sign, and suchlike. Assuming there is such a capacity, I never got to that level. I generally can't make heads or tails of someone until I engage with them.

But I know a mind-fuck when I bite into it, and once I taste that junk, I won't hesitate to spit it out right then and there. I don't feel any obligation to give it another moment. These people know exactly what they're doing, and I have not the time nor the patience for it, even if it means I'm walking away from a shitload of money—which, of course, they almost invariably tend to claim is ready to burst out of their wallet if only you can manage to play your cards just right.

My response to the mind-fuck is disappearing-act. I will get up midsentence, theirs or mine, and walk away without another word. If I'm going to get involved in something challenging, I'd much rather deal with a different set of issues because this one, specifically, takes form within a very complex construct of worldview, ego, and attitude toward relating. Although, once, I tackled the topic and had a brief, real conversation with a young, still-malleable guy, I generally regard it as a can of worms better left unopened.

Significantly, I also have to concede that because stripping has always been something I do for fun and cash stash rather than for a real living, I have had the incredible luxury of walking away from the possibility of money without much consequence (although, doing it only one night a week, as I now do, means that a bum night equals a whole bum week!). Depending on your customers in this business for your living essentials, your staples of survival, puts you in a much tighter spot, at least psychologically, and can lead to a large amount of bitterness and resentment toward those who want to work you over. And as I said, there are always those who do. Also, because sexuality—the basis of the business—is such a personal thing, it's not necessarily a difficult enterprise for a determined individual to get under a girl's skin in one way or another.

One Halloween, in keeping with my vampire costume, I theatrically slithered up to a customer, threatening to suck the life out of him. I had thought it was a humorous dramatization, all in good fun, of the Stripper from Hell—but he did not, and proceeded to verbally clean my clockwork. It was obvious, he snarled, what a foul, malicious, cold-blooded creature I was and that he saw right through my wicked game (I hadn't realized my imitation was *that* good). Utterly blindsided, I spent the next twenty minutes skulking behind the plastic tree in the corner, regaining my composure.

Another time, I fell for a real snow job by a guy who screwed me out of a significant amount of money, just before reporting me to the police for stealing his wallet. This one backfired nicely, though. Following my interrogation by the officer, I kicked back and watched him get a personal police escort out of the club down to the city jail.

While this kind of stuff (and much worse) goes down, I still think one of the most striking observations I've made has to do with the nature of dramatization. After a significant period of time working in this industry, I found myself cogitating on an intriguing phenomenon. I wondered why I always seemed to miss out on all the crazy action down at the club. There were such wild stories constantly flying around about the outrageous goings-on about the place, yet whenever I was there, things seemed remarkably subdued, with a minor conflagration here and there.

What I finally figured is that the apparent significance of any given event was more a measure of the quality of reaction and the quantity of attention given to it than the actual size of it and that the former is something people simply inflate for sheer entertainment value.

I do see a lot of overreaction taking place in many situations, admittedly, as a result of the hypercharged atmosphere of sexuality mixed with alcohol and money combined with the big-picture drama around sex that exists under wraps everywhere. And ultimately, my conclusion about the common impression that "these kinds of places" harbor more than their share of delinquent or perverse individuals is that it has to do with the inflated reactions and overdramatized stories that originate therein. People love making mountains out of molehills, especially in juicy domains! It's the same people everywhere; it just boils down to what erupts in a given environment, like the classic broken-windows theory in criminology.

New Attitude

I could never have expected to escape from such an experience—particularly given the length of time I have continued stripping—without getting grazed by the crossfire in some other places, and I did not.

Early on, one man decided he had to read me the riot act for not entirely shaving off my pubic hair (I've always chosen to leave a generous "landing pad"—my *whoopie* cushion—by fervent request of my partner). This was a strip club, goddammit, clean up your junk! Another man told me my breasts looked like I'd had children (which I have not), and I had to grapple with the impact of that for quite some time.

Although the former was aggressively emotional about it, the second one stated his observation very matter-of-factly, apparently more interested in making an assessment about my personal history than my physical attractiveness. Yet another man enthusiastically exclaimed how he had always considered himself a breast man, but after seeing my ass, he was thoroughly converted. So does this come off as another slam against my poor little titties, or as a whopping compliment to my assets in the rear? How these things landed really depended on me, so it constantly kept me light on my toes.

(Now, this is a supremely important, highly relevant discussion here, so please set aside any reservations about the issue of objectification, because we're going to hammer that one out shortly, I promise.)

I chose to regard all this kind of input, to the best of my ability, as scientific data. Earlier, I mentioned the importance of extricating self-worth from the highly critical and limited ideas we have about sex appeal, and one of the best ways to do this is to *gather data*. Raw data, because of its objective nature, is the best crowbar in town for dislodging the obstinate mind-sets we have about our bodies regarding how they do or don't measure up to our trivial ideas about what is and isn't sexually desirable (generally the result of highly subjective processes). Using this tool, however, requires committing to the practice of *objectivity toward one's own body*, something extremely difficult to manifest successfully, especially amid confused notions about the meaning of objectification.

For years I had practiced asking for feedback of this nature and worked to understand this part of my own psychological and emotional relationship with my body and my sexuality. I had worked to oust my narrow, critical judgments in favor of an enlightened reality-based perspective that listed toward the philosophy of "different strokes for different folks" in terms of the features that turn people on sexually.

But, in the most critical areas, I really had not accepted this very deeply; I simply had not been convinced out of my most ingrained beliefs and staunch positions. I think many of us fall into the sneaky bear trap of thinking we have the authoritative verdict on these matters. Somewhere we have picked up varying notions that have become our spoken and unspoken maxims, such as "men prefer large breasts," "women want great big penises," "blondes have more fun," "more flesh is less attractive," or specifically, as in my case, "my butt is ugly," and so forth. Well, nothing came close to the education I got about the ins and outs of all this from stripping.

In this environment, I have worked with other women of—absolutely—all shapes and sizes (fat, slender, muscular, emaciated;

real tits, fake ones, nipples-only; tall, short, miniature; all-made-up and au naturel). Observing the behavior and (frequently discussing) the responses generated among all sorts of customers, both male and female, gave me an inundating landslide of firsthand information about the huge range of sexual preferences among the general populace. The jury is in, and the verdict is, truly and incontrovertibly, *different strokes for different folks*. No more crafty dismissal of this conclusion as a euphemistic phrase designed to appease those of us endowed with the "less than ideal" genetic attributes.

It's also true that some people adhere to very clearly defined preferences, while others are ecstatic to enjoy the full range of variation among different bodies and types. I watched customers go wild over dancers I was certain were homely, too thin or overly rotund. I watched numerous men go nuts over enormous boob jobs and listened to many disapproving complaints about them. For every man that expressed disinterest in pubic hair, there were many more who expressed appreciation for it—those who demanded I shave it and those who begged me never to do so.

For myself, I even discovered that in spite of my occasionally obsessive interest in leanness, when I tune into my personal homosexual responses, I actually find rounded, voluptuous women more sexually alluring. So looking directly at that alone forces me to alter my evaluation of the standards to which I hold myself, sometimes too harshly. In further support of my softening standards, at one point, when I pared myself down to the weight to which I had always aspired, a longstanding regular complained that I'd become too thin. I make a note. Another customer prefers it. I make a note. A handsome, ripped thirtysomething at the gym admits, in a conversation with my partner, his own growing sexual preferences for a little "junk in the trunk." I make note. (I've also noticed my own sexual preferences in men, over time, shifting away from the hard and ultra-lean toward the more meaty hunks.)

Interestingly enough, what happens frequently is that when it's right in front of us—unless we're really stuck in the head—many preferences sort of get forgotten or overlooked, and sometimes (like the tits-to-ass convert), an appreciation for something new and different is discovered. It's because sex itself functions according to quite different parameters than our thinking minds caught up in various limiting and conflicting agendas. And our thinking minds have been immoderately influenced and shaped to favor the prevailing public ideal provided by the media.

Just beneath the marketed ideal of sex appeal lies the truth about what *really* appeals to us sexually, which is far more accommodating than that familiar product image. (Take a visual survey of the vast selection of pornographic themes in an adult store to get the point!) Understanding this requires really paying attention both to the world around us and the world within us, and it gives us a much better sense of reality around the definition of sex appeal. And it's also why exposure to having it right in front of us is very important, in addition to gaining experience and examining our own standards.

The fact of the matter is that for *everyone* there will be a certain percentage of the population that will respond to them sexually. Yes, of course, there will be the genetically blessed "hotties" and not-considered-so-hotties of the world, but everyone will have a *distribution of percentages* that they cannot second-guess. And nobody can please them all, although insecurity demands zero-sum thinking. The hot girl who gets her breasts augmented will gain a new set of admirers and simultaneously lose another. No matter what she looks like (or what St. Paul has proposed for himself), she can never be all things to all men. Some guys will come around who only see the girl we never thought twice about. There is no way around it. Different strokes.

And women respond to sexual objects in just the same way as men do. When a friend of mine put up a pole in his little bar and held a ladies night with some bold local men putting their amateur skills to the test, I was ecstatic to see the boys step into the role. One young stallion was a sculpted piece of eye candy, a special treat with a frothy topping of youthful enthusiasm and a cherry of innocence. Another was a fair bit older, slightly soft in the middle, but was so erotically composed that his performance was positively ballistic. Watching both men and women dance erotically—and engaging with both men and women in this context—I confirmed, for myself, that a sizable chunk of the appeal resides heavily in the way someone inhabits, embodies, and expresses their sexuality.

Stripping, I learned that of the men who verbalize their appreciation of my body, a large percentage will particularly like my ass, a comparable number will find my nipples arousing, fewer (yet indeed some) will be focused on my breasts, and some will appreciate the whole package. And then there's the section who will have absolutely no interest at all and may even be completely turned off. Regarding how I inhabit and express myself, some will be attracted to my exuberant performance, while others will prefer the more aloof and unrevealing type.

Finally I was able to take the data to heart and take that crowbar to my ass. All my life I was convinced that my buttocks were distinctly unattractive—in fact, I was quite self-conscious about what I'd decided was an overly generous helping of gluteal meat—and it took an overwhelming cascade of definitive feedback to the contrary for me to relinquish this mind-set. Now I'm as sly as any she-fox when it comes to this stuff and I'll come up with any half-baked excuse to cling to my self-critical persuasions. So it's totally not okay for me to write this off just because booty is hot now…because the fashion for roundness in the rear is just having its brief moment in the sun before something else comes along. Meanwhile, we have to live with ourselves over the course of a lifetime, and that's much more fun when we give ourselves more space around our definition of sexy. Besides, *sex is one thing that fashion can never define or confine, no matter how much it tries.*

To be clear, the lesson here is not about seeking external validation but about how the outside data reflects on inner, poorly lit processes, bringing to them the light of day and allowing us to air them out in a more conscious, open-minded realm. We *must* look at the things we take as factual that are merely (usually fallacious) assessments we have made based on (typically) extremely limited, often distorted, data, and we carry these things around with us, so confident in our convictions. We have to stop and look directly at these things, taking a good, long, hard look to see what's really going on. It will simply not work to shrug about our self-critical judgments, rationalizing them away as superficially meaningless—because this is not truly the experience of it. The truth is, we can be relentlessly plagued by these stubborn little things we may have never even questioned, and to successfully overcome their influence, we have to be aggressively proactive, with our feet firmly planted on the ground.

Once, I met a sensitive man who had been a photographer for *Playboy* magazine, and through the course of our conversation, he expressed to me his troubled astonishment at what he observed about women's relationships with their bodies. He was stupefied by his discovery that *every single one* of these models he encountered expressed dissatisfaction with her body in one way or another. He simply didn't know what to do with this. I mean, this is la crème de la crème, right? And yet it's just you and me, worried about this, that, or the other thing, which we've decided is *less than Playboy-perfect* and, therefore, unacceptable. (How about that for a crowbar?)

In a conversation with my mother about my stripping experiences, it was evident that she held some of the typical discomfort about the issue of female *objectification*. In fact, I've found that many people are unable to share my gassy enthusiasm for the discoveries I presented above, because it all falls within that precarious territory.

As a worker—male or female—in the sex industry, you are, beyond the shadow of a doubt, a sexual object (in fact, it cannot be otherwise). You have chosen to be so, and you are much better off if you have a healthy relationship with that fact. That relationship becomes your own shelter from the storm, and rather than preventing you from being a whole human being in your work, it keeps you intact and impervious to feelings of degradation in the face of the reality of objectification.

Of course, to have a healthy relationship with sexual objectification requires not only an intact sense of self-worth but also—*and actually even more importantly*—an understanding about sex and sexuality that most of us are lacking. And this piece goes way beyond the sex industry and deep into the wider realm of human sexual existence. Therefore, part of sexual recovery as a whole involves getting acquainted with the ins and outs of what we (mostly inappropriately) lump into the objectionable category of objectification, so we can discern the pieces and disentangle what has become wadded into an awful mess.

The topic itself has become a massive object and there are extremely important things to be said about it so I best stop gathering moss and get rolling. We have to dismember the whole thing from soup to nuts. First, we have to ask what is objectification, and then we have to ask why it is a problem.

To answer the first question simply, Webster's definition of *objectify* is: "to present as an object, especially of sight, touch, or other physical sense; make objective; externalize."[123]

Addressing the second question is more complex and has three parts—historical, psychological, and sexual—that have gotten all jumbled up (the definition from my Mac Dictionary illustrates this: *"degrade to the status of mere object: a deeply sexist attitude that objectifies women"*). Truthfully, only the first two parts are problematic on their own. The problem with the third one is just that it's gotten in with a bad crowd.

History is one hell of a problem. For millennia, objectification has been employed as a way of *dehumanizing* groups of people to aid ruthless ambitions, from militant oppression to slavery and genocide, so, from a global humanitarian perspective, we are smart to be wary of it. In this vein, women have been objectified, or basically treated as livestock for the purpose of driving the economics of patriarchal society. Through this background, and the efforts of women's lib, the term *objectification* has become casually defined (as in my Mac) as an act of degradation, most commonly as a sexist attitude toward women, and so now, as a result, we recoil with aversion and distrust at the mere mention of it. The atrocities of history infuse shock-horror emotion into our ideas about objectification, causing people to adopt steely stances highly resistant to cross-examination in this area.

---

[123] Webster's New Universal Unabridged Dictionary (New York: Barnes & Noble Publishing Inc., 2003), 1336.

And then, to make matters worse, history has packaged and delivered to us a sexuality so persecuted, perverted, and pathologized that we can't even look it straight in the eye without getting the willies.

Next problem. Now we're deep into the psychology (start drinking heavily). When we regard something within as perverted, defective, or suspicious, our psychology protects us (ego defense) by externalizing it (dissociation, projection) into something that is outside, or *not us* (for one example, demonizing the objects of your sexual desire when you view lust as the temptation of the devil). When it comes to sex, this is the basis of neurosis, since—for the sweeping majority of us—we simply cannot sanely deny and successfully divorce ourselves from the meat and marrow of our own humanity, try as we might. And, sexually, this is really what we have in our society: a neurotic scourge. This is what drives the fanatical zealot, the over-protective parent (regarding sex, most are), our sexual attitudes, and, as a result, all the bloodshed in the bedroom.

The third part of the problem—sex itself—extricated from the horrors of the first two, now shines with pristine simplicity...except that it's still hard to see it through the lingering fog of confusion (because the history and psychology hang so thick and heavy). So, in order to see it for what it really is, and keep sorting out the shady business of objectification, we need to develop a whole new attitude. At the end, it will be clear that the only problem all along was due to the fact that *we've been conflating a pathological phenomenon with a natural sexual process.*

Fleshing out this new attitude will involve taking everything I've discussed up to this point (even rehashing some of it) and turning the idea of sexual objectification from a dreaded artifact of history and mental derangement into something we can actually work with that honors the facts of sexual desire and functioning.

Material Girl

What are these facts of sexual desire and functioning? It all boils down to the single fact that sexual response is quite material:

we are turned on or off sexually by the physical features of an object that appeal to the senses. These objects can be human, non-human, even inanimate. Sticking to the first of these three, the point that another human being possesses other significant nonphysical attributes—intellectual, emotional, spiritual, democratically accorded "unalienable rights," et cetera—does nothing to alter this fact. And, like the earlier discussion about rape, honoring the material facts underlying sexual response does not imply consent to behaviors (like human trafficking, for example) that turn people into faceless commodities. Rather, honoring the facts is about growing up as human beings, plain and simple.

Through a sexually damaged culture informed by the cruelty of history, we've learned that appreciating the physical is downright despicable (at best, it's considered shallow, and we use the pejorative terms "materialistic" and "superficial" to describe its loathsome limitations). Then, infused with the spirit of self-righteous indignation, we go on incubating these ideas within and among ourselves as we go forth laying out more and more politically correct rules along the way. Women have pointed a collective finger at men for objectifying them, while men have recognized and recoiled from the collective folly of their gender's predecessors. We're trying so hard but getting ourselves deeper into trouble because we're still missing the most important point, which is the one incontrovertible fact of sex: *sexuality runs, and can only run, in the playground of objects.* In our confusion, many of the things we label as objectification are pure and natural sexual desire and response.

We have decided that *male* sexual nature, straight out of the *Animal House*, naturally bends toward the nasty habit of objectification because we believe, thanks to evolutionary psychology, that they are the sexual savages who respond more to their "coarser" senses (those *p.i.g. pigs!*—as she squawks in the movie)[124], while *females*, more "refined" in our sensual appreciations, desire sex from a place less carnal and more civilized (a biological marvel...do you smell

---

[124] *Animal House*, directed by John Landis, 1978.

something funny?). Then, as women, since our sexuality is supposed to *be* less physical than a man's, we expect it to be *treated* that way out of basic human decency. So, of course, all the strenuous work we do training them to perform those romantic overtures (to acquit them of all charges for sexual motive) seems totally sensible instead of just plain silly. Naturally, this sends us running faster and faster around the old the hamster wheel, reinforcing the imaginary division between "us" and "them."

In all reality though, the historical problem of the objectification of women is *not* a direct result of men's *sexual nature*, but a by-product of their *social power struggle*, so we have to be extremely careful in making the convenient associations that evolutionary psychology presents, because it's driving us all to ruin. It's high time to finally come to terms with the fact that having sexual desire and response to *physical objects* (which we have and are), and having sexual motive and intent toward manifesting the act of sex based on those responses, has nothing to do with *degrading people* to mere objects for the sake of exploitation. It is, rather, an innocent human impulse.

It's also important to recognize that women participate in the objectification of men in our own culturally conditioned ways. We just don't like to call it that. Women turn men into objects of our own desire: for security, for status, for validation, for gratification of any of the myriad desires we look to men to fulfill, without really admitting that the projection often has little to do with the human being himself (and because it's not focused on *getting sex*, per se, but about getting all the other feel-good goodies, we feel somehow more noble). This is called the "romantic fantasy." That fantasy is, by definition, not real, but we attempt to make it real by playing out our role in the fairy-tale romance, and by expecting—often demanding—that he perform his role according to its theme and plot. Needless to say, this is no more a noble venture than what we think men are doing to us. It's just another way of using one another to get what we want (or in this case, what we *think* we want, because of our social training as females).

Nevertheless, we all continue to rationalize and glorify the destructive emotionalization of sex trained into women, now taking it a step further by raising it as a politically correct model for modern men to aspire toward, thus training *their* sensitivities down the same dead end and neutering us all. Although I hate to rain on the parade of good intentions (I certainly don't think PC is malicious), I'm afraid it's got us marching down the pavement to just where those ambitions lead! Ultimately, the misguided attempt to right the wrong only hurtles our world along another uncharitable trajectory.

The modern media culture has successfully pulled young men equally into the self-conscious vanity fair now capitalizing on the insecurities of both genders, with sexuality at front and center. This may put these men in a position (squeezed into limited ideals with restricted outlets of expression) more similar to that in which women have been, creating in them, too, that vacuous need for a sexuality padded with the comforting platitudes of romantic emotionality. This is not a healthy direction in which to be going.

Now, what I'm pointing to is adjusting the course of the progressive movement by coming to terms with the basic facts of life, because we have overlaid history and neurosis onto sexuality so that the result is this completely nonsensical "common sense" we carry around about the evils of sexual objectification and everything it represents. This nonsense has never worked in bringing anyone into alignment with these basic facts of life, and therefore, it has never led to any sense of contentment, sexually or otherwise.

When I had moved from rural Oregon to the California Bay Area to start school, I encountered a breed of male influenced by the emerging "progressive" PC culture to such an extent that my sexual escapades were brought to a screeching deceleration. I found males who appeared to have become socially castrated as I barreled into a bog of uptight, palpably contrived, sexual intransigence that left me confused, disheartened, and sexually frustrated. I missed my "real" men from Oregon, who recognized that sex could be something casual, racy, and fun.

Most of these Californians were of the twenty-something age bracket—white, middle-class young men raised with an elevated social conscience. And, at a time when they truly ought to be seeking sexy escapades of their own, they were astoundingly stuffy about it. Others were the middle-aged men of this same social strata, who had been involved in the New Age mind-set, also identifying as progressive.

I, for one, do not view this as social progress, but rather as another in a long string of dubious repercussions stemming from ignorance about sexuality and an incomplete understanding of history. I saw boys trying to be men, and men trying to be "appropriate," in a world that has taken from them a grounded connection with their sexual being in any given social context, one that has cut away all sexual suggestion, and agency, in order to render them innocent of their gender's historical indictment.

In the process of trying to be "woke" people, building a more humane world for ourselves and posterity, we have condemned the material nature of our sexuality (which, through stifling our natural responses, inevitably squelches casual sex) and tried to pretend that we (men and women both) remain sexlessly unmoved by it, and by each other physically. But, nevertheless, that old elephant is still galumphing about in the room, and the emperor's weathered genitalia are still flapping in the breeze. Political correctness is just a flimsy disguise for the underlying problem that remains to be addressed: society's sexual attitude problem.[125]

We cannot solve the problem by training more and more people to dissociate from their own inherent sexuality (which is what all the PC training actually is, which is why it's digging us deeper and deeper into dementia). Instead, absolutely the contrary, we have to bring it all back inside and finally pull ourselves together to heal all shame and judgment around the aspects of ourselves we've learned to condemn.

---

[125] Bill Maher, American comedian, political commentator, and TV host defines political correctness as "the elevation of sensitivity over truth," saying "we're not getting to the truth because we're too sensitive." (David Marchese, "Bill Maher on the Perils of Political Correctness," *New York Times*, Talk, Sept. 30, 2019).

With all this uncomfortably in place, where can we possibly put such things as nude entertainment? In the current wider cultural environment, it is naturally going to be suspect and our responses to it are going to be ambivalent, at best.

Bad, Bad Thing

Some women do feel it is a degrading livelihood—I have heard them use these very words. Others (many, in my experience) find it fun and empowering, and not because they are ignorant of deeper implications but because they simply don't carry the burden of the designated stigma. Some women turn to stripping as a last-resort means of making money; many others, like myself, out of a sheer desire to do it. Some women feel "ruined" by the experience. Others rewarded. I heard a tender minor assert that, through stripping, she had gratefully learned about what actually turns her on, and she felt like a much more sexually embodied woman as a result. I saw another fall deep into the allure of drugs and alcohol.

In all reality, the women involved in the industry are little other than a cross-section of fairly ordinary humanity (as are the customers themselves), and so, to an insider, the stereotypes are mostly laughable. The negative aspects that (can and do) get inflamed in that context are merely the symptoms of a much greater problem, a consequence of the sexual dysfunction ubiquitous in society as a whole. The environment itself merely provokes the troublesome elements into action, but, to recall the wisdom of psychologist, author, and spiritual teacher Ram Dass, *nothing can fuck with you if there's nothing to fuck with*. The fault is to be found well beyond the walls of the facility.

In the sex industry, the feeling of degradation that some women take on from stripping generates not from the fact that it *is* inherently degrading but rather from the *belief* that it is. That belief, fostered by men and women both, and sometimes manifested by men in their treatment of the women in this industry (either by chastising them or by trying to father them—patronizing or paternalizing), is tied up in all the twisted attitudes around sexuality that I've been discussing throughout this book. The woman taking on this belief and its shame might attribute it to the mainstream condemnation of her "ill-reputed" livelihood, the red letter it brands into her, and the fact that she is not at all comfortable letting others (especially, sometimes, those closest to her) know how she earns a living. If she has indeed turned to it because her preferred options have not panned out successfully, were it not for the stigma and censure in our neurotic society around anything sexual, it should be no more of a blow to her stature or self-esteem than resigning herself to any of her other less-preferable options of employment.

My mother articulated her objection, stating what a shameful comment on society it is that working as a stripper should pay better than, say, a job waitressing. Overlooking the fact that waitressing might to many (myself first among them) be a far less appealing option to begin with, I'll move straight to the point that money simply follows what society values, and, the bottom line is that—underneath all the public disclaimers and distorted manifestations—we value sex. Immensely. It's just who we are, and it motivates us to throw our money around the way nothing else can (even prompt, polite table service). The real shameful comment to be made is about how the most vital feature of our humanity has been violated and putrefied to such an extent that we cannot even function as healthy human beings and admit the honest truth about sex.

The consumption of pornography, popularly considered a politically incorrect and generally immoral pastime, due to its blatant (inherent, really) objectification of sexuality, offers measurable proof of the immensity of our valuation of sex. As a matter of fact, consuming pornography is just as popular as condemning it (even among the same people), just not so readily admitted. My partner loves pointing out that the roughly ten-billion-dollar-per-year porn industry in the US[126] is not supported by *ten* people spending a billion dollars per

---

[126] In 2006, the estimated yearly revenue of the porn industry in the US was $13.33 billion, coming in at around $44.67 per capita, according to a global

year but, probably, more like *two hundred million* people spending about fifty dollars per year. This is an important thing to recognize and accept in order to remove the shame and judgment that surrounds the matter as though it were actually an aberrant paraphilia: dude, it's you and your next-door neighbor![127] And it's not a pathology—either individually or societally.

Marty Klein, sex/couples therapist for thirty-five years, discusses how hurt, angry conversations about porn have spiked in his practice since the turn of the millennium, with the availability of porn via broadband internet. It's heartbreaking, he says, because the suffering is so unnecessary. He attributes it to the "porn panic" spread by "moral entrepreneurs who have given themselves the job of alerting everybody to this supposedly horrifying, dangerous thing" and giving them "false information about what's harmful and what's not." He explains that "moral panics tend to arise in times of social change. The country was completely unprepared for 24/7 porn in everybody's home." So, people freaked out about the purported menace, with catastrophic visions of society overrun with violent crime, depressed erections, and the destruction of happy homes. (But, he says, rates of sexual violence, child molestation, and divorce have actually all gone down since the year 2000, according to FBI reports and divorce records.)

Pathologizing porn is just another way of pointing the finger at something "evil" outside ourselves rather than turning within to figure out what healthy functioning actually looks like. Klein says of porn "addiction," as a diagnosis, that it keeps people from getting appropriate help for underlying issues by focusing on *porn* as the problem rather than the person and how they're using it. He says,

---

analysis utilized by organizations selling internet filtering products and services (http://internet-filter- review.toptenreviews.com).

[127] Even America's "golden boy," Patriots quarterback Tom Brady, doesn't bat an eye about searching the internet for porn, just doing "the same shit every 27-year-old guy does," he said in a 2005 interview with *GQ* magazine (David Kamp, "The Best There Ever Was?" *Gentlemen's Quarterly*, August 9, 2005, gq.com/story/tom-brady-patriots).

"People who claim to treat porn 'addiction' rarely offer a model of healthy porn use or healthy passionate sexuality."[128]

It seems fairly obvious that if sex were not otherwise so indiscriminately condemned and strictly constrained by the pious and puritanical authors of our moral constitution, the outlets provided now by the sex industry would certainly have a less supercharged reason to exist. Who desperately needs an "outlet" when you can simply "let it out" without a hitch and hoopla? (So much for those well-meaning church ladies, ignorant of the profound error and hypocrisy of their position, who frequent the strip club dressing rooms showering gifts and prayers for the lost souls working therein. Call it bilateral job security, I suppose!)

In a PBS Frontline story about pornography, Danni Ashe (ex stripper, model, and proprietor of the hugely profitable soft-core porn site Danni's Hard Drive), demonstrates an elegant understanding of the wildly various, often disturbing, aspects of sexuality found in pornography—including the violence, the aggression, the "depravity." She simply says, "It is a reflection of who we are" and that an environment of sexual repression tends to exacerbate the aggressive anger that fuels some of the kinds of violent images that appeal to people. She is largely correct. And, for all the ruffled feathers and self-righteous discomposure among the religious contingent, they would do well to examine their central, leading role in the obsessive and violent aspects of the pornographic feature.

We would all do well, in fact, to examine Western religious moralism as the primary basis of our messy situation and to fully acknowledge how we have all been condemned to a life of sexual repression based on prejudice and willfully ignorant misinformation. This hell, as usual, is the creation of human minds, and will not relent until our minds are truly changed. So let's come right out and call it what it is, pointing the index finger back in the right direction. Then let's point

---

[128] Martha Ross, "Sex Therapist Counsels Couples on 'the Porn Problem,'" *San Jose Mercury News*, February 19, 2017 (an article interviewing Marty Klein after the publication of his latest book, *His Porn, Her Pain: Confronting America's Porn Panic with Honest Talk About Sex*).

the middle finger skyward, taking its literal directive upon ourselves, and happily fuck our way out of the paper bag we're in!

On the other hand, we would also do well to recognize and rein in the misguided aspects of feminism. In the blog of one of my favorite porn actresses, Amarna Miller,[129] some worked-up women offered their critical assessment, "informing" her that the men consuming her image online do not, in fact, value her at all and will not hesitate, after jacking off, to dismiss her altogether with a single click of the mouse (how abusive…not even a virtual hug!) to move on to the next exciting image for their monstrous chauvinistic appetite. I suppose this was presented to enlighten what they assume is her naive ignorance about the reality of how pornography is actually used as well as to express their disgust with it. Instead, to someone like her—hardly naive, remarkably enlightened for her age, and evidently quite sexually liberated—their comments would likely reveal these women's own ignorance of the real issue. Hidden under the smothering blanket of pseudo-suffragette morality lies that sexual insecurity that is due to both the damage done to women specifically and people's relationship with sex in general.

Since we've succeeded in making sex into such a degenerate thing, we now have to wrap it all up in an emotional security blanket to reassure us that *even though we are involved in it, we are still okay*, which looks like making believe that having sex is about so many other meaningful things besides "merely" having sex. In this way, to double your trouble, sexuality has been prostituted in the reverse—by *subject-ification*, or insisting that every aspect of its physical manifestation must reflect the whole kit and caboodle of one's emotional being, heart and soul.

The constant demand for these absurd reassurances is simply pandering to an emotional frailty that needs to be seriously examined, thoroughly understood, and permanently resolved. The root of

---

[129] amarnamiller.com (Ms. Miller is no longer actively working in the sex industry. She is coming out with a book, through Spanish publisher *Temas de Hoy*, exploring the experiences of women using anecdotes from her own life.)

the problem goes back, again, to the disempowerment resulting from females' trained disconnect with our sexual bodies, teaching us to completely emotionalize something that is physical or physiological. When we're out of touch with our own bodies, we are incapable of understanding how sex actually works, which makes us susceptible to such distorted ideas about what is and what is not meaningful and relevant to sex, sexual identity, and sexual relationships. We can't possibly comprehend the fact that the body responds *sexually* to another body—not to an intellect, a heart, or a soul—and that this response is normal and healthy rather than perverted, demeaning, and inhumane. If we insist that it must be based upon non-physical attributes, we simply cannot appropriately value sex, and if we can't do that, we certainly can't make healthy evaluations about our own sexuality or our sexual relationships. When we cannot understand these things, we are disenfranchised as full (social-sexual) human beings and we have to scramble around patching ourselves together with a mishmash of other makeshift pieces, which sends us straight up the pole—and *not* the sexy brass one.

We then find ourselves trying to squeeze sexual expression into one perfect politically, emotionally, and morally correct tidy package, while creating an obscene mess—since our politics, our emotions, and our morals are systemically infested with a confused and fundamentally incorrect view of sex. (And, if we really want the clearest vision of sex, we cannot try to mix it up with our political/emotional/moral package at all, even if that collection weren't so out of sorts.)

The strip club offers deliverance from the stifling atmosphere of political correctness, where people of all walks and genders can enjoy the ease of a more fresh, unguarded expression. Yes, the emphasis is on the physical, bodily aspects that stimulate sexual excitation. It's a place where this kind of indulgence is fostered and relished. Men find great relief and happy freedom in a context where they can openly admire a woman's body; in a male "review," the women go wild without a worry about demeaning the objects of their desire. It's just pure sexual response. What could be more desirable, more healthful, more good, clean fun?

With things more comfortably and reasonably in place, a woman as a female entertainer can, even if it is not her ideal line of work, function within such a venue (as many indeed already do), free from the belief that it is an inherently debasing and fundamentally fucked-up activity. Instead, she can celebrate the joys involved in the pure sexual expression of her work. In addition, with all these other binding strings untied, those onlookers on the outside can let go of petty concerns and critiques about the betrayal of women's liberation represented by the industry, focusing instead on issues more pertinent to real liberation, like screwing our heads back on about sex.

Understanding our own sexual bodies and coming to terms with the implications of that understanding—as largely quite different from what we have learned—is pivotal to arriving at a wholesome and practical sense of self (forming the basic substructure of personal empowerment mandatory for our liberation). It is foundational to appropriately valuing ourselves and others and, therefore, naturally paves the way toward healthy human relationships, on and off the stage. What more could we ask for?

Little Wing

I loved the Magic Mike movies. While I was enchanted just watching those boys move their bodies, it was also great, as a female entertainer, to see a representation of the shoe on the other foot.

Sometimes men come to the gentlemen's club with bitterness toward women making money from stripping. (This has always fascinated me, since that's what you're going to find happening at a strip club.) These guys take direct personal affront to being actually charged for a lap dance, as though they thought if the women in there were truly decent people, they would offer the services for free. I assume much of this reflects on the rotten male-female dynamic happening outside the club where some men are undoubtedly taken to the cleaners financially by entitled, often vindictive women who may be using sex calculatingly as currency to buy favors. Yet why the man who feels sexually frustrated and so manipulated would venture straight into a venue where fee-for-service is the undisguised *basis* of the business, looking for refuge and recompense is, to me, one of the more curious manifestations of human behavior. In part, I have conjectured that perhaps these angry gentlemen enter—knowing precisely what they will find—in search of the conclusive proof of female indecency, to fan the flames of their own misogynistic fury with just this very definitive piece of righteous justification. Ouch. (I'd love to be wrong, but I haven't been able to come up with a better explanation for this phenomenon.)

So one of the things I especially relished in the Magic Mike movies (particularly shown in the first one) was the portrayal of these men *working it* for the tips: working the crowd of women, figuring out how to thrill them into emptying their purses. And what fun it was! The ladies, screaming like banshees, were ecstatic to do so. It showed, reassuringly that this hustling attitude is the nature of the business rather than the noisome nature of conniving women. Every man teetering on this suspicion should see *Magic Mike* for that reason alone.

In the second movie, a talented young man tells his comrades that as male entertainers, they are actually healers. He recognizes the healing power of the role he plays in wholeheartedly giving of his sensual self to his female customers. He sees that injury has been done to them somewhere along the way (by the injurious state of our intimate relational and sexual affairs) and that his services offer a balm of real value.

Now, in my experience, some people refuse to acknowledge and accept this aspect of the industry because of the *money* involved. To me, this is like somebody coming into my massage practice, getting onto my table, and bracing against my touch for the entire session because, since they know they're just paying me to do it, I can't possibly have their best interest at heart. So, of course, they get very little of the nourishing and therapeutic benefits of the massage. Although everyone has varying abilities to really trust and relax, most people don't have that attitude toward massage therapy, and therapists, because *it isn't sex* and thus does not directly stir up the disabling sexual psychology and distrust hidden inside.

However, one could easily make similar arguments and judgments about both. For example, we could say that we should have enough affectionately caring people in our lives to not have to pay someone else to give us a massage, that people in the massage business are preying on the unfortunate folks who do not or cannot get their needs for healing touch nourished organically in their lives. In the sex industry, just exchange the words *sex* and *sensuality* for healing touch (much the same, anyway). Yet in both professions, there are a set of skills and a particular environment involved that can help to meet these needs in a unique way.

And yes, there *is* too often a dearth of healing touch and sexuality, and it is not only okay *but it is a very important thing* that these services are available to satisfy those needs. A monetary transaction does not negate the real value of what is provided in exchange. (Your psychotherapist gets paid, yet the service is gratefully accepted—and the payment unquestioned—in a world that fosters psychological and emotional dysfunction. Your doctor, too, works for money, yet few will question the value of the service in a world, no less, of widespread illness and disease hardly remedied via prayerful beseeches to that loving Creator.)

I've had customers at the club who have had the luxury of abundant female sexual attention throughout their lives, those who have *never* had sex they didn't have to pay for, and everything in between. They all enjoy receiving the services at the strip club, and I strive to offer all the same quality of attention. The truth is, despite the verbal slaughterhouse of the dressing room, and although I still see a lot of the stereotypical drama between men and women at the club, so many of these ladies do, by all means, step into a very openhearted role in servicing their customers. As a result, so many of these patrons benefit greatly.

I can tell immediately whether a customer is embracing the experience or *bracing against* it, and they also know how present and engaged the dancer is in her work. The energies mix or do not mix accordingly, and under the right conditions, a lap dance can be a richly sensual experience offering the very healing and balancing qualities of sex. The most important piece in creating these conditions is found under the ribcage.

Sweet Honey

The secret to a good lap dance is in the diaphragm! In a lap dance, hands down (hee hee), the one who breathes the most receives the most. I know a customer is letting go and *letting it in* during a lap dance when they are breathing. (I've learned to watch for this as a massage therapist, because the same is true in that setting.) If they are holding their breath, they are holding back, and they are missing out big-time.

I've also learned that when I allow myself to breathe during a dance, I am much more present and relaxed (so I always start out with a big sigh in order to get off on the right foot). And I can only be fluid and uninhibited when I'm not bumping up against a customer's resistance or wrestling with their wayward hands.

I think one of the most difficult parts of receiving a lap dance—having experienced this myself—is learning to follow the rules, and in most clubs (whether followed or not), the top rule is, no touching the dancer. It's not the most natural response (to say the least) to just sit there and not touch back, so it takes practice. I think that, oftentimes, enforcing this bodily restraint inadvertently causes a person to hold the breath, quite unconsciously. But when the recipient can break that connection and allow the breath full freedom from restraint, then that sweet honey can flow, and the bodily restraint of the appendages can be more easily forgotten.

I've had customers who sigh like the wind set free so that I feel like rain falling on parched desert earth. That's pure poetry, and I call it the Zen of the lap dance. It is total surrender to the fullness of what *is* happening without fixating on the frustrating desire for what is *not* happening!

Some people are natural experts at this, some have to learn, and some never get it. Sometimes unpleasant odors or truly mismatched chemistry prevent the flow. Sometimes the dancer herself just doesn't have the presence or the energy to give much. Most secrets are not a panacea.

All the Young Dudes

When I first came to live with Steve, I had a recurring theme in my night dreams about hot sex with young guys. The reason for this was transparent: as I mentioned earlier, one of my points of contention about entering into a monogamous relationship with him was that I undeniably wanted a younger version of him.

Dancing at the club gave me lots of exposure to—and attention from—some hot young dudes, and this, no doubt, fanned that flame. For the most part, I deliberately channeled my own attentions back to Steve, but *most* is generally not enough, and so it came to pass that at some point I found myself quite distracted.

I had a particularly strong overall response to an exquisitely attractive young regular who, one day via text message, invited me over for a frolic. (I establish phone contact with regulars I trust so that I can keep them abreast of my erratic schedule.) I was polishing off a tub of frozen yogurt when the text came in and immediately responded with a friendly decline, briefly explaining my situation.

That sequence went off without a hitch, but what followed was what got under my skin. Irresistibly, I began to visualize what that could have looked like with him, and it made me perspire. Steve happened to be out of town, I had the time, I had the desire, he was there ready for me…It occurred to me that this is how these things happen, and suddenly, those stories of surreptitious affairs that *other* people get involved in became very immediately personal. The nearness of the possibility startled me, and part of the distress was in how much it intrigued me, as well as how much it aroused me.

I did not bodily take action on it, but my mind had slipped into the sands of a dangerous territory, and my desire ballooned into a distraction that had a palpable impact on my relationship with Steve. Thoughts of this guy would bubble up while having sex, and I found that these thoughts stirred up my preferences—the yearning for that youthfulness and that novelty that Steve could never satisfy. My sexual responses became noticeably obstructed; my attention became fractured. It wasn't pleasant for either of us, particularly so for Steve. We talked about it a number of times, and he finally asked me if I needed to go have sex with this guy. I seriously contemplated it.

Now, this is where the significance of the truly authentic openness of his suggestion shines. He did not shoot that question at me with barbs of accusation, daring me to destroy the intention of our monogamous commitment, but offered it up in complete vulnerability, having no sure idea of the answer at which I would arrive. He *expected* me to seriously contemplate it and handed me full responsibility to make the choice I needed to make for myself, regardless of how that might affect him, or us, or align with his vision of what was or was not appropriate at this juncture.

Finally, I chose not to have sex with this guy, not from a knee-jerk position that said, "Of course, I can't do that because we're monogamous, and that's not our agreement" (which, I have to say, was my first inclination), but from the place of seriously, unassumingly tuning into the matter at hand at every level within myself to sense the real significance of it and to allow a more anchored, deeply rooted judgment to surface. What arose was a clear realization that I really, badly *wanted to* but that I really, honestly did not *need* to.

Now this may sound like a very simple thing, but to have access to a truly grounded judgment of that nature actually involves a lot of practiced acquaintance with discriminating between our own needs and desires, which requires a reflective, aware, honest, and healthy relationship with ourselves and, of course, with sexuality.

And if the wrong choice is made in a situation like this—like if I really *did* need to do it to complete an emotional, sexual, or psychological gestalt or if, conversely, mistaking the strength of my desire for a need, I really *didn't* need to do it but merely indulged myself— the fallout will be the "dirty laundry" issue, which will stink up the whole house at some point later on down the line.

This kind of circumstance is precisely where nasty little spooks will creep into relationship, so I want to paint out the picture somewhat. The former scenario (restraining or repressing a necessary action) may result in a seed of unfinished business or resentment that may grow into something overblown with time. The latter (taking an unwarranted action) may create complexities or complications that were altogether unnecessary for us to endure, draining energy away from what we are working to manifest between us.

Had Steve come from the less pliable stance of shoving our agreement down my throat to stifle my process and control my behavior, and had I needed to do it and did not, from that same rigid position, I wind up not taking the deepest level of responsibility for my life, which compromises my autonomy and my vitality (as I so sharply learned years ago), and in creeps that subtle resentment. And here's the biggest rub: even in the case where an action is not truly needed—as in this instance with me, Steve, and Hotstuff—if it is not looked at squarely and seriously, the loose ends of that alone may cause turbulence and unrest later on, simply because it was left as an *unknown*, on some level. Sneaky business.

In this situation with us, because I had already previously allowed myself a widely untethered exploration of sex with various men, I had amassed enough hard data to inform my entire being with a complete enough perspective on sex as a whole to create within myself a sense of appeased contentment that, even if not right at the surface, was there to be accessed with a bit of effort. In other words, with sufficient experience, there is the realization that there is no end to the desires that will arise (insatiability), but when enough of those desires have been individually explored, the curiosity need not *necessarily* be attended to (yet even here, we must still be careful to avoid any foregone conclusions). Until this point, however, the curiosity (component of a healthy sexual vitality), unfulfilled, will leave troublesome tracks across the carpet that may be difficult, if not impossible, to remove.

Through honestly tuning into the question at this level and locating a genuine "body-yes" kind of answer (body-yes, in somatic therapy involves a whole mind-body sense of rightness), I was able to put it down and move on without any of the residue that would have remained if I hadn't given myself the depth of permission to take full responsibility for my decision. (I've done enough things inappropriately to have amassed *that* data as well!) I still think of the guy occasionally with a rascally smile but without any lingering lustful longing, wistfully wondering about what goodies I missed out on.

This is serious business, and because sex is such a commanding force of integral significance to personal and relational well-being, it must be regarded with utmost respect.

These are the moments where we take the biggest risks in vulnerability and intimacy, and it's called *being alone together*. What that means is that we are first and foremost alone, as I described in the section "Higher Love." *Then* we are together—in agreement, commitment, companionship. Living up to this requires a fundamental understanding of the principle (the fact of our aloneness), in addition to constant awareness and intention around the way our choices are being made. Relationship unfolds with a much greater depth of pristine harmony when we do not foist upon one another the responsibility for our own well-being. Then the "we" is not an attempted or forced amalgamation but a genuine collaboration between two individuals who understand what it means to be fully responsible for oneself and one's own deepest welfare. And as I described in the chapter on love, this position actually forces us into functioning intimately, because in order to do it, we actually have to tell the truth about who we really are and what we really want and need.

This very basic mode of operation brings us face-to-face with the larger reality that life, if it is to be truly lived, demands a dynamic, active intelligence firing on all pistons, rather than resting on established rules and codes of conduct. Monogamy often lulls us into complacency by offering a deceptive "practical simplicity" to an aspect of life that requires a more sophisticated fluidity. To be handled appropriately, it cannot be tucked smugly into a box and stowed away in a closet, for there it will gather dust and get chewed by moths and mice while we blithely attend to other pressing matters.

Beyond this first instance, successfully hurdled, there were a number of others who stood out over the years. The adorable Berkeley Boy—had I been twenty years younger and unattached—I would have joined promptly after my shift for journeys northward.

Montana Man, a massive hunk of burning bronze, made me lubricate just by entering the establishment, pressing up hot and hard against my established boundaries. "Monet" was not so easy on the eyes but surprised me with a wild chemistry that left me reeling for weeks. The "Saver," who, unfathomably, looked like a cross between Vin Diesel and Dwayne Johnson—*so* easy on the eyes I was nervous as a preteen to approach—was the sweetest sensation of all, literally inspiring me to recite poetry in parting.

And with one delicious darling, I actually had to cut off the lap dances, because I knew just one more song and I'd be making out with him. He had come up to the stage as my set began, and we instantly locked into each other, spontaneously declaring in unison, a visceral agreement of powerful attraction. "Ooh, yeahh." That moment felt like sex, my words and his, coming through my body like a velvet orgasm, and I will never forget that moment of pure sexual response and raw, potent connection. Fascinatingly, this moment smacks of that fantasy I used to endlessly simmer in my vat of indulgent adolescent romanticism. Back then I would have taken it to mean so many things. Now, however, I was able to enjoy it as a magnificent, mutual, steaming-hot moment, and nothing more.

These were some of the most memorable provocations, and they all gave me lessons in balancing the openness with restraint, allowing others to inspire me (both above and below the waistline) without disrupting the finite bounds of a greater commitment; in appreciating fully the awesome beauty of other men and gracefully letting them go; in bringing the arousal back into the relationship at hand, staying settled (with hard work) and intimately attuned within its parameters; in coming to terms with the insatiability of desire (*so many men, so little me!*); and finally, in recognizing that the *body* does not understand sexual restraint, so if there's going to be an unpolluted, untangled emergence from this kind of jungle, there had better be some serious depth of emotional, psychological, and philosophical understanding to sort it all out (as well as a full and healthy physical outlet—in other words, *sex* with my partner).

Superstition

I have a confession. At the time of this writing, I have still not entirely allowed the identity of my alter ego full, unchecked freedom outside the closet. Yes, my family knows and my friends all know… but when my bank teller eyes my fistfuls of cash, wondering aloud if I'm a waitress, I smile and say softly, "Mm, something like that."

When our beloved realtor gasps her breathless dismay about her son driving around with *strippers in his car*, as she transports us—in her car—to an open house, we jab each other with ironic elbows, still opting to keep the puss in the pouch.

When people ask me *what I do*, rather than telling them I rustle up dollar bills dancing on dicks, I generally offer up my more conservative occupation as a therapist. I do this to blend in, to slip under the radar, and also to avoid potential glitches showing up because of the snap judgments that may surface as a result of stating that I'm a *stripper* (plus, my additional remaining aversion, for fairly obvious reasons, to telling people in the same breath that I am both a massage therapist *and* a stripper).

Off the stage, I enjoy the underappreciated privilege of being possibly one of the most inconspicuous entities you are ever liable to forget, and I have viewed protecting that anonymity as a component of stealthy efficiency. I am generally not interested in the undue attention and explanations involved, inviting unwelcome gestures my way, being labeled, marked, judged, suspiciously eyeballed, or inordinately waylaid.

I enjoy judiciously exposing the juicier data here and there at my own discretion, when I'm feeling curious, rambunctious, and adventurous, or otherwise up to contending with whatever might ensue as a result. Many times, choosing this route has resulted in very positive, real, and lively interactions, but positive or negative, I'm usually just interested in a quick, smooth, in-and-out style of business as I move through my daily world.

My vigilance is also calculated in response to the fact that a stripper does run into acute stereotyping. When I was just becoming acquainted with a now-close friend of mine and we got to the part about me being a stripper, his first response was that oh, he could see why I would wind up doing that, given my struggles with self-esteem. Poor me. I just burst out laughing, because his assumption about my involvement in stripping—the inevitable result of a malignant attraction to an inherently degrading activity—was so utterly and absurdly off the mark. (Of course, I came to it only as I began to really *step into* my self-esteem, only able to dare making that kind of ballsy expression as a *result* of my growing confidence, and to value myself enough to aggressively prevent living with regrets.)

My friend's assumption echoes that same attitude I encountered among the women in my liberal college circle twenty-five years ago. These echoes are hokum reflecting off the walls inside a claustral box in which there's little room to stretch the elbows beyond trite moralistic conclusions, and they come from both left and right. That liberal bunch views you as a traitor to the cause of female emancipation from the tyrannies of patriarchy—you are willingly undermining feminist progress by playing yourself into the hands of their manipulative, objectifying domain and thus feeding into the male tradition of female degradation. The conservative bunch, on the other hand, views you as evil incarnate—you are succumbing to the devil that pleads from your nasty vaginal groin, spoiling God's plan, destroying the fabric of the nation, and so forth. Then, in an uppish gesture of magnanimity, the two parties join hands to pity you, as a casualty of the tragic dehumanizing commoditization of people in the sex industry.

Together, both camps transform the character of ordinary women into extreme, polar caricatures—from unscrupulous scandal or wicked demon to pitiful victim of circumstance. But hey, it makes everyone more comfortable when things are back to black and white. And then here we are hating one another again.

The smug certainty that leeches onto the package of presumptions that constitute a stereotype is deceivingly cozy and is certain, in time, to render its host a fool. It doesn't take Einstein to recognize it. Every stripper knows the customer who swaggers into her personal space like the self-appointed patron saint of the damned, making statements that go along with every sort of assumption about how damaged and desperate—not to mention lacking in the smarts department—she certainly must be in order to do what she does. I can tell from a mile away when I'm being pigeonholed because of the certainty of the assumptions and the flagrant irrelevance of the statements. Once somebody has me stereotyped, we're no longer people having an interaction. Paradoxically, that's when I know I've truly been turned into an object, and the only time I feel annoyed by it. At some point, like the mind-fuck, I just have to walk away.

Suffragette City

I see, however, that my reticence about making full disclosure of my multifaceted identity, anytime and anywhere, is actually a disservice to my sisters-in-arms. True commitment to the cause requires a trooper ready and willing to walk straight into the line of fire and deal with anything and everything that comes along with that. (Perhaps writing this book can offer me a little slice of redemption?)

Intriguingly, paying attention to women in porn reveals a number of intrepid feminine soldiers—*femme fatales* for the ultimate destruction of female sexual repression. Nina Hartley, my idol who's been rocking the porn world for over thirty years, is surely one of these heroines of our day. In the course of her hearty activism as a sex-positive feminist, she says people frequently ask her how she can be a *feminist* and do what she does. Her response: "Easy. My body, my rules."[130] Period. She also shines a beacon into that darkness (and simultaneously challenges that adversarial attitude about sex) by pointing out that "sex isn't something men do to you. It isn't something men get out of you. Sex is something you dive into with gusto and like it every bit as much as he does."[131]

One of my most longstanding regulars (and friend) from the club introduced me to the material of the adorable Spanish porn starlet Amarna Miller, whom I mentioned earlier. Perusing her blog, I found the intellectual extension of her persona addressing, along with a large bulk of adoringly positive feedback (from both men and

---

[130] *X-Rated 2: The Greatest Adult Stars of All Time* (Showtime, 2016).

[131] en.wikipedia.org/wiki/Nina_Hartley#Sex_positive_activism.

women), a deluge (also from both men and women) of the same old overripe slurry that people like to dump out of their festering bowels onto women who boldly buck sexual convention. Coming from women, this excrement smells like misery demanding company (which I'll explore in the next chapter), whereas from men, the odor reeks of fearful control. But who wins here?

Well, frankly, those (the damned) daring dames do, because once they have stepped over the threshold onto the other side, it's obvious whose ass is truly hanging out. Once a woman has her head on straight, it's very easy to see clearly. I'd say we're just laughing *our* asses off, but that's only half the woeful story, because when you really understand the tragic immensity of the big joke with the whole of your being, it brings up grief and anger as well, which takes all the fun out of winning.

That's why young Miriam Weeks (porn actress Belle Knox), notoriously exposed as the Duke University school-girl-gone-bad, is "defending herself in every forum that will have her."[132] The intelligent law student says, "Normally when a sex scandal happens, a girl gets outed, she gets shamed, and then she goes into hiding. But I refuse to be shamed." (I immediately think of Monica Lewinsky, who, in order to escape from the persecuting masses after the inordinate presidential scandal, retreated to the UK to live, study, and put her life back together. She says that scarlet letter "A"—albatross—is hung around your neck and once it's there, "it's a bitch to remove."[133]) That's also why Weeks was inspired, through her experience in and out of porn, to become a lawyer who fights for the rights of women and sex workers.[134]

---

[132] "The School of Hard-Core Knox," *Penthouse Magazine*, Women's Studies, June 2014.

[133] www.vanityfair.com/style/society/2014/06/monica-lewinsky-humiliation-culture.

[134] In the course of her academic studies, she was rejected from volunteering at a clinic overseas on the basis that "it would be inappropriate for her to work with children" because obviously such a woman is a grave danger, lacking in the decent humanity required for humanitarian work, particularly with our beloved *asexual* children who will certainly be putrefied by her very presence.

It's not at all surprising that some of the most enlightened and level-headed feminists (and, therefore, the most powerful and effective advocates for women's liberation) are actually the women happily involved in the very things that traditional libbers despise most. Take a moment to think about the implications of that. It indicates that there is certainly a most discomforting flaw in the "liberal" thinking, a flaw involving female sexual identity and expression that needs to be investigated and rectified. And I believe it is hidden within the us-versus-them paradigm at the heart of the ongoing gender conflict.

The original feminists rightfully identified a problem in female sexual objectification under the domination of an oppressive patriarchy and then (a certain contingent) wrongly focused, reactively, on censorship and condemnation of the sex trade rather than—through a progressive and enlightened understanding of sex—transforming the industry from the inside out (which now many more "radical" feminists, internationally, are actively working to do). This censorship-and-condemnation approach is as futile and backward as trying to outlaw abortion and prostitution and prohibit the consumption of alcohol and drugs. It creates a dangerous and costly "criminal" world of black-market, pimp-riddled, back-alley recourses.

The militant side of feminism that has emerged in the fight for equal rights is only a natural backlash, and an inevitable part, in the process of demanding freedom from militant oppressors reluctant to relinquish that stance. It has a reason and serves a purpose in time and place. But facing off in a military manner leaves its trails of hostility, such as the us-against-them tension that continues to haunt our daily lives. Nowadays, from what I see, truly radical feminism is not militant man-hating (the equivalent of desperate "suckers" that shoot off a troubled tree trunk) but strong, sex-positive feminine forces that are going back to heal the *root* of our shared human sexuality by openly, aggressively, and unabashedly reclaiming female eroticism. It's obvious that when women discover what is really available within themselves sexually, it's a big deal (which is why it has been so feared and fiercely controlled) and it's worth a lot. It is vitally empowering and overwhelmingly positive.

The wonderfully terrifying truth about the sexual empowerment of women is that, ultimately, everybody wins. I say "terrifying" because often the thought of ending the fight is actually scary when being a soldier is all you think you know (as represented by the gays and East Germans I highlighted in an earlier chapter). Putting the war behind us and coagulating ourselves into a new peacetime identity is a grandiose reinventing of our social and sexual landscape, inside and out, for the good of all. Warren Farrell, the soft-spoken, warmhearted (ironic) center of the crunchy, hardened movement the MRA (men's rights activism), states the obvious: "All women's issues are to some degree men's issues and all men's issues are to some degree women's issues, because when either sex wins unilaterally, both sexes lose."[135] What could be more simple and clear?

Furthermore, in *Sex at Dawn*, the authors point out that in studies of extant matriarchies, where women are "in power," the consistent observation is that of a highly egalitarian and openly sexual overall sociopolitical structure. They do not, as many expect, tend to be a "mirror image of patriarchy," and this is due to "the differing ways males and females conceptualize and wield power." They go on to say, "Societies in which women have lots of autonomy and authority tend to be decidedly male-friendly, relaxed, tolerant, and plenty sexy. Got that, fellas?"[136]

So while the fear is a natural response to any pivotal change, it is unfounded on both sides. I believe, *in theory*, we could be well on our way toward that kind of society if only we can, each of us, manage to undo the inordinate damage incurred to our sexual, and thus gender, identities. This means becoming peaceful warriors, which means instead of fighting *each other*, we're fighting the good, hard fight for *sexual freedom*. This situation cannot (and will not) resolve itself unless (and until) the "us" that we have become is transformed into a different entity altogether. Then (and only then) can it fall away.

And, again, this is really a one-by-one affair, solitary and sometimes lonely at the outset. The new peaceful warriors of this "move-

---

[135] warrenfarrell.com.

[136] Ryan and Jetha, 133–34.

ment" (if I may!) must possess and cultivate the inner strength and integrity to meet this truth and persevere.

Glory Box

I see the reality of this potential win-win scenario manifest in my work as a stripper. What it involves is a kind of innocence and nothing else. It's a truly gorgeous thing that bubbles up in those women who have tapped into their erotic reservoir and enjoy the art of expressing it. That innocence is a generous, wholehearted, sexually embodied and empowered spirit of the "giveaway" (in the Native American sense of thanksgiving, from the abundance model). In this context, what is being given is the openhearted, straightforward expression of relating, personally and sensually, to another human being, sympathetically, with no presumptions, suspicions, or hidden agendas. What this allows, and fosters, is the like reflection that resides within the other person—often hidden, guarded, buried, and forgotten—beneath the protective armor shielding that innocence along their own bumpy journey through life. This gesture alone can be so disarming that it melts away any misgivings one may have harbored against the openly transactional environment of the strip club. (Again, the exchange of money is not the problem here.)

Now, imagine how many grievances, injuries, misgivings, and hostilities will melt away in the environment of everyday relations when we can crawl out of our protective shells and enjoy an unencumbered sexuality together, beyond all the exasperating adversity.

RIP HER TO SHREDS

But for the serious suffragettes to gain and maintain solid footing, we need much more *solidarity*. There's too much catfighting going on in our midst that I think is actually the result of historical oppression combined with sexual immaturity. What I'm saying is, on a certain level, *we have met the enemy and they is us!*

When I was sixteen, in a desperate attempt to escape from the intolerable tyranny of my older sister, I arranged to finish high school as an exchange student overseas. Since I already suffered a lonely alienation from my American peers, I could see no wisdom in traveling to a country in which a language barrier would present an even further sense of isolation, so I chose the little British Commonwealth country of New Zealand. It was attractively situated about as far away from my miserable life as I could envision on the globe, and it was intriguingly off the mainstream radar—as opposed to Australia, which smacked to me at the time of a more rowdy, hayseed kind of place to which I felt I'd had enough exposure in my rural-Oregon neck of the woods. I knew nothing from *nada*, but I felt an affectionate allure toward that little squiggle of earth protruding from the far South Pacific.

I learned I would be living on the east coast of the South Island, attending an all-girls school in the small town of Oamaru, about a three hours' drive south of Christchurch. I remember the sinking feeling around knowing I would be attending school without boys, who represented both a source of excitement and stability to me at that time of my life. I had no idea what to expect, but it was certainly daunting since I'd observed many of my female peers, from a safe (yet painfully lonely) distance, to be horrifyingly catty, conniving, and cutthroat.

So what's up with those girls anyway? Many sources observe that while males within peer groups manifest a high degree of rather volatile competitive aggression among themselves, theirs tends to be pretty direct, straightforward, and swiftly forgotten, with little impact on the overall peer social structure. Females, on the other hand, appear to function with more indirect and relational aggression, their rivalries insisting on the maintenance of a stern status quo, with fierce sororities cultivating deeply punitive grudges that may result in permanent ostracism of a member who upsets the group tempo.

This kind of precarious social environment exaggerates the development of a deep, baseline insecurity, because even if you are decidedly *in* the in-group, you know how it works and that to maintain status requires strictly adhering to the rules, which squelches individuality and expression. This, added to the subtle-but-ubiquitous undercurrent of (and sometimes blatantly overt) cultural discrimination of her gender, her anatomy, and her inmost sexuality, leads all too frequently to profound levels of dysfunction centered upon such deep-seated insecurity. Although this vulnerability can, and often does, *drive* a particular type-A kind of woman to excel in the world, she cannot thrive so much internally and relationally with such a deeply hidden insecurity driving her. If in place, this kind of insecurity can end up being a handicap to realizing one's full potential and balanced well-being.

Phyllis Chesler, an old-school American feminist and author of *Woman's Inhumanity to Woman* (for which she received sharp criticism from her feminist contemporaries for focusing and elaborating on the darker side of women), reveals many anecdotal accounts of women's calculating, devious, manipulative, and underhanded attacks upon one another, even within the solidarity of the women's movement. She points out, with female rivalries tending to support the status quo, that "in order to improve their own lot, most women, like men, collude in the subordination of women as a class," psychologically taming one another into conformity.[137]

Not shockingly, she calls in the primates, as many seekers will do to find an explanation for our perplexing behaviors hidden in the genes of our furry Darwinian ancestors. You have undoubtedly noticed that I am not a squealing fan of evolutionary psychology. I find it to be a far too speculative and presumptuous approach to a field concerning something so malleable and highly susceptible to social, cultural, environmental—and even totally random—circumstances. I don't believe one itty-bitty smidgen that we are programmed by genetic evolution to be such snide sisters. (Chesler admits that she, also, does not conclude this.) I do not deny the nearly identical nature of our primate genetics, but again, our social behaviors are a far more direct reflection (barring clinical pathology) of socialization and social climate rather than genetic blueprint. Even apes show this behavioral malleability, while study after study of human behavior has shown its highly contextual nature.[138] As social creatures, natural selection has favored this social pliability. In other words, we "survive" as social creatures by shaping our behavior in response to outward conditions.

With all this in mind, it appears that the patterns of woman-to-woman hostility *are rooted in a culture of gender inequality and sexual disempowerment* that contribute to a rampant sense of deep-seated insecurity. Chesler suggests that as an oppressed group, women need one another too much emotionally—need the security of other women's overt conformity for a sense of empowerment in solidarity—and are far less tolerant and forgiving of the trespasses of other women

---

[137] Phyllis Chesler, *Woman's Inhumanity to Woman* (New York: Thunder's Mouth Press / Nation Books, 2001), 37.

[138] Jane Goodall's studies revealed dramatic behavioral shifts among chimps in the wild as a result of altered feeding patterns that in turn change the chimp's social dynamics and hierarchy; the "broken windows" theory illustrates the way humans' criminal behavior can be elicited by unkempt surroundings; the Stanford Prison Experiment is a common example of how people's behavior can be distorted beyond their own self-recognition by the circumstances in which they function.

than those of men (upon whom they feel more dependent in other ways), thus *upholding* the odious double standards. This security dynamic among women is anything but empowering; it ultimately amounts to a sister-squelching system that fears and attacks another woman's strength, truth, and individuality (and the *sense of solidarity* is just that, an airy feeling with no solidity).

The sexual disempowerment of women is perpetuated to the third degree through this discouraging system. According to scientists at McMaster University, their research shows that women themselves effectively suppress one another's sexuality, fiercely stigmatizing female promiscuity through the infamous "slut-shaming" often blamed on men. They say that with sex coveted by men, women accordingly "limit access as a way of maintaining advantage in the negotiation of this resource" and that "women who make sex too readily available compromise the power-holding position of the group, which is why many women are particularly intolerant of women who are, *or seem to be*, promiscuous."[139] (Flashback to my best friend in the professional environment, where her mere unconventional presence was enough to aggravate her female colleagues. And I am fortunate to have been quite comfortable—beyond awkward adolescence—being a fringe-dweller, for I would have had some real struggles trying to function as an adult within a large social circle once I endeavored a boldly open sexual lifestyle.)

This brings us full circle back to my comment in the first chapter about the power of women in our society often being relegated to a willingness or reluctance to acquiesce sexually. And here we are, looking straight into the face of our own complicity in this predicament. This is the manifestation of *modern sexism* and represents one example of the many ways women have unknowingly internalized sexist values. Chesler writes about cross-cultural studies that have "shown that grown women target and shun other women, most often for violating patriarchal norms."[140] In Islamic culture, women's own gossip

---

[139] John Tierney, "A Cold War Fought by Women," *New York Times*, November 18, 2013.

[140] Chesler, 151.

actually "creates the climate in which the [honor killing] of a young woman is inevitable,"[141] and this is just an extreme example of how the casual behavior of women actively participating in the "rumor system" are "faithful collaborators [who uphold] the oppressive traditions of the patriarchal regime which are directed against them."[142] She makes it very clear in her book that this type of female-female dynamic directly aids the perpetuation of the inequality of women in the patriarchal arrangement and that, therefore, in order to finally bring about the equality we desire, this behavior must stop.

Obviously, the happiest way (perhaps even the *only* way) out of this baleful state of affairs is to fully uncover the basic fact that men are not the only human animals that covet sex, that the female sexual appetite is, with its estrogen-softened edges, equally grandiose. And the way to do that is to just start digging and removing one heaping shovelful at a time from the towering landfill that sits on top of it (Yes, it *is* hard walkin' on that stuff, Porky Pine!)[143]

This will shift the sexual economy out of our deluded and outdated scarcity-model belief system and, as a result, bring us closer to the overall achievement of gender equality.

My first observations of the social landscape at Oamaru's Waitaki Girls High School revealed two radically distinct cultures of females, comprised of the "day girls" and the "boarders," who obviously took little interest in one another. Even through the thick kiwi accent, to which I was not yet acclimated, I could immediately detect the universal vernacular of the snarl behind their references to one another.

Nevertheless, Waitaki turned out to be my saving grace as an insecure, awkward teenager. The girls from both camps were friendly and accepting: as an exchange student hosted by families living in town, I came and left the school campus to the rhythm of the day

---

[141] Chesler, 161.

[142] Chesler, 164.

[143] From Walt Kelly's 1970 Earth Day poster featuring characters from his comic strip *Pogo,* including the line, "We have met the enemy and he is us," a parody of a famous dispatch from the US Navy commander in the war of 1812.

culture, yet being away from my own home and family, I was also akin to the boarder bunch, just boarding off campus.

The boarders became my inner circle of sisters, as they drew me in most warmly to their saucy, irreverent, close-knit family of peers in a way I had not experienced before. I could scarcely believe my fortune at finding myself part of a nuclear group of smart, edgy girls whom I found both fun and admirable. (In fact, I was so filled with happy contentment at finally *not* feeling like a lonely outsider among my female peers that I do not remember once missing the presence of boys that year. I was making up for lost girl-time!)

Within their group, the girls were just a mass of friends and acquaintances, some closer than others, some with more friction than others. But I never witnessed the kind of nasty backstabbing and gossip that took place among the American girls at home. These girls just seemed more stable and content within their own skin, in my estimation, and I felt at ease with them. Even the rift between the boarders and day girls didn't involve any inordinate drama beyond a chafed disinterest.

The school environment was uniquely dynamic and politic. I watched in awe the peer mentoring system at work among the girls at school and was deeply impressed watching the older girls graciously step into their big-sister guidance roles. Although it was an official program promoted by the school, it was obvious that the girls took pride and initiative in both its organization and institution.

I do believe that the absence of boys on campus likely streamlined the girls' attention, enhancing the efficacy of their endorsement of one another. But I also believe that such mentorship programs would help foster an attitude of support and camaraderie among young women in co-ed schools as well and that, along with faculty guidance, it should be seriously developed and implemented. This approach shifts the students' energies from competition to teamwork while developing worthwhile social (and rudimentary professional) skills rather than childish initiation rituals for the humiliation and degradation of "lower classmen" upon which many American high school students expend their creative resources.

Transferring to Waitaki, I stepped into an altogether different world from my rural American high school. The level of maturity, both socially and academically, expected of these students was far above anything I'd encountered at Baker High. My seventh-form music instructor literally looked at me cross-eyed before immediately transferring me to the third-form curriculum in music theory, which translates as a high school senior taking eighth-grade level instruction. I barely managed to keep my feet up with the approaching pavement in my English class, as I was expected to write intelligent critical analyses of Shakespeare, which had never even been so much as required reading material in my entire education. I was so far behind these kids it was preposterous.

It was clear that the faculty treated their subjects and their students with a level of respect and seriousness that challenged students and invited them to step forward into an advanced level of personal and intellectual responsibility. I was not used to this; it scared me, and it impressed me.

Go Sister, Soul Sister

It would be totally inappropriate, and highly inaccurate, to draw broad cultural inferences from my experience at Waitaki, but my simple conclusion is that in many environments (though certainly not all), maturity fosters maturity.

If we cultivate maturity within ourselves and *expect* a level of social maturity among one another, it will spread. This is thanks to that innate social malleability that got us into the sexual mess in the first place! Only now we're taking charge of it instead of being led around on a leash by it.

If we respect one another's individuality—appearance, intelligence, expression, sexuality—rather than fearing it as a threat, we will nurture that in one another and face its challenges within ourselves. Facing inner challenges, rather than retreating or trying to condemn, control, and manipulate others, results in inner strength and personal power that enable greater capacity and higher functioning across all areas of life. This kind of "core" strength is a dignity and an integrity that cannot itself be manipulated or taken away. With regard to how we treat each other as women, we urgently need to change our tune if we really want to manifest true feminist empowerment for ourselves.

When I think of that gorgeous orgy of women I watched on video, I think of how different our lives as women would be if we could love our own and one another's sexuality so wholeheartedly. But, orgy or no orgy, we have to embrace our sisters as ourselves, turn our pockets inside out, and together heal all forms of internalized misogyny. It is up to each woman, one by one, to simply opt out. Ending the (un)sisterly rivalry is a matter of willfully and deliberately stepping outside the fray. That means no further participation in the juicy drama of the "girlfriend" culture and, instead, digging our heels into the rich soil of emotional and relational maturity. Just like the forethought in the flammable environment at the strip club, a little reflective awareness goes a long way.

Chesler's final chapter is worth a lot, and she says that women have been internalizing sexism for so long that this value structure will not disappear immediately. She explains that the practice of sisterhood is a *psychological and ethical discipline* that requires a strong and independent mind and spirit, self-love, and the courage of perseverance. Finally, she concludes, "Woman's inhumanity to woman is painful, powerful, and paralyzing. I would like women to learn to use their power in generous, not envious ways."[144]

She says it all but the one thing nobody will say. And this is that the solution lies in *sexual* healing and *sexual* empowerment. Nobody is willing to dive headlong into this bucket of sauce the way I'm doing, because *real* sexual healing and empowerment entails, well, sex. Lots of sex (gitchi yaya *mama*!)[145]. And, evidently, that's just awfully unpleasant. Am I missing something? Anyone? Anyone?

---

[144] Chesler, 473–5.

[145] "Gitche yaya dada" meant "get your sex, daddy" in Labelle's song, "Lady Marmalade," Epic, 1974

ROCK ON

In Belarus, during World War II, the Bielski brothers (Tuvia, Zus, and Asael) fled from the Nazi regime into the forest where they aided the survival of roughly 1,200 of their fellow Jews over a period of about three years, from 1941 to 1944. In the cinematic portrayal of the story, *Defiance*, Zus chooses to fight for a while, blood for blood, by joining the Russian army. At first—enraged by the atrocities that claimed his mother, father, wife, and child—he denigrates his older brother for "hiding out." But Tuvia stays to lead the refugee community, saying, "Our revenge is our survival."

During their time in the forest, the members of the camp were forbidden to procreate, allowing them to concentrate their resources on their own survival. By bringing new lives into their untenable situation, they would jeopardize their own success, and therefore, any new life bore nothing but the burden of casualty. They had to understand this very clearly and practice it unshakeably. Since World War II, however, the survivors who emerged from the forest of Belarus have reproduced over five generations, resulting in some nineteen thousand Jews who were "never supposed to exist."[146]

Likewise, everything we do to piece together a viable entity from the fragments of our war-torn sexuality and turn ourselves into whole, healthy sexual beings is defiance against the forces that struggle incessantly to defeat us. Resurrection of our vibrant sexual selves is our shining requital. And just like the camp of survivors, as we

---

[146] Interviews with Robert Bielski, son of Tuvia, and Zvi Bielski, son of Zus. *Defiance*, 2008, DVD bonus features.

struggle to heal a tattered and persecuted sexuality, tending vigilantly to our own shoddy business must come first before we can imagine that we are doing any favors to anyone else, let alone our children. The pithy, sage advice, that we must *become the change we wish to see,* has become quasi cliché on the surface but harbors radical revolutionary truth, and the only real durable solution.

For our "daughters," we need to reinvent the feminine legacy by becoming sexually enlightened role models, and that means learning how to be that which we were not taught. Achieving this—and using our power—requires us to literally take back our bodies and our minds, reclaiming and restoring all the forbidden territories of our anatomical, physiological, emotional, psychological, and social existence as sexual creatures. Such effort will gradually begin to revive, repair, and reshape the entire social landscape, so we've got to be smart about it. All the nonsexual issues must be addressed in order to get the sexual stuff right. And we have to get the sexual points in question ironed out, or else all the other garbage will find itself reinvested more deeply into our beings. To update an old saying from the women's movement, "taking back the night" should not be viewed merely as reference to reclaiming our safety to walk the streets after dark, but should be understood as a call to arms against all the dark, unenlightened elements we carry inside ourselves, sexual and otherwise.

This is not a battle of women against men, or women against women. It's an internal campaign against all that separates us from our deeper, inner, natural selves. It's the struggle of a single aware entity, surfacing through all the muck and mire that has been overlaid for centuries on top of us all. Time to rise, and take a deep breath of fresh air.

This is, in all respects, a full-time job (the activist quintet Sweet Honey in the Rock sing, "*we who believe in freedom cannot rest*"). But we're talking about rock and roll, baby—I mean, how much more fun could a job be?

From this time, unchained,
We're all looking for a different picture.
Through this new frame of mind
A thousand flowers could bloom.
Move over and give us some room.

—Portishead, "Glory Box"

PLAYLIST

*The Blues had an illegitimate baby and
we named it Rock 'n Roll.*

—Little Richard

**In the early 1950s, Cleveland radio disc jockey,
Alan Freed, popularized the term "rock 'n roll,"
which was black slang for having sex.**

Hot Blooded, Foreigner
Under Pressure, Queen & David Bowie
Swinging, Tom Petty
What's Going On, Marvin Gaye
Beast of Burden, The Rolling Stones
I'm a Lover, Not a Fighter, The Kinks (original blues standard by Lazy Lester)
Witchy Woman, The Eagles
Dead End Justice, Joan Jett
Us and Them, Pink Floyd
Let the Children Play, Santana
Communication Breakdown, Led Zeppelin
Paint it Black, The Rolling Stones
American Girl, Tom Petty
Ball of Confusion, The Temptations
A Life of Illusion, Joe Walsh
L.A. Woman (Mr. Mojo Risin'), The Doors
Mama Weer All Crazy Now, Joan Jett

Like a Virgin, Madonna
Cherry Pie, Warrant
Brilliant Disguise, Bruce Springsteen
Here Comes My Girl, Tom Petty
Train in Vain, The Clash
Stairway to Heaven, Led Zeppelin
Highway to Hell, AC/DC
Have a Cigar, Pink Floyd
Vive L'Amour, Harvard Krokodiloes
Don't Do Me Like That, Tom Petty
Born to be Wild, Steppenwolf
First Flash of Freedom, Tom Petty
Go Ask Alice, Jefferson Airplane
Free Fallin', Tom Petty
Goodbye, Yellow Brick Road, Elton John
Yellow Brick Road, Kris Delmhorst
Higher Love, Steve Winwood
Goodbye Stranger, Supertramp
Dirty Laundry, Don Henley
Such a Woman, Neil Young
Into the Great Wide Open, Tom Petty
I Shall Be Released, Bob Dylan
Bad Reputation, Joan Jett
Thorn Tree in the Garden, Derek and The Dominoes
Red Headed Stranger, Willie Nelson
Call Me Super Bad, James Brown
Tougher Than the Rest, Bruce Springsteen
Oh Woe is Me, Joan Jett
Wouldn't it Be Nice, The Beach Boys
Dear Mr. Fantasy, Traffic
Tell the Truth, Derek and the Dominoes
What's Love Got to do With It, Tina Turner
It's Raining Men, The Weather Girls
Waiting for a Miracle, Leonard Cohen
Wild is the Wind, David Bowie
Rusty Cage, Johnny Cash

I Want a New Drug, Huey Lewis & The News
Love Stinks, J. Geils Band
Addicted to Love, Robert Palmer
Super Freak, Rick James
(I Can't Get No) Satisfaction, The Rolling Stones
When Doves Cry, Prince
Breakdown, Tom Petty
She's Not There, Santana (originally by The Zombies)
Janie's got a Gun, Aerosmith
Little Red Corvette, Prince
Boys and Girls, Blur
Take It to the Limit, The Eagles
Let's Get It On, Marvin Gaye
Speak to Me, Pink Floyd
The Thrill is Gone, B.B. King
Walking on Broken Glass, Annie Lennox
Sexual Healing, Marvin Gaye
My Generation, The Who
Won't Get Fooled Again, The Who
Good Morning Little School Girl, Johnny Lang
Lost in the Supermarket, The Clash
The Boxer, Simon & Garfunkel
Louder Than Words, Pink Floyd
Burning Down the House, The Talking Heads
I Need to Know, Tom Petty
One of My Kind, INXS
Across the Universe, The Beatles
Come Together, The Beatles
Freedom, Richie Havens (inspired from the Afro-American spiritual, "Motherless Child")
Who Are You, The Who
(What's So Funny 'Bout) Peace, Love, and Understanding, Elvis Costello
This Is Your Life, The Dust Brothers
Main Man, T. Rex
Jump!, Van Halen

I and I, Bob Dylan
Stuck With You, Huey Lewis & The News
Let's Get it Started, The Black Eyed Peas
As Tears Go By, The Rolling Stones
Eyesight to the Blind, Aerosmith
Stroke Me, Billy Squier
Eyes on the Prize, Mavis Staples
More Bounce to the Ounce, Zapp & Roger
Sex Machine, James Brown
You Shook Me All Night Long, AC/DC
Roadhouse Blues, The Doors
Pressure Drop, The Clash (originally by Toots & The Maytals)
Just Like a Woman, Bob Dylan
I Get By, Everlast
With a Little Help from My Friends, The Beatles
We Can Be Heroes, David Bowie
All She Wants to Do is Dance, Don Henley
I Need a Man, Eurythmics
Strange Brew, Cream
Hey Lawdy Mama, Buddy Moss
Shake Your Money Maker, The Black Crowes (original blues standard by Elmore James)
Time Waits for No One, The Rolling Stones
What It's Like, Everlast
She Works Hard for the Money, Donna Summer
Money For Nothin', Dire Straits
Sweetheart Like You, Bob Dylan
Shelter From the Storm, Bob Dylan
It Ain't Me Babe, Bob Dylan
New Attitude, Patti LaBelle
Material Girl, Madonna
Bad, Bad Thing, Chris Isaak
Little Wing, Jimi Hendrix
Sweet Honey, Slightly Stoopid
All the Young Dudes, David Bowie
Superstition, Stevie Wonder

Suffragette City, David Bowie
Glory Box, Portis Head
Rip Her to Shreds, Blondie
Lady Marmalade, Labelle
I Fought the Law, The Clash
Ella's Song, Sweet Honey In the Rock
Rock On, David Essex

APPENDIX

I FOUGHT THE LAW

If you really want to get agitated about something, look into the criminalization of your sexuality. Go straight out and locate *America's War on Sex*, by Marty Klein, and read it cover to cover. You'll be going cross-eyed, emitting steam, ready to go on a personal mission to make a statement of any kind.

That's exactly what Steve and I did, with Klein's book just adding a nice hefty kick to an impetus that had been building up in us both for quite some time. (It also added massively to the growing pressure behind doing my own expressive writing as an outlet, resulting in this book.) Based upon the data we were able to acquire about the specific laws restricting sexual expression between consenting adults in each state across the nation, we outlined a plan to travel to each one of these states (and the capital) in order to break every single one of those laws that pertained to us. Following is a list of what we found. (It is the list we worked from; it is now outdated, but at the time, we believed it to be accurate.)

Among consenting adults,
(28) *adultery* is illegal in twenty-eight states,[147]
(9) *unmarried sex* is illegal in nine,[148]

---

[147] AL, AZ, CA, CO, FL, GA, ID, IL, KS, MD, MA, MI, MN, MS, NE, NV, NH, NY, NC, ND, OK, RI, SC, TN, UT, VA, WV, WI.
[148] GA, ID, MA, MS, NC, RI, SC, UT, VA.

> (8) eight states have a law against *unmarried people living together*,[149]
>
> (32) *sex and/or marriage with a first cousin* is illegal in thirty-two,[150]
>
> (28) twenty-eight states outlaw *pornography*,[151]
>
> (19) having a *visible erection* (even while clothed) is against the law in nineteen states,[152]
>
> (17) seventeen states outlaw *oral sex* with either the same or opposite gender,[153]
>
> (7) seven deem *oral sex* illegal only with the same sex,[154]
>
> (15) fifteen states outlaw *anal sex* with either gender,[155]
>
> (9) in nine states *anal sex* is illegal with the same sex only,[156] and
>
> (49) *prostitution* is outlawed in all states but Nevada.

Of these eleven laws, there amounted to five that applied directly to us, that we could confront within the bounds of our arrangement. And so we set out across the nation, by plane and by automobile, having oral, anal, unmarried sex, flaunting visible erections, and enhancing our saucy capers with a variety of pornographic materials along the way. One by one, we crossed off all the forty-one states with any of those five laws in place.

It took us four years to complete our mission, since we had to proceed according to the scope of our sexual repertoire as it unfolded along its own course. While we tacked on a variety of spectacular excursions to explore some of the regions we were visiting, we took

---

[149] AZ, FL, ID, MI, MS, NM, NC, VA (Florida reversed this law in 2016).

[150] AK, AZ, AR, CA, DE, FL, HI, ID, IL, IN, IA, KS, KY, MI, MN, MO, MT, NE, NV, NH, NY, ND, OH, OR, PA, SD, UT, WA, WV, WI, WY, DC.

[151] AR, CO, CT, GA, HI, ID, IA, LA, ME, MI, MN, MO, MT, ND, NE, NV, NJ, OH, OK, OR, RI, SD, TX, VA, WA, WV, WI, WY.

[152] AZ, FL, GA, ID, IN, MA, MS, NE, NV, NY, OH, OK, OR, SD, TN, UT, WA, WI, VT.

[153] AL, AZ, FL, GA, ID, KS, LA, MA, MN, MS, NC, OK, OR, RI, SC, UT, DC.

[154] AR, MD, MT, MS, NV, TN, TX.

[155] AL, AZ, FL, GA, ID, LA, MN, MS, NC, OK, RI, SC, UT, VA, DC.

[156] AR, KS, MD, MA, MO, MT, NV, TN, TX.

great care to remain mindful of the primary objective of our travels: *to spit in the face of laws that have no business existing.*

We wandered among bison in Oklahoma, through the dazzling corridors of the Biltmore mansion in North Carolina, on the Appalachian Trail along Skyline Drive, and down enchanted Savannah streets lined with moss-draped trees. We traipsed in and out of the Grand Canyon, rambled endless spectacular miles through Bryce Canyon and Capitol Reef, ate fancy food in Cour d'Alene, and toured teeming alligator swamps in Louisiana. We stormed the Alamo.

We visited a little porn shop in a rather desolate sprawl of Denver, Colorado, where we rented a private viewing room to watch remarkably bad porn videos.

At a grocery store in Arkansas, when Steve asked where we could buy magazines like *Hustler* and *Playboy*, the clerk was utterly aghast and begrudgingly gestured vaguely across the tracks, literally, toward the other side of town. We found ourselves in a slightly run-down neighborhood in a little market where the pornography was stashed out of public view, underneath and behind the checkout counter. The cashier eyeballed us warily, behaving as though we were engaging in an illicit drug deal. We took our ignominious purchase to enjoy, innocuously enough, sprawling in the grass under the shade trees on the Arkansas State University campus.

We sat on a bench along the waterfront, after sunset on the Mississippi River, as I stroked his mettlesome erection and the unwitting public strolled casually by.

We had sex in national parks and at national monuments. My favorite was under the magnificent stony-eyed surveillance of our nation's greatest figures peering out of the Black Hills at Mount Rushmore. Who could better appreciate the exercise of personal liberty!

One of our favorite little bonus tactics that Steve deviously devised (and which we continue to this day) is the insertion, in those ubiquitous hotel-room Bibles, of pornographic clips between the pages of Leviticus 18 and 20, where the LORD spake to Moses outlining all the abominations of the flesh, punishable by death, and which form the literal basis of the whole fanatical moral fiasco we find ourselves up against. It's a nice touch, I feel, reaching into the deepest layers of the persecution of human sexuality.

But why is it, in a democratic society of freedom and justice for all that emphasizes, on one partisan side, the separation of church and state, and on the other side, the minimization and circumscription of government, that we find ourselves facing the legal regulation on religious moral grounds of our most deeply personal human impulse, in activities affecting no one but another interested and willing party?

Marty Klein points out how sexuality is targeted for criminalization in order to outlaw for *everyone* something that makes *some* people uncomfortable. People who become obsessive about their sexual discomfort will see obscenity everywhere they look, feeling as though their world is being invaded—and they personally violated—by all of it. So, reactively, they lash out at a world they perceive is aggressively assaulting them, while in reality the problem is the result of an internal neurosis. He says, "Those who fear sex conceptualize all sex as public. They have a well-worn list of ways that private, consensual, adult sexual behavior supposedly affects the community, and is therefore not really private."[157]

That list:

- hurts children (*always tops the list*);
- undermines other people's conventional marriages (*how this actually works is always unclear*);
- encourages "sex addiction";
- exploits women;
- disrespects the God-fearing community; and finally,
- encourages masturbation (*a very bad thing*).

"People who believe this," he says, "think your sexuality is their business." Propping up the list are the basic assumptions (all unproven and some even *dis*proven by real scientific, statistical, and

---

[157] Klein, 170.

historical research) about the imminent dangers of sexuality from which we all must be protected.[158]

Klein says, given the depth of our guilt and shame about sex, that problems and anxiety make more sense to us than real facts, which "might tell us that our kids, our property values, and our bodies are safer than we think," and so we will disregard the facts and gravitate emotionally to the "faux expertise" offered by the ex-addicts and reformed perverts who qualify to testify in the government hearings that "periodically bless the latest problem from which we must defend our families."

Ultimately, he says, people come to believe that "feeling scared about sexuality is responsible citizenship and common sense."[159]

Corroborating Klein's assessment is Dr. Wilhelm Reich—case in point—found guilty of espousing and promoting revolutionary sexual ideas, who was incarcerated and subsequently died in a federal penitentiary. Reich calls the overall cultural notions of sex "a caricature of sexuality," being a grotesque distortion of healthy sexuality. He says that it is often the real experiences of the *disturbed* that drive public discourse and sway public policy and that this represents "the typical reactions of sexually unhealthy individuals to the fight for sexual happiness on the part of healthy individuals."[160]

Reich's central thesis is that it is the energy of suppressed genital sexuality (from infancy through puberty and sexual adulthood) that provides the fuel for the "bio-pathological scourge" of human neuroticism.

---

[158] A typical "moral panic" publication (Catholic Church flier) about "What the Church Teaches on Pornography" details the profound harm of pornography on viewers and society (mentioning, but failing to cite, a meta-analysis proving that damage). The invocation reads, "As citizens, we have the right and the obligation to demand that our governmental authorities create laws which… place 'reasonable restrictions on the depiction of the human body and human intimacy.' Contact your representatives on local, state, and national levels" (Our Sunday Visitor Inc., 2007).

[159] Klein, 52–3.

[160] Wilhelm Reich, *The Discovery of the Orgone: The Function of the Orgasm*, trans. Theodore P. Wolfe (New York: The Noonday Press, 1942, 1948, 1961), 164.

However, it's important to acknowledge the fact (something Klein also points out) that the healthy individuals—out of both a cultured shyness around the topic of sex and a lack of vivid recognition of the serious extent of the problem—are not really putting up much of a fight.

William Butler Yeats said, "*The best lack all conviction, while the worst are full of passionate intensity.*" In the politics of sexuality, the relevance of this statement is immense, and—in order to formulate a stance of conviction—it is imminently important to seriously acknowledge how badly out of line the issue is and to really understand how personal the offense is.

So this is why we fought the law, playing the silent, underground Bonnie and Clyde of our own solitary sexual revolution. Still waters run deep, and taking this action, in willful defiance of circumstances we find abominably abhorrent, has been a deeply meaningful gesture affecting us both profoundly. It is a statement that has created a powerful resonance in my own being, strengthening my own conviction, like an anchor sunk deep into the murky floor far beneath the churning ocean with all its writhing of beasts and gnashing of teeth.

One might say "the law won," since we did nothing to change the legal policies themselves, but...

If you merely change the lens through which you view it (say to a wide-angle one), you will see that *sex* is actually the law of the land, the immutable, enduring law that governs from within, and it is this kind of law that always wins, regardless of what constraints are put upon it. In the long run, the judicial laws fluctuate with the changing tides of political favor, and yet some things remain ungovernable.

Attempting to govern the ungovernable ultimately always leads to trouble, requiring further damage control, more laws, more unrest, more fighting. It is important to climb to such a vantage point that we can see which ones these are.

Our politicians have not ascended, and possibly will not ascend, to the heights necessary to take in the whole scope of sexuality, so it is up to us to do the job, climb the mountain, and gain the perspective that will allow us to simply cross over the line onto the winning side and establish ourselves there with full, wholehearted conviction. From there, we quietly go about our subversive business that affirms the lives and the well-being of the individuals of our species, from the inside out. In this way we come out on top, as we have affirmed it for ourselves and, in spite of all the obstacles devised to prevent it, stepped—with conviction—courageously into the glory of our birthright. (Then, maybe we'll even vote in politicians who represent that appropriately.)

ABOUT THE AUTHOR

Karin Grace has dedicated her life to personal growth pivoting on sexual understanding, healing, and expression. She has worked in the sex industry as an entertainer for over ten years, been a guest speaker for college-level human sexuality classes and assisted both formal and informal psychotherapy workshops. She graduated summa cum laude in biology, has practiced as a licensed massage therapist for twenty-five years, and is a published scientific illustrator and artist. Her life's focused endeavors,  combining both deeply thoughtful reflection and active engagement, coalesce to give her a practical and dynamic background in the workings of the mind and body, and an integrated view of their complex interface.

Her website is www.hotbloodedstudies.com.

www.ingramcontent.com/pod-product-compliance
Lightning Source LLC
Chambersburg PA
CBHW051433250726
48655CB00001B/42